WISCONSIN DAY TRIPS

BY THEME

BY MARY M. BAUER

Adventure Publications, Inc.
Cambridge, MN

Acknowledgements

Thanks to my dedicated daytrippers who rode shotgun with me: Mom, Dad, Kenny, Shelly, Chris, Susie. You guys rule! Thanks to Judi and Sue at the Hudson Travel Information Center—the best rest area in Wisconsin and always my first stop before any day trip adventure! And a big thank you to the talented, hard-working folks at Adventure Publications for bringing dreams into reality, especially Gordon, Gerri and Kathy. It's been a pleasure writing Day Trips.

About the Author

A full-blooded Irish lass, Mary M. Bauer was born and raised in Lutefisk Country. She and her husband jumped the state line over a dozen years ago and bought a Wisconsin dairy farm. Her two children ran off to college, then found careers, to avoid baling hay and fence painting. A former nurse and interior designer, Mary began her writing career as a weekly columnist for a regional newspaper. She discovered ranting in public and getting paid for it is a lot of fun. She is the author of Adventure Publication's *Minnesota Day Trips by Theme*. Besides family, her major loves are traveling, hiking, books, decrepit Christmas decorations, and Reese's Peanut Butter Cups. She is a dog and cat person, and is thinking about adopting a pig.

Book design by Jonathan Norberg

10 9 8 7 6 5 4 3 2

Copyright 2005 by Mary M. Bauer
Published by Adventure Publications, Inc.
820 Cleveland St S
Cambridge, MN 55008
1-800-678-7006
www.adventurepublications.net
Printed in the United States of America
ISBN-10: 1-59193-113-4
ISBN-13: 978-1-59193-113-3

WISCONSIN DAY TRIPS

BY THEME

INTRODUCTION

The Badger State is also the nation's Dairy State and loaded with cheese and Cheeseheads, but that's not all. Wisconsin is the birthplace of famed architect Frank Lloyd Wright, children's author Laura Ingalls Wilder, escape artist Harry Houdini, the Harley-Davidson road hogs and the rails-to-trails system. Wisconsinite inventions the world can't live without include the supercomputer, bathtub, snowmobile, hydroelectric power and ice cream sundae. The Green Bay Packers are the nation's only public-owned professional football team and something Cheeseheads can't live without. Annually, 2½ million people travel to the Wisconsin Dells, making it the Midwest's number one vacation hot spot. If that's not reason enough to check out Wisconsin, then perhaps the two Great Lakes, Mississippi River, Door County and the Apostle Islands will clinch it.

Okay, now you're overwhelmed. A vacation in Wisconsin sounds great, but who wants to sort through all the brochures? *Wisconsin Day Trips* takes the information overload out of planning an excursion. Each chapter offers a number of attractions based on themes such as lighthouses, garden tours, family day and so on. Simply turn to the chapters that appeal and bypass the rest if you like. All the information is right at your fingertips.

So go ahead and have a grilled bratwurst while you tailgate; wash it down with a Wisconsin brewski. Discover covered bridges and round barns on scenic Rustic Roads. Tour the state's museums and historic sites, Muskie fish in the Northwoods, join an archeology dig, buy a freshly baked pie at an Amish farm, whitewater raft Class 5 rivers or simply laze the day away on one of the thousands of miles of lakeshore beaches. Wisconsin is your getaway destination!

Table of Contents

Table of Contents

Table of Contents

Steeped in a bygone era, the Amish are known for their traditional pacifist ways, horse and buggy travel, colorful handmade quilts and plain clothes. Wisconsin has the fourth largest population of Amish in the US, with the first families moving to Medford in 1920. Overcrowding in the east and increasing land prices make an ongoing relocation to Wisconsin an attractive alternative for the growing community.

Based on their concept of Christian humility, the Amish adopt a "plain lifestyle," foregoing modern conveniences such as electricity, cars, telephones, computers, etc. Many of the Amish operate small bakeries, furniture shops and quilt shops on their farms. Watch for signs detailing business hours; they are not open on Sundays. For a more personal glimpse into the Amish lifestyle, there are several tours available. See the Amish Tours section in this chapter for information. If you'd like to know more about the Amish, log onto www.Amish.net. The web site features an informative FAQ section.

Amish Country

Amish Tours

Shops That Sell Amish Products

Amish Getaways

Amish Tours

NOTE: The Amish prefer not to have their pictures taken. Please respect their privacy.

Augusta Wisconsin Standard Amish Countryside Tours

The Wood Shed, 105 W Lincoln St, Augusta; 715-286-5404; www.woodshedheirlooms.com

Board a bus (14 people) for two regularly scheduled tours that depart daily from The Wood Shed, M-Sa. Stops include a bakery shop, woodworking shop, candy shop, home and farm. The tour takes approximately 1½–2 hours. Step-on guides are also available for 3-hour coach bus tours. Call ahead for times, cost and reservations.

Bonduel Wisconsin Standard Amish Countryside Tours

The Wood Shed, 126 E Green Bay St, Bonduel; 715-758-6096; www.woodshedheirlooms.com

A guide rides with you for an informative 1½–2 hour tour of the Amish community. Stops include a harness shop, two bulk food markets and an Amish home and farm. The cost is per car, per van or for groups of 6 or more. Step-on guides are also available for 3-hour coach bus tours. Call ahead to make a reservation.

Down A Country Road

2 miles east of Cashton on a corner along Hwy 33; 608-654-5318;
www.downacountryroadamish.com

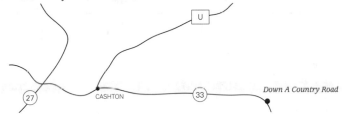

Your "Englisher" guides Chuck and Kathy Kuderer and their children live on a farm in the heart of one of the largest Amish settlements in Wisconsin. Learn about the history and customs of these gentle people on a personal tour of the Amish community. Your guide will ride with you in your vehicle for 1½ hours as you visit farmsteads. Tours May-Oct are scheduled by appointment M-Sa. Call for times and cost.

Rustic Road 56

Ontario (Vernon County)

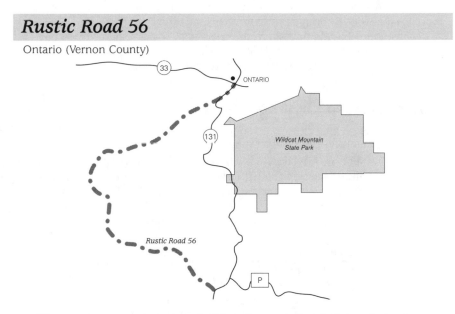

The scenic paved route travels 8⅗ miles past Amish farms, log cabins, a round barn, examples of contour farming and Wildcat Mountain State Park. Travel west on Hwy 14 to Hwy 131. Drive north on Hwy 131 approximately 20 miles to Dutch Hollow Rd, Sand Hill Rd, Hoff Valley Rd and Lower Ridge Rd. Rustic Road 56 (R56) begins at the intersection of Dutch Hollow Rd and Hwy 131, extending to the intersection of Lower Ridge Rd and Hwy 131.

Rustic Road 73

Curtis (Clark County)

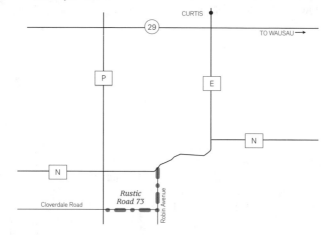

The 2½-mile gravel road traverses woodlands and dairy farms. A 1-lane wooden bridge on Robin Ave spans the railroad tracks. View a pasture of buffalo and share the road with horse-drawn Amish buggies. Travel Hwy 29 west from Wausau to Cty P just past Curtis. Go south on Cty P to Cloverdale Rd and east to Robin Ave.

Tomah Area Driving Tours

Tomah Chamber/CVB Office, 805 Superior Ave, Tomah 54660; 800-94-TOMAH or 608-372-2166; www.tomahwisconsin.com

The Tomah area Amish live mostly south and west of town. Request an Adventure Map Self-Guided Driving Tour through Amish Country. The free maps are available through the Tomah Chamber or you can download them online. Other maps available include a driving tour of Cranberry Country and the Mill Bluff Coulee Region.

Trempealeau Car Tours

Trempealeau County; 715-538-4045; www.trempealeaucountytours.com/amish_tour.htm

Not quite 15 miles in length, the self-guided hour-long tour includes many Amish farms with retail shops such as bakeries, leather goods, furniture and fabric shops. See a sawmill, furrier and buggy shop. Shops closed Su. Download the audio tour and map for free online; CDs or tapes are available for a fee.

Tour Directions: Start in Whitehall and drive northeast about 2 miles on Hwy 53 to the junction with Cty S at the village of Coral City. Turn right on Cty S, continue southeast 2½ miles to Shelly Ridge Rd, turn right (south). Drive southeast 2 miles to rejoin Cty S, turn left and follow north and west to the junction with Larkin Valley Rd (which you passed by earlier). Turn left (south) on Larkin Valley Rd, drive 2½ miles past Rat Rd to Snake Coulee Rd, turn right (west). Drive to Schansberg Rd, turn north, drive 4 miles to the junction with Hwy 53. Tour ends here.

Westby Self-Guided Biking and Driving Tours

PO Box 94, Westby 54667; 866-493-7829 or 608-634-4011; e-mail westbycoc@mwt.net

The 24-mile self-guided, moderate difficulty trail leads through the largest Amish community in Wisconsin. Pick up a free brochure at the Stabbur, Westby Information Center or call 866-4-WESTBY. Free download also available at www.westbywi.com.

Shops That Sell Amish Products

A & J's Amish Oak Furniture

1120 N Broadway (¾ mile south of I-94, Exit 41 onto Hwy 25/12, which is N Broadway; A&J's is next to Napa Auto Parts), Menomonie; 715-235-1261

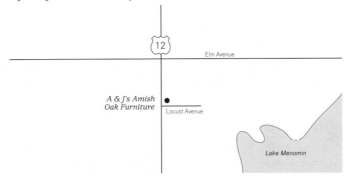

Giant 6,400' showroom filled with Amish oak and cherry furniture and gift items. Open year-round M-Sa. Call for hours.

Amish Country Corner

1101 Superior Ave, Tomah; 608-372-3222

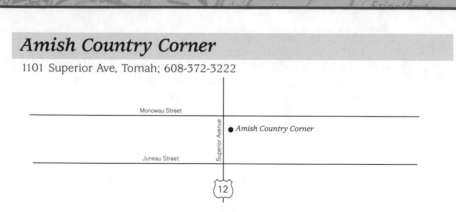

Handcrafted Amish and Mennonite oak and pine furniture, crafts, quilts, rugs, baskets and candles. Open year-round M-Sa. Call for hours.

Amish Country Quilts and Furniture

N2030 Spring St, Stockholm; 715-442-2015

Nice selection of quilts, wall hangings and handcrafted oak, pine and cherry furniture. Open Feb-Dec. Call for hours.

Amish House

Cty F, Lakewood 54138 (go east of Lakewood on Cty F, about 1 mile, then turn south into McCauslin Brook Golf & Country Club); 715-276-7769

Amish furniture in oak, cherry, pine, hickory, maple, pine log, white and red cedar; quilts, faceless dolls, baskets, jewelry chests, quilt racks and more. Handicap accessible. Open daily year-round. Call for hours.

NOTE: Amish House has a second location at 221 W Main St, Wautoma; 920-787-3491. At the Hwy 139 and 51 intersection take the Coloma exit. Drive east on Hwy 21 for 13 miles, take a left on Hwy 22 for 2 blocks, then right on Hwy 21 for 4 blocks. Open year-round F & Sa. Call for hours.

Amish Quilt Show & Sale

4599 Hwy 57 (held at Institute Saloon Hall, 4 miles north of Sturgeon Bay at the corner of Hwy 57 and Cty P), Jacksonport; 920-823-2288

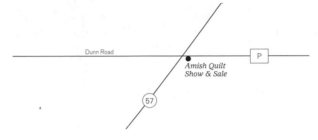

The annual show features traditional Amish quilts, rugs, wall hangings, table quilts and books about the Amish. Handicap accessible. Call for show hours (1 week in Jul & Oct). Admission charged.

Amish Stone House

302 N River St, Spooner; 715-635-8016

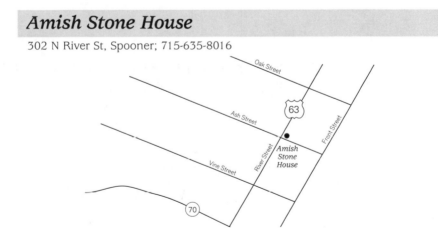

Amish furniture and crafts. Open year-round M-Sa. Call for hours.

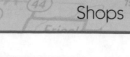

Cashton Mercantile

1237 Front St, Cashton; 608-654-5387

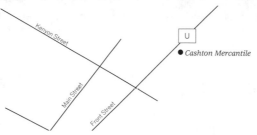

Cashton Mercantile

The Mercantile features Amish and Ocoach Mountain Artisans, hand-woven baskets, rugs, homemade soap, maple syrup, candy and more. Open daily year-round. Call for hours.

Donan Furniture & Art Gallery

129 E Division Ave (in Barron on Hwy 8; 14 miles east of St. Croix Casino), Barron; 800-644-2653 or 715-537-5775; www.amishoakfurniture.com

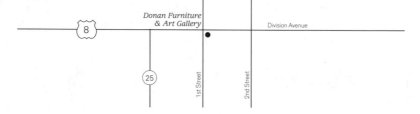

Over 5,200' of limited edition art prints, collectibles, lace, bulk food and handcrafted Amish furniture and crafts. Open year-round M-Sa. Call for hours.

Down A Country Road

Two miles east of Cashton on a corner along Hwy 33; 608-654-5318; www.downacountryroadamish.com

The quaint country shop was built by the Amish and features books on Amish weddings, school, dress, etc. Also cookbooks, syrup, baskets, candies, jellies and jams, quilts, dolls and Amish-made crafts. Open May-Oct Th-Sa, closed Su, other days by appointment or by chance year-round. See map page 9.

NOTE: Down A Country Road also offers Amish tours. See page 9 for information and the map.

Hustler Cheese Shop & Torkleson Natural Valle

110 Omaha St (4 miles west of New Lisbon via Cty A or 3 miles south of Camp Douglas via Cty H), Hustler; 608-427-6907

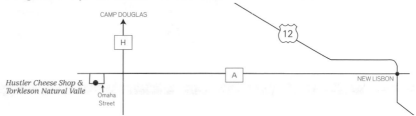

Amish cheese and gifts. Watch production of Muenster cheese through the observation window. Open year-round Tu-Sa. Call for hours.

Jacksonport Craft Cottage

6275 Hwy 57 (Door County; about 1 block south of the intersection of Hwy 57 and Cty V), Jacksonport; 920-823-2288; www.jacksonportcraftcottage.com

The 1860s-era log home features handcrafted original gifts by over 70 artists, including Amish quilts, wall hangings, table runners, rugs and more. Original Door County lighthouse pin collector series. Open daily mid-May-mid-Oct. Call for hours.

Kaitlin's Amish Goods

227 Broad St N, Prescott; 715-262-4321

Three floors of Amish and Mennonite furniture, accessories, candles, quilts, dolls and gifts. Open daily year-round. Call for hours.

Montello Two-Mile Fair

Hwy 22 (2 miles south of town on Hwy 22), Montello; 920-394-3203

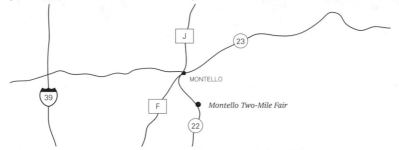

Large outdoor flea market with arts and crafts, antiques, clothes, toys, farmers market, freshly made doughnut holes, Amish baked goods and more. Open mid-Apr-Oct F-Su. Call for hours. Free admission.

Old Country Cheese (shop)

5 miles southeast of Cashton on Cty D (take I-90 until Sparta, exit Hwy 27 S, follow to Cashton, take Hwy 33 east a few miles to Cty D, go 5 miles), Cashton; 608-654-5411; www.oldcountrycheese.com

One of the few cheese factories left in the US that handles fresh canned milk from 230 Amish producers. Watch the cheesemaking process through an observation window. Fourteen varieties of cheese, Amish furniture, crafts, jams, jellies, pickles, preserves, baskets and more. Open year-round M-Sa. Call for hours.

NOTE: Old Country Cheese has a second location at 2434 Rose St in La Crosse; 608-781-8089. Take Exit 3 off I-94 to Hwy 53 S, which becomes Rose St. Open daily year-round. Call for hours.

Sandee's Treasures

400 Broadway, Ste 11 & 12, Wisconsin Dells; 608-253-7747

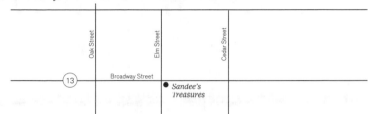

Locally made Amish furniture (including log furniture), quilts and crafts, glassware, textures, antiques, artwork and more. They will do custom furniture orders. Open year-round. Shorter winter hours.

Simply Amish Furniture

512 Oak St, Baraboo; 800-292-6474 or 608-356-7858

Handcrafted solid wood furniture, specializing in tables and chairs. Oak, cherry, walnut, pine, maple and hickory. Custom orders welcome. Delivery available. Open daily year-round. Call for hours.

The Treasure Mill

211 W Main St, La Valle; 608-985-7300

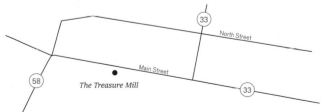

Antiques, old coins (selling and appraisal), Amish furniture, homemade Amish candies, herbal soaps and salts, bird feed and supplies, arts and crafts. Open daily year-round. Call for hours.

The Vintage Shoppes

W7461 Hwy 21 and 73E, Wautoma; 920-787-2303

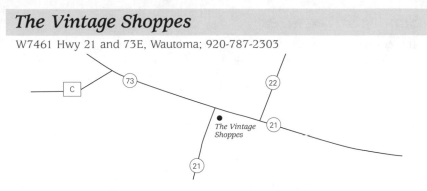

Amish furniture and folk art, needlework, prints, gifts and Christmas shop. Handicap accessible. Open year-round daily. Call for hours.

NOTE: The Vintage Shoppes has a second location at 124 Main St, Ripon; 920-748-7487. Open daily. Call for hours.

The Wood Shed

105 W Lincoln St (Hwy 12), Augusta; 715-286-5404; www.woodshedheirlooms.com

Huge selection of handcrafted Amish and Mennonite furniture, quilts, crafts, jams, jellies, baskets, candles and more. Handicap accessible. Open year-round M-Sa. Call for hours. See map page 8.

NOTE: The Wood Shed has two other locations: 101 W Main St, Cambridge; 608-423-4504 (open daily year-round); and 126 E Green Bay St, Bonduel; 715-758-6096 (open year-round M-Sa). Amish tours are available in Augusta and Bonduel. See the Augusta and Bonduel Wisconsin Standard Amish Countryside tours on page 8 for more information and maps.

Amish Getaways

Ages Past Bed & Breakfast and The Back Door Cafe

1223 Front St, Cashton; 888-322-5494 or 608-654-5950; www.agespast.net

Ages Past Bed & Breakfast
and The Back Door Cafe

The elegant historic country inn and restaurant was once a Catholic rectory. Meticulously restored, antique furniture dates to the 1600s. Stained glass, oak staircase, claw foot bathtubs, terry robes and slippers, fresh cut flowers (in season), gourmet dining and wine. Located in the heart of Amish Country, take your breakfast on the front porch and watch Amish horse and buggies clip-clop past. Area attractions include Sparta-Elroy Bike Trail, Amish community and shopping, hiking, Wildcat Mountain State Park, canoeing, Kickapoo River, antiques, horseback riding, two 18-hole golf courses. Call ahead for reservations.

Country Pleasures Bed & Breakfast

S1075 Weister Creek Rd, Cashton; 608-839-4915; www.countrypleasuresbandb.com

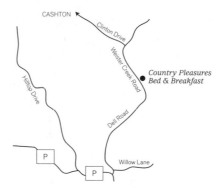

Country Pleasures
Bed & Breakfast

The 5-bedroom, 4-bathroom Amish homestead is in the middle of Amish Country. Hike the wooded trails, explore two ponds or just sit back and enjoy the sunset. Families are welcome. Special Scrapbooking Weekends available. Area attractions include canoeing the Kickapoo River, hiking and biking. Call ahead for reservations.

You knew there'd be a chapter about cheese. After all, Wisconsin is the Dairy State and home to the crazy, but fabulous Cheeseheads. Wisconsin is number one in cheese production, claiming 27 percent of the country's total supply. The state's 290 factories produce more than 2 billion pounds of cheese in 250 varieties (brick and colby are Wisconsin originals). That's enough mozzarella for 900 million pizzas, more than three for everyone in America. Many cheese factories have observation windows or offer tours, but get there early as most cheese-makers begin work before sunup.

To find out how the most important ingredient—milk—gets to the cheese factory, book a stay at a "vacation" farm. From the first fresh, creamy squirt to bulk tank storage, you'll learn all about milk production and what it takes to be a Wisconsin dairy farmer.

Dairyland

Cheese Factories and Farms

Farm Vacations

Cheese Factories and Farms

Bass Lake Cheese Factory

598 Valley View Trl, Somerset 54025; 800-368-2437 or 715-247-5586;
www.blcheese.com

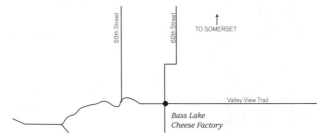

The award-winning cheese factory specializes in many varieties of
cheeses made from cow, sheep and goat milk. They have an observation window, cheesemaking video, self-guided tours, a retail store
and dairy antiques. Open M–Sa. Call for hours.

> **Option:** Thanks to the Apple River, Somerset is the "tubing capi-
> tal of the world." It's also known as the "frog leg capital of the
> world." Campgrounds, water parks, tube rentals and deep-fried
> frog legs—check out the **River's Edge Supper Club** for all of the
> above; 715-247-3305.

Carr Valley Cheese Factory

S3797 Cty G, La Valle 53941 (take Hwy 33 west through Reedsburg to
La Valle, turn left on Hwy 58 through Ironton to Cty G, left on G);
800-462-7258 or 608-986-2781

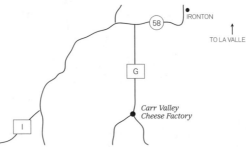

Carr Valley Cheese Factory is a century-old family cheesemaking
operation specializing in cheddar, colby, monterey jack, pepper jack,
veggie jack and curds. Watch the cheesemaking process through an
observation window at scheduled times. Curds fresh from the vats for
sale when available. Store open M–Sa. Call for hours.

Cedar Grove Cheese Inc

E5904 Mill Rd, Plain 53577 (from Plain, drive east on Cty B for ½ mile, turn left on Mill Rd); 800-200-6020 or 608-546-5284; www.cedargrovecheese.com

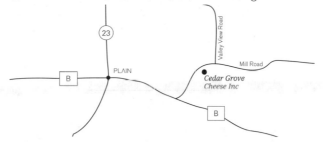

These folks have been making specialty and organic cheeses for more than a century. Tours include their fascinating "Living Machine" water treatment system. Tours M–Sa. Fee charged. Reserve ahead if you have more than six in your group. Call for hours.

Green County Welcome Center

2108 7th Ave, Monroe 53566 (in the old Milwaukee train depot); 608-325-4636

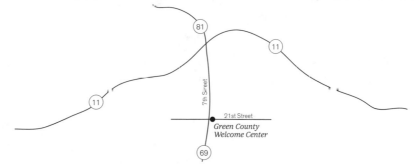

There are approximately 30 cheese masters in Wisconsin, and Green County has nine of them. Cheese masters work as licensed cheesemakers for a minimum of ten years before they become certified in a particular cheese, which usually takes another three years. It's safe to say the folks in Green County definitely know their cheese, so it's no shock to find that the Welcome Center's main attraction is their Historic Cheesemaking Center—a replica cheese factory display. Open year-round. Fee charged.

Options: Monroe County is home to the **Chalet Cheese Cooperative** (the last place in the state to make Limburger) and **Alp & Dell** (the only factory still using copper vats). To arrange a tour of the Chalet Cheese Coop call 608-325-4343; Alp & Dell 608-328-3355.

Lakeview Farms

E19241 83rd St, Bristol 53104 (in Bristol, east on 83rd St to 194th Ave, use the southwest entrance); 800-806-6952 or 262-857-2316; www.lakeviewfarms.com

Tours M–F at scheduled times. No reservations required for groups of ten or less. Open daily. Call for hours and tour times.

> **Option:** Grab your corsets, full-body armor and princess hats, then head to the **Bristol Renaissance Fair**—30 acres of sixteenth-century life. Fifteen stages and 200 artisans joust, juggle and demonstrate their wares. The Faire is at 124020 128th St (from Kenosha, take I-94 S to Exit 347, which is Russell Rd, and follow the signs); 847-395-7773. Open mid-Jun–Aug rain or shine. Admission charged. Call for hours.

Nelson Cheese Factory

S237 S Main St, Nelson 54756; 715-673-4725

Nestled along the bluffs of the mighty Mississippi, Nelson is one picturesque little cheese factory. The family-owned, 1850 creamery produces cheddar, colby, monterey jack and fresh curds. The old-fashioned store sells a nice selection of wines as well as dairy and meat products, but is especially popular for ice cream. Indoor and outdoor eating areas, plus a cozy fireplace room for wine and cheese sampling. Observation window; call to pre-arrange a tour. Open daily. Call for hours.

Springside Cheese Corp

7989 Arndt Rd, Oconto Falls 54154; 920-829-6395

Springside is one busy cheese factory and a great place to learn the ins and outs of cheesemaking. They produce more than 25 varieties including cheddar, farmers and low-sodium cheeses. They have three observation windows and request that you call ahead for a guided tour. The store is open daily. Call for hours.

Union Star Cheese Factory

7742 Cty Rd II, Fremont 54940 (in Zittau, 4 miles southeast of Fremont on Cty Rd II); 800-354-3373 or 920-836-2804

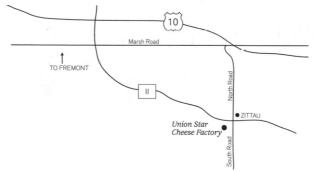

If you're super serious about learning the cheesemaking process, the folks at Union Star can help you out. Watch them make Muenster, cheddar, colby, string cheese and curds. They conduct tours year-round M–Sa at scheduled times; call ahead for groups over six. Open daily. Call for hours.

Farm Vacations

Dorset Ridge Guest House

22259 King Rd, Wilton 54670; 608-463-7375

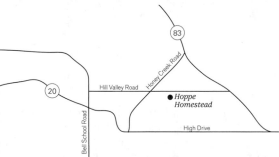

Dorset Ridge is 400 acres of fresh country air sitting smack in the middle of Amish Country. Sixty dairy cows and a flock of chickens will have you up bright and early for the morning milking. The famous 32-mile Elroy-Sparta State Bike Trail is nearby as are opportunities for canoeing and horseback riding. The separate farmhouse sleeps eight. Open year-round. Reservations required.

Hoppe Homestead

33701 Hill Valley Rd, East Troy 53120; 262-534-6480; www.hoppehomestead.com

The 300-acre Hoppe family spread has been in operation since 1866. Milk a cow or bulk up those muscles by helping with the chores, then head to the house for a mountain man Sunday morning breakfast. The Hoppe Farm has horse-drawn hayrides and sleigh rides. Open Mar–Dec. Reservations required.

Palmquist's "The Farm"

N5136 River Rd, Brantwood 54513; 800-519-2558 or 715-564-2558;
www.palmquistfarm.com

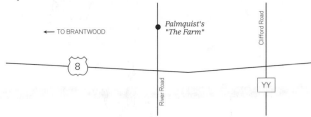

This is not a dairy farm, but it is a great getaway. And getaway you shall on
this 800-acre beef and timber farm. Oh, there are still plenty of chores to do,
but there are also scenic hiking and biking trails, fishing ponds, a Finnish
sauna, hayrides, nightly cookouts and winter cross-country ski trails. Hunt
year-round on the 600-acre licensed deer farm or hire a guide and do a little
grouse hunting. Accommodations include suites, cabins, the farmhouse and
horse lodging. Open year-round. Reservations required.

Room to Roam Farm Vacations

W656 Veraguth Dr, Fountain City 54629; 608-687-8575

After four generations, they're still milking registered Holstcins on the
century-old Room to Roam dairy farm. Gather morning eggs or bot-
tle-feed a calf. Stroll a freshly mowed hayfield or watch as farmer Jess
harvests his crops. The separate 2-story farmhouse sits on top of the
river bluffs overlooking the Mississippi River—a prime vantage point
for watching Bald Eagles. There's a garden behind the house for the
picking, and real dairy butter in the fridge. A tire swing, fire pit and
hayrides are all part of the Room to Roam experience. Open year-
round. Reservations required.

Dubbed "Cape Cod of the Midwest," the 75-mile-long Door peninsula captivates 2 million visitors each year, and it's easy to see why. Door County boasts more coastline than any other county in America, 5 state parks, 18 county parks, 10 golf courses, 12 lighthouses, 100 galleries, 41 surrounding islands and unparalleled sunsets. It ranks third in cherry production behind Utah (second) and Michigan (first).

Door County truly is Wisconsin's most romantic and scenic getaway. Around mid-May thousands of acres of cherry trees explode in fragrant full bloom. The lazy days of summer are anything but, with all the hiking, salmon and trout fishing, swimming, boating, golfing, shopping, fish boils, outdoor theaters, antiques and wineries. The autumn hillsides explode with brilliant color, and the powdered cross-country and snowmobile trails are the stuff of a winter enthusiast's dreams. It's little wonder *Money Magazine* named Door County one of the top ten vacation destinations in North America.

Door County

Adventures for Kids

Explore the Parks

Golf Door County

The Famous Door County Lighthouses

Museums

Romantic Door County

Theater

Wineries

Island Hopping: Washington Island

Island Hopping: Rock Island

Door County Odds & Ends

Adventures For Kids

You've dreamed about it. All of your friends and neighbors have been there. Now here you are in beautiful Door County with the kids, and they don't want to shop. And you don't want to take them to the wineries. What can you do here with kids? Frankly, a lot—here are a few ideas.

Al Johnson's Swedish Restaurant

IS THAT A HOOF ON THE ROOF?

702 Bay Shore Dr, Sister Bay; 920-854-2626

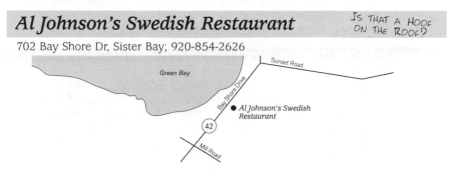

Al Johnson's is to Door County what the Eiffel Tower is to France—an icon you have to see. From the start, Al Johnson's had a sod roof and served up tasty Swedish cuisine, but the restaurant wasn't as busy as Al would've liked. As a practical joke on the morning of Al's wedding, his best man put a few goats on top of the restaurant's roof. When Al showed up to get them down, he noticed a large crowd staring at the goats. This was an "ah-ha" moment for Al. There have been goats on the roof ever since, and the place is always packed. Al's has a log cabin atmosphere with Swedish cuisine and Scandinavian-clad servers. Customer favorites include Swedish pancakes and Swedish meatballs, but beware—pickled herring and homemade pickled beets are also on the menu. Open daily. Call for hours. They don't take reservations. The goats graze the roof from mid-morning until afternoon during the summer months.

Country Ovens Cherry De-Lite

CHOCOLATE COVERED CHERRIES, ANYONE?

PO Box 195, 229 E Main St, Forestville 54213; 800-544-1003 or 920-856-6767; www.countryovens.com

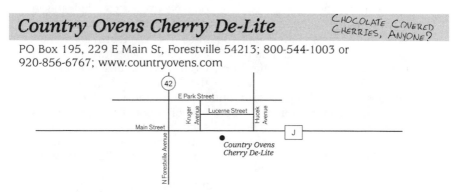

Cherry pie, cherry wine, cherry salsa, cherry cheese spread, cherry

pancakes, cherry spitting contests. The point is, cherries are a big deal in Door County. In fact, the county ranks third nationally in the cherry industry. Former dairy farmers Mike and Kathy Johnson know all about the Door County cherry industry, because they are in the business of dehydrating the tasty fruit. Country Ovens began in 1987 on a very modest scale. Kathy used to dry a few cherries for friends and neighbors with her $15 garage sale Electro-Sun dehydrator. Word spread and life for the Johnson's is now a factory full of cherries. See the ovens and watch the packaging process through the observation window. Open year-round. Call for hours. Gift store and free tastings.

Option: **Forestville Dam County Park** is a couple blocks from Country Ovens, but in the opposite direction. Specifically, take County J west to the edge of town. This is a wonderful little park with a picturesque lake held back by a dam with a hiking trail across it. Swimming is allowed, but there is no lifeguard on duty. Picnic, fish, playground, restrooms. The park is part of the Ahnapee State Trail.

Dairy View Country Store & Schopf's Hilltop Dairy

WHERE DOES MILK COME FROM?

5167 Cty I, Carlsville (take Hwy 42 north of Sturgeon Bay to Carlsville, then east on Cty I); 920-743-9779; www.dairyview.com

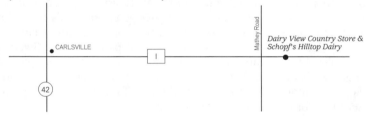

You're in the Dairy State, therefore you have to take your kids to see a real working dairy farm. Schopf's Hilltop Dairy is a cool place to show them how a modern dairy operates. This is a fourth-generation family farm, milking around 600 Holstein cows. Take the self-guided tour and see the cows as they're milked through an observation window. After watching two videos that explain the whole dairy operation and milking process, putting the milking machine on the mechanical cow should be a snap... Uh-huh, right. The tour includes many interesting, hands-on displays such as the one that compares a cow's stomach to a human's. The store carries every flavor of ice cream—all made right on the premises—from Blue Moon to Strawberry Shortcake. The busy folks at Schopf's also make their own fudge. The best seller is a caramel-chocolate-vanilla blend, aptly named "Udder Delight." Once everyone's got their fudge and cones, head outdoors for a challenging hike through the 22-acre corn maze (beginning of Aug). Admission charged. Corn maze admission is an extra charge.

NOTE: Call for time the cows are getting milked so you can plan your trip accordingly.

Door County Living Classrooms

BOOK AN ECO-EXPERIENCE

5880 Cedar Creek Pl, Sturgeon Bay 54235; 920-746-0056; www.dcecoadventure.com

Do you want to show the kids the real Door County? Then give Door County Living Classrooms a call. Guides Brian and Jaime are life-long Door County residents and know just about every inch of the peninsula from the lush forests to the thick bogs and scenic overlooks. They customize outdoor adventures perfect for your family, whether it's a twilight hike to watch animals prepare for the night or a canoe trip on an inland lake. You tell them what you want to see, and they take care of the rest. There is a charge per person for a 2-hour adventure. There is also a charge per person for canoe or kayak adventures plus equipment fee.

Door County Stables

RIDE 'EM COWBOY!

See Horseback Riding in the Odds & Ends section of this chapter for Door County horse stables

Is there a kid alive who hasn't spent at least one birthday wish on a horse? Door County is a great place to take the kids on a horseback riding adventure—wooded walk trails, scenic brooks and streams, gentle horses. The stables offer everything from a 1-hour ride to camping out; Kurtz Corral even has winter rides that end in a cup of cider around the fireplace. Most offer lessons. Price range is $20/hr and up.

Egg Harbor Fun Park

AMUSEMENT PARK

1 ½ miles south of Egg Harbor on Hwy 42; 920-868-9417

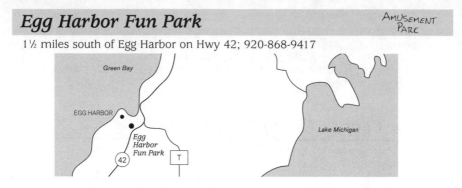

The Egg Harbor Fun Park is the largest arcade in Door County. If that isn't enough, they also have Water Wars, which pretty much means you're going to get soaked. Miniature golf course, pizza made to order, ice cream, hot dogs—this is kid heaven!

The Farm

4285 Hwy 57, PO Box 44 (4 miles north of Sturgeon Bay on Hwy 57), Sturgeon Bay 54235; 920-743-6666

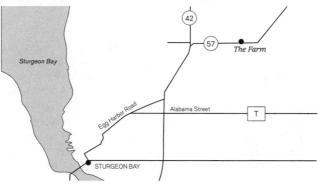

Advertised as a "living museum of rural America," the 40-acre Farm is the perfect place to bring the kids for a day of goat milking, kitten holding, hatching chicks, bottle feeding lambs and piglets and learning about farm life. Hike trails and explore log buildings full of antiques and old farm tools. Stroll the gardens and climb on antique equipment—everything is pretty much hands-on. Pack a picnic lunch and stay for the day because the kids will not want to leave! Open daily Memorial Day–mid-Oct. Admission charged. Call for hours.

Hands On Art Studio

THE ART BARN

1.75 miles east of Hwy 42 on Peninsula Players Rd, Egg Harbor; 920-868-9311
www.handsonartstudio.com

Is your child the next Leonardo da Vinci or does he just like to play in the mud? It doesn't matter, because all kids have a blast at the Hands On Art Studio. The do-it-yourself studio is located in a 1960-ish round-roofed barn. They offer numerous projects from ceramics to glass fusing to metal sculpture. The folks at Hands On welcome kids and have lots of projects and programs designed with them in mind such as creating their own special birthday plate. One of the friendly Art Helpers will explain all the options and get the kids started. Open year-round. Call for winter hours. Hands On is a "walk-in" art studio and reservations are not required.

Option: Hands On also has a special **"Express Yourself!" Night** for grown-ups. The Art Barn becomes a stress-free, music-filled creative place for "adults to reconnect with their creative spirits." Paint a T-shirt, a martini glass or whatever project thrills you. It's BYOB and snacks to share. Every F night. Call for hours. Reservations are not required, but you must be 21 or older. There's a flat fee plus project cost.

PC Junction

ALL ABOARD!

Corner of Hwy A and E, Peninsula Center, Baileys Harbor; 920-839-2048

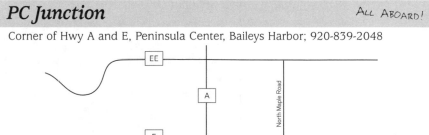

Toot! Toot! The train's a-comin' and—hey, it's hauling food! Train paraphernalia rules at PC Junction and so does fun. Kids love it here. The train circles the bar, so try to sit there. The counter is cool anyway because it's made from old wooden doors. When you hear a train whistle your food is done and on the run down the tracks to you. Open daily. There is also an outside bar and a playground.

The Ridges Sanctuary

8288 Cty Rd Q; PO Box 152, Baileys Harbor (½ mile north of Baileys Harbor on Cty Rd Q); 920-839-2802; www.ridgesanctuary.org

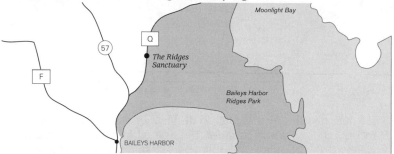

Established in 1937, The Ridges Sanctuary was the first National Natural Landmark in Wisconsin. Living within the 1,200-acre nature preserve are all 23 native Wisconsin orchids, 13 endangered plant species and the federally endangered Hines Emerald Dragonfly. Boardwalks and bridges trail through bogs, swamps and dunes. Naturalist-led tours leave at scheduled times M–Sa during summer months. Trails open sunrise–sunset year-round. The sanctuary also has a trail for the visually handicapped. Weekly summer lecture series, snowshoe hikes and family programs. No pets, picnicking, smoking, baby strollers or bikes on trails due to the fragile nature of the environment. The nature center is open daily mid-May–mid-Oct. Call for hours. Admission charged.

Sally's Soft Serve

1514 Michigan St, Sturgeon Bay; 920-743-9661

Just when you think you've seen everything, a place such as Sally's Soft Serve comes along to prove you haven't. It dishes up wickedly wonderful chocolate shakes, but the truly remarkable thing about Sally's is that dogs and cats eat here for free. How cool is that! Sally's has drive-through and walk-up service, soft serve and sugar-free ice cream and fat-free yogurt. No shoes, no shirt, no problem, say the folks at Sally's. Hmm. Sounds like they listen to a lot of Jimmy Buffet.

Skyway Drive-In Theatre

LET'S GO TO THE DRIVE-IN

Hwy 42 between Fish Creek and Ephraim; 920-854-9938

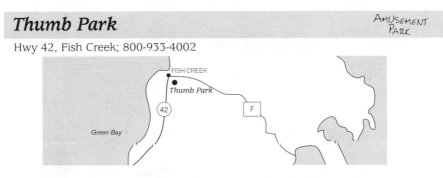

Do you want to show your kids what a trip to the movies was like when you were their ages? Take them to The Skyway—one of the last drive-in movie theaters in the state. The drive-in opened in 1950 and is still going strong. Memories will stir when you order popcorn from the snack bar and tune in the old radio sound. Double features nightly Jun–Labor Day and weekends in May & Sep.

Thumb Park

AMUSEMENT PARK

Hwy 42, Fish Creek; 800-933-4002

Thumb Park is a combination water park and fairgrounds. Water slides, go-carts, bumper boats, mini golf, haunted mansion, fair food and fair rides. The kids will love it.

Explore the Parks

Door County seems graced with more than its fair share of parks, but who's complaining? Breathtaking scenery combined with all the outdoor activities nature has to offer is a-okay in just about everyone's book.

Combined, the **5 State Parks** encompass over 8,000 acres in Door County and have close to 100 miles of hiking trails, 20 miles of undeveloped shoreline and over 600 campsites. They are critical habitats for the threatened Dwarf Lake Iris and Dune Thistle. Each park features self-guided nature trails, nature centers with changing exhibits and naturalists and trained volunteers who conduct interpretive programs.

There are **18 Door County Parks** (18!) totaling 792 acres, 12 miles of groomed trails, 7 launching ramps, 4 swimming beaches, 14 restrooms and numerous picnic and playground facilities. You might ask who is responsible for taking care of all of this wonderfulness? That would be the energetic folks at the Door County Parks Department and you can thank them (or ask them any of your questions) by calling 920-746-9959; e-mail dcparks1@codoor.wi.us; 3538 Park Dr, Sturgeon Bay 54235; http://map.co.door.wi.us/parks.

Ahnapee State Trail Park

Access the trail at Forestville Dam County Park or at 1820 S Neenah Ave, Sturgeon Bay

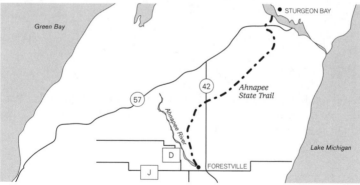

Open year-round, the Door County side of the Ahnapee State Trail consists of 12 miles of abandoned railroad grade for hiking, biking, snowmobiling and horseback riding. It features a picturesque bridge, stone quarry, woods, an orchard and a swamp. It's a light-use free trail, but donations are accepted. Restrooms are at Forestville, Maplewood and Sturgeon Bay.

NOTE: The trail also extends 18 miles south to Casco in Kewaunee County for a total of 30 miles.

Baileys Harbor Ridges Park

2301 Ridges Rd, Baileys Harbor

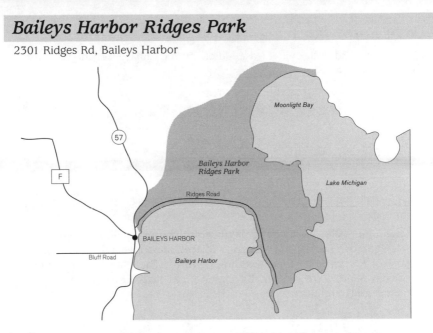

The county park has 30 acres of sand beach on Lake Michigan, two lighthouses, a habitat for endangered plants and animals, swimming, hiking and a picnic area. Adjacent to The Ridges Sanctuary (see the Adventures for Kids section in this chapter).

Robert M. Carmody Park

3570 Cty CC, Gardner

Robert M. Carmody Park opened in the fall of 2004. The beautiful park overlooks the waters of Green Bay and is already considered a fisherperson's paradise. Fishing pier, 6-lane boat launch and picnic area.

Cave Point Park

5360 Schauer Rd, Jacksonport (east end of Cty WD, adjacent to the Whitefish Dunes State Park)

Cave Point offer 19 acres of picturesque shoreline cliffs along Lake Michigan. It's no surprise why so many bridal couples take full advantage of the view for their wedding pictures. The park's underwater sea caves are a major draw for experienced scuba divers. Enjoy the hiking trails and picnic areas.

Chaudoir's Dock Park

1552 Cty N, Namur

The 5-acre Chaudoir's isn't much more than a place to launch your boat, but hey, it's a good one if that's what you're looking for. It has a protected harbor with stairs, a picnic area and handicap accessibility to the dock.

Door Bluff Headlands

12900 Door Bluff Rd

For those really into nature but not into crowds, this is your park. The undeveloped 155 acres has limited access except for a road to the interior. Natural hiking trails (bring the bug spray). Woods and cliffs overlook Green Bay.

Ellison Bluff County Park

12050 Ellison Bluff Rd (Hwy 42 to Porcupine Bay Rd, then west, follow signs)

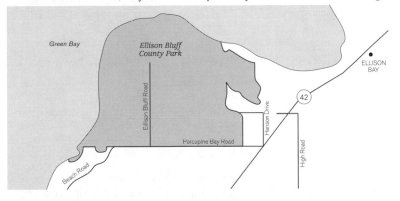

Half the pleasure of this 174-acre park is the spectacular winding drive through forest and fern glades to the waters of Green Bay. If you're into gorgeous sunsets, this little known park is probably one of the best places in Door County to watch the nightly event. The wood bench at the scenic overlook faces west across the bay. Pick up a nice bottle of wine from one of the many local wineries and toast the end of a perfect day. The park has hiking trails and a picnic area.

Forestville Dam County Park

475 Mill Rd, Forestville

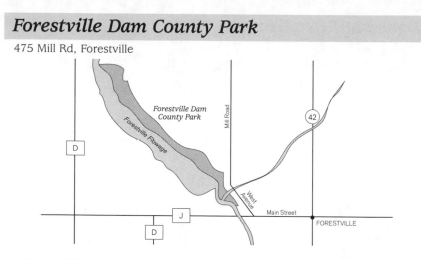

Forestville Dam County Park is roughly mid-point on the 30-mile Ahnapee River Trail. The 79-acre park has a millpond, pavilion rentals, dock, boat launch, playground, picnic area and restrooms.

Percy Johnson Memorial Park

640 Lake View Rd, Washington Island (take ferry from Gills Rock)

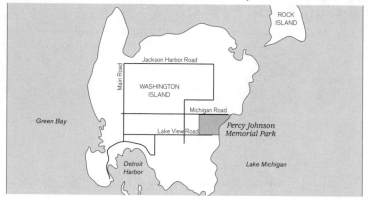

Percy Johnson Memorial Park has 5 acres of beautiful sand beach, perfect for swimming, sunbathing, picnicking and relaxing. For more attractions, see the Island Hopping section of this chapter.

Robert La Salle Park

408 Cty U, Clay Banks

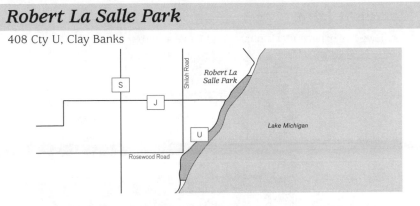

Explore the trails of the 3-tiered, 8-acre park—Lake Michigan shoreline, grassy upland and higher wooded upland. All three areas are separated by steep, sand bluffs accessed by stairs. A small stream cuts through a sandy ravine and a historical marker commemorates the 1679 landing of French explorer Robert de La Salle. Volleyball court, playground and picnic area.

Lily Bay Park

E4449 Cty T (northeast of Sturgeon Bay)

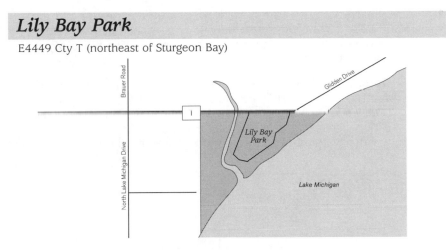

The 1-acre park is the smallest in the county system and used exclusively as a Lake Michigan fair weather boat launch. No facilities.

Meridian Park

6799 Hwy 57, between Jacksonport and Baileys Harbor

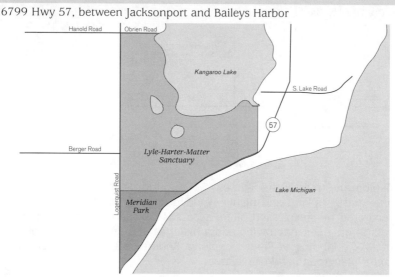

The 92-acre Meridian Park is halfway between the equator and the North Pole. It's also the second largest undeveloped park and adjacent to the Lyle-Harter-Matter Sanctuary. The wayside has a picnic area and restrooms.

Option: The **Lyle-Harter-Matter Sanctuary** is adjacent to and accessed from Meridian Park. The 40-acre rugged park ranges from woods to wetlands. No facilities and no road access, but the park is a great way to let the naturalist in you enjoy nature's beauty virtually undisturbed by the more conventional hiker.

John Miles Park

812 N 14th Ave, Sturgeon Bay

The 59-acre park hosts the annual County Fair in early Aug and stock car races on Sa nights, May–Sep. Soccer fields, picnic area and playground.

Frank E. Murphy Park

7119 Bay Shore Dr, Egg Harbor (Cty Hwy G)

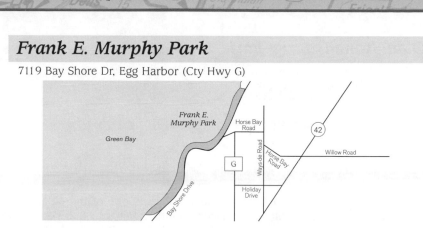

Only 14 acres, Frank E. Murphy Park is the most extensively used in the county park system. It has a nice sand beach and dock on Green Bay, a 2-lane boat launch, playground, volleyball court, picnic area, pavilion rental, swimming and changing rooms.

Newport State Park

475 Cty Rd NP, Ellison Bay 54210; 920-854-2500

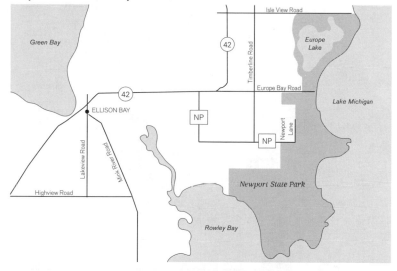

Newport is Wisconsin's only formally designated wilderness park. The trails are perfect for those who love challenging hikes. The 2,400-acre park has 11 miles of Lake Michigan shoreline (3 miles of which are beautiful sand beaches) 30 miles of hiking trails, 15 miles of mountain bike trails, 16 backpack campsites, fishing, 23 miles of cross-country skiing, 6½ miles of snowshoeing, winter camping, candlelight skiing and year-round interpretive programs. The park also has a gun hunt and late bow hunt season for deer.

Olde Stone Quarry Park

4879 Bay Shore Dr on Cty B 4½ miles north of Sturgeon Bay

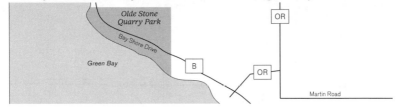

The impressive 9-acre Olde Stone Quarry Park is one of the oldest and largest limestone quarries in Door County. It takes 13,000 years to make 1" of limestone. Care to fathom a guess as to the age of the quarry? Well, take the depth times the width and er, uh—you do the math. It's old. The park is a favorite for fishermen. It has a boat launch, fishing pier and picnic area.

Peninsula State Park

9462 Shore Rd, Fish Creek 54212-0218; 920-868-3258

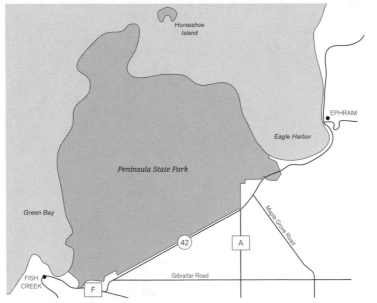

Established in 1909, Peninsula State Park is Wisconsin's most popular camping destination. The 3,776-acre park has it all—nature center, 75' lookout tower, 1868 Eagle Bluff Lighthouse, professional theater, an 18-hole scenic golf course, tennis court, old cemetery, fishing, excellent swimming, 20 miles of hiking, 19 miles of off-road biking, 18 miles of snowmobiling, 16 miles of cross-country skiing, 5 miles of snowshoeing, candlelight skiing, 469 family campsites (100 electric), handicapped-accessible cabin and winter camping. The golf course's No. 17 fairway serves as a sledding and tubing hill. In 2003, *Midwest Living Magazine* listed Nicolet Beach number seven out of 100 best beaches. It has concessions and bike rental; sailboat and other water craft rental available from a concessionaire near the beach. Horseshoe Island is also part of the park. Explore, hike and picnic on the island, but no fires or overnight camping allowed.

Potawatomi State Park

3740 Cty Hwy PD, Sturgeon Bay 54235; 920-746-2890

The 1,178-acre Potawatomi State Park has 2 miles of shoreline. Climb the 75' observation tower for a panoramic view stretching 16 miles across the bay that includes a spectacular view of the old limestone quarry. The park has a small, hands-on nature center where kids learn to make animal tracks in the sand. The camp store has concessions and canoe, kayak and bicycle rentals. No swimming, but excellent fishing. Trails include 9 miles of hiking, 8 miles of off-road biking, 8 miles of snowmobiling, 8½ miles of cross-country skiing, snowshoeing, candlelight skiing and adjacent downhill skiing. There are 123 family campsites (25 electric) and an accessible cabin. Winter camping is available.

NOTE: When the last of the glaciers melted 10,000 years ago, they left behind a radically altered landscape. Nowhere is the evidence of the ice age better preserved than across Wisconsin. The east end of the **Ice Age National Scenic Trail** begins at the observation tower in Potawatomi State Park. The 1,000-mile path follows the route of the Wisconsin Glacier from Sturgeon Bay south between Madison and Milwaukee, loops north to the Northern Highland-American Legion State Forest and continues west to Interstate Park near St. Croix Falls.

Rock Island State Park

Rte 1, Box 118A, Washington Island 54246; summer 920-847-2235; off-season 920-847-3156

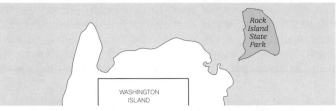

If you've ever wanted to own an island but didn't want to cough up the cash for one, this is your chance to at least feel like an island owner. Rock Island is 906 acres of beautiful, nearly secluded, rustic adventure. Foot traffic only, the park is Wisconsin's farthest northeast point and has 3 old cemeteries, ½ mile of beautiful sand shoreline, stone water tower, former fishing village site and Thordarson Estate with its massive stone Viking Hall. It also boasts the oldest lighthouse in Wisconsin (Potawatomi Lighthouse, 1836—contact the park ranger for info about special tours). Nature center, 1-mile self-guided nature trail, 9½ miles of hiking, 35 primitive family campsites, 5 backpack campsites, good fishing and swimming.

NOTE: Rock Island State Park is accessible via a 15-minute ferry ride from Jackson Harbor (free parking) on Washington Island. Daily schedule runs from end of May–mid-Oct. Admission. Rock Island Ferry 920-847-3322 or 920-535-0122.

Sugar Creek Park

2349 Cty N, Namur

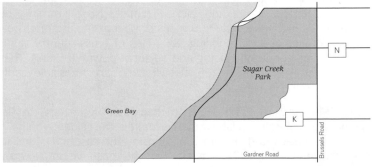

For those of you who love a challenge during a boat launch, check out Sugar Creek. More exposed than other coves, wind and strong currents are a large factor.

Tornado Memorial Park

8518 Hwy 57, 10 miles south of Sturgeon Bay

The 3-acre wayside has the added distinction of being the first Door County park. A historical marker tells of a former village nearby destroyed by an 1871 "tornado" of fire, killing 128 people. Picnic area and restrooms.

Whitefish Dunes State Park

3275 Clark Lake Rd (Cty Hwy WD), Sturgeon Bay 54235; 920-823-2400

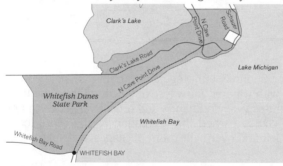

Whitefish Dunes has more visitors within its 847 acres than any other day-use park in Wisconsin, and it certainly is one of the most unique. The park is famous for numerous sand dunes such as Old Baldy, which rises 93' above Lake Michigan, but it's also one of the few places on earth where you can see the rare Dwarf Lake Iris and Dune Thistle. Both plants are on the government's "threatened" list. Whitefish Dunes was the site of two archeological digs that unearthed an ancient village. The village was reconstructed along one of the hiking trails. Stop by the nature center for a booklet about the digs and discoveries. While you're there, pick up the checklists for wildflowers, birds, wildlife and fungi. Year-round naturalist activities, 15 miles of hiking, 1½ miles of biking, 9 miles of cross-country skiing, snowshoeing and candlelight skiing. The awesome sand beach has wheelchair access via a boardwalk and grid system map.

CAUTION: Lake Michigan can produce severe rip currents, so heed the no-swim zones.

Golf Door County

Fore! This is a pre-warning. Door County golf courses are not only challenging, they're exquisitely beautiful as many overlook the mesmerizing waters of Lake Michigan and Green Bay. You're going to have all you can do to keep your eye on the ball.

Unless specified, all courses are open to the public daily, have a golf/pro shop, hand carts, power carts, club rental and require tee time reservations. Peak season is mid-Jun–Sep. There's a discount for weekday, off-season and twilight play. Most offer junior/student and senior rates.

Alpine Golf Course and Resort

7670 Co. Rd G, PO Box 200, Egg Harbor 54209; 877-318-8773 or 920-868-3232; www.alpineresort.com

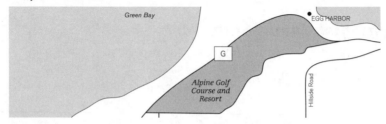

Alpine Golf is Door County's only regulation, public 27-hole course. It's mostly woods with watered fairways with a tram lift up the bluff. The bar & grill features weekend bands and orchestras. The 9th hole on the Blue Nine course earned the reputation as the most scenic hole in the state. Golf and overnight room packages available.

Bay Ridge Golf Course

1116 Little Sister Rd, Sister Bay 54234; 920-854-4085; www.bayridgegolf.com

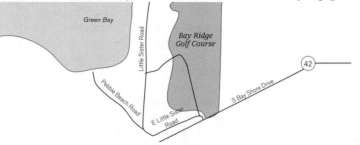

Bay Ridge is a 9-hole course with watered fairways and spectacular flower gardens. Clubhouse fare includes wine, beer, snacks and hot dogs. No reservations required.

Cherry Hills Golf Course and Resort

5905 Dunn Rd, Sturgeon Bay 54235; 800-545-2307 or 920-743-3240; www.cherryhillsgolf.com

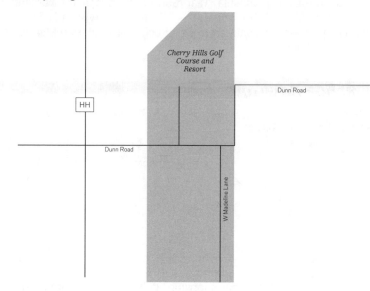

Cherry Hills is an 18-hole championship course with PGA pro lessons, clinics and schools. The gourmet restaurant is open daily from breakfast to dinner and is famous for its outstanding Sunday brunches. Cherry Hills offers room and golf packages along with golf and dining specials.

Deer Run Golf Course and Resort

Rt 1, Box 11D, Main and Michigan Rd, Washington Island 54246; 920-847-2017; e-mail deerrungolf4@hotmail.com

The 9-hole course is a 20-minute ferry ride across Lake Michigan to relaxing Washington Island. Deer Run features a pond, motel with golf packages and a restaurant. No tee times required. Free shuttle from Washington Island ferry dock to course. For those less serious

about their long game, check out the 18-hole mini golf course on the premises.

NOTE: Catch the **Washington Island Ferry** at Northport Pier located at the tip of the Door peninsula. Year-round daily departure. Passenger fee charged; 800-223-2094 or 920-847-2546; www.wisferry.com. The **Island Clipper** departs daily from Gills Rock, seasonal; 920-854-2972; www.islandclipper.com

Horseshoe Bay Golf Club

5335 Horseshoe Bay Rd, Egg Harbor 54209; 877-599-GOLF or 920-868-9141; www.horseshoebayfarms.net

The stunning 18-hole championship golf course, located on an impeccably manicured historic farm, went private as of the 2004 season. *Golf Digest* rated Horseshoe Bay the number three private club in Wisconsin.

Established in 1916 as a working farm, Frank E. Murphy and his nephew, Eldridge, had broader dreams and set out to create a world-class golf facility. Unsuccessful in the venture, the original clubhouse was torn down in 1975 and Horseshoe Bay turned to the dairy industry with its most notable cow ranking third largest milk producer in the world. The farm became the county's largest employer and the nation's largest fruit producer (apples, cherries and plums). In 1995 the Murphy descendants developed some of the farmland for home sites, then built the Horseshoe Bay Golf Club bringing alive Frank and Eldridge's dream. Today, just a small portion of the land is farmed and the only animals left are gorgeous riding horses. Gourmet restaurant, spacious and elegant club cottages and golf packages make Horseshoe Bay a popular resort destination. For more information, call 877-599-STAY.

IdleWild Golf Course

4146 Golf Valley Dr, Sturgeon Bay 54235; 920-743-3334; ww.idlewildgolfclub.com

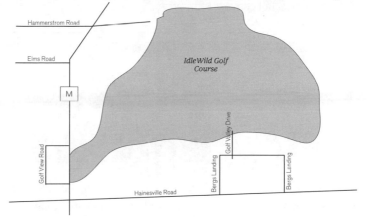

Rated 4 stars by *Golf Digest*, IdleWild features a lake-studded 18-hole championship course, an island green with a fishing hole, golf lessons and the Solarium Lounge & Grill.

Maxwelton Braes Golf Course

7670 Hwy 57, PO Box 399, Baileys Harbor 54202; 920-839-2321; www.maxwelton-braes.com

The 18-hole championship golf course comprises 200 acres of rolling hillsides reminiscent of Scottish braes. Maxwelton Braes has a USGA rating of 68.7, offers 5-day lessons with PGA pros, a heated pool, restaurant and hotel cottages.

The Orchards at Egg Harbor Golf Course

8125 Elm Rd, Egg Harbor 54209; 888-463-GOLF or 920-868-2483;
e-mail theorchards@itol.com

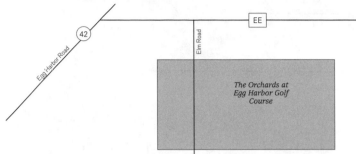

Get a real taste of Door County's stunning beauty at this challenging
18-hole course with its pristine lake, woods, orchards and grassy meadows. The bar & grill is open daily.

Peninsula State Park Golf Course

9775 Water St, Ephraim 54211 (PO Box 275, Fish Creek 54212); 920-854-5791;
www.peninsulagolf.org

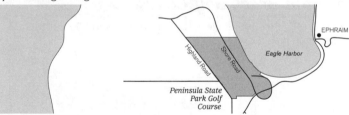

Folks can't wait to golf the Peninsula State Park Golf Course, and
that's no lie. Most mail in their preferred tee time and green fees to
the DNR by Feb. First opened in 1921, the course enjoys a renowned
fame for its spectacular views of Eagle Harbor and the quaint village
of Ephraim. Watered fairways, driving range, golf lessons; restaurant
serves breakfast as well as burgers and sandwiches. No phone reservations accepted prior to Mar 1. Include a self-addressed stamped
envelope when reserving by mail.

Stonehedge Golf Course and Driving Range

9320 Cty Rd E, Egg Harbor 54209; 920-868-2566

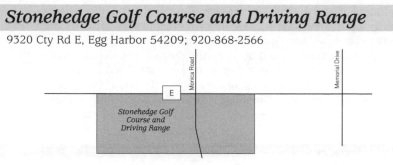

Established in 1993, the 9-hole, par-35 Stonehedge course has watered fairways, gorgeous scenery and a bar & grill. Open daily.

The Famous Door County Lighthouses

There's probably nothing more nostalgically romantic than the lighthouse. They and their keepers are sturdy beacons in a raging storm. A visit to a lighthouse is a glimpse of a bygone era that seems almost magical to the "wannabe" sailors in all of us. Wisconsin has more than 55 historic lighthouses and 12 of them are found in Door County. That's more than any other county in the nation! Special access to each lighthouse is offered the third weekend in May during the annual Door County Lighthouse Walk. An admission is charged for the self-guided tours, but other options include shuttle buses, trolley trips and lake cruises. Contact the Door County Maritime Museum & Lighthouse Preservation Society for more information on the lighthouses, including tours and hours of operation; 120 N Madison Ave, Sturgeon Bay 54235; 920-743-5958; www.dcmm.org. To view photos of the lighthouses, log onto www.lighthousefriends.com.

Baileys Harbor Range Lights

Ridges Rd, north side of Baileys Harbor

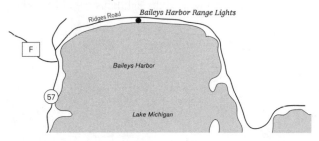

Built 1869; automated 1923; lights removed 1969. In 1867, Baileys Harbor was the only harbor refuge north of Milwaukee. Although a light existed on the east side, the numerous shoals at the harbor's entrance made it nearly impossible to navigate at night, so a pair of range lights were added. The front tower height was about 12' and the rear tower rose above the attached keeper's dwelling for a total of 21'. Progress marched on and by 1923 the range lights were converted to electricity. A few years later Immanuel Lutheran Church took over the keeper's dwelling as a parsonage until 1956. In 1965, the Coast Guard leased the dwelling to The Ridges Sanctuary. The lighting equipment is long gone, but the towers still stand. A boardwalk connects the two.

Boyer Bluff

West side of Washington Island, at the northern tip

While visiting Door County, you're going to hear a lot about their "10" lighthouses, but in actuality there are at least two more—Boyer Bluff is one of them. At 210' high, the pyramidal skeletal tower is the tallest light on the Great Lakes. Owned and operated by the Coast Guard, Boyer Bluff is still active, but not open for viewing.

Cana Island Lighthouse

Baileys Harbor; take Hwy 57 north to Q, then take Cana Island Rd (Rustic Road 38) to the causeway; park and walk to the lighthouse; 920-743-5958

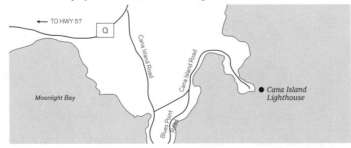

Built 1869; automated 1944. Cana Island is the county's most photographed lighthouse. When built, the 81' white tower with its

1½-story keeper's dwelling was the tallest brick structure in Door County. The light, now powered by electricity, is still used today. Call for hours. Admission charged.

Chambers Island Lighthouse

Chambers Island (7½ miles northwest of Fish Creek, 11½ miles northeast of Marinette)

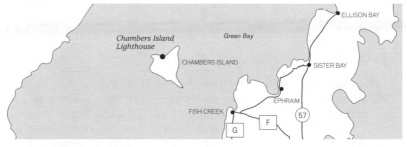

Built 1868; automated 1961. In May of 1867, the US government purchased a 40-acre peninsula on the northwest side of Chambers Island at the staggering cost of $250 for the purpose of building a lighthouse. The 67' tower and keeper's house was rumored to be haunted until the prayers of a visiting nun released the spirit from his earth bond. The lantern is gone and the lens is in a folk museum in Nebraska. Accessed by boat, tours are limited to when the caretakers are present. Admission is charged.

Dunlap Reef Lighthouse

400 S Fourth Ave, Sturgeon Bay

Built 1881; deactivated 1924; moved 1925. Dunlap Reef is another of those bonus lighthouses you won't find on official maps. Originally built north of Michigan Bridge, the light had a 2-story keeper's dwelling with a square frame tower on the roof. It's now a private residence relocated to Fourth Ave and is minus the tower.

Eagle Bluff Lighthouse

Peninsula State Park, Fish Creek; 920-743-5958

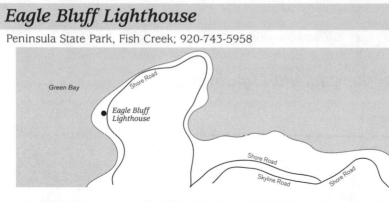

Built 1868; automated 1926. The Eagle Bluff light is the twin of the Chambers Island Light, except the towers were built differently so mariners could distinguish between the two. A popular tourist attraction, Eagle Bluff is 43' tall and constructed of cream-colored Milwaukee brick. The light is still in active use. On-site museum. Daily tours Jun–mid-Oct. Call for hours. Admission fee charged. Reserve ahead for large groups.

Old Baileys Harbor Lighthouse

Eastern side of Baileys Harbor on Lighthouse Island. Turn at the Sandpiper Restaurant on the corner of Hwy 57. Follow Ridges Rd past the yacht club to the point where the road takes a sharp left turn. At this turn you will see the lake ahead at the end of a gravel road. Take the road approximately 300'; the light-house is on the island to your right.

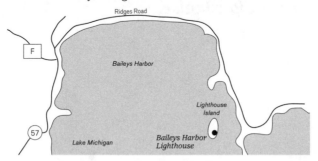

Built 1851; never automated—closed 1869. In 1848, Captain Justice Bailey found shelter from a fierce storm in a cove on the eastern side of Door County. The cove is now the town of Baileys Harbor and the first settlement in Door County. Interestingly, Baileys Harbor is still the only designated Harbor of Refuge on the lakeside of the peninsula. Captain Bailey and the shipping company owner persuaded the government to build a lighthouse at the harbor's entrance. The lighthouse has a 52' tower capped with a rare birdcage-style lantern room, but is in such bad condition that if something isn't done soon the entire structure will collapse. The lighthouse was added to the Doomsday List in 2001. It sits on private grounds with no public access.

Pilot Island Lighthouse

Pilot Island (northeast of Gills Rock; far eastern entrance)

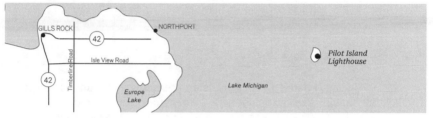

Built 1858; automated 1962. The original lighthouse was built on Plum Island in 1846, but moved to Pilot Island, where it was put to better use. Pilot Island was originally named Port des Morts (French for "Door of the Dead"). A combination of rough Lake Michigan waters and a dreary, fog-shrouded landscape made this lighthouse somewhat depressing for its keepers. A solar-powered lantern still guides mariners, but the grounds are overgrown and seagulls have pretty much taken over the island. The tower is 41' high and accessible by boat only.

Plum Island Range Lights

Plum Island (northeast of Gills Rock)

Built 1895; automated 1969. In 1895 Plum Island was the largest station in Door County, boasting a pair of range lights, a fog signal, keeper's dwelling, barn, boathouse and several piers. But by 1964 most of the station had been dismantled and the original wooden front range light tower was replaced with a steel skeletal tower still in use today. Accessed by boat, the foundation ruins of the 65' stone tower are visible near the rear range light.

Pottawatomie Lighthouse

Rock Island (the easternmost point in Wisconsin)

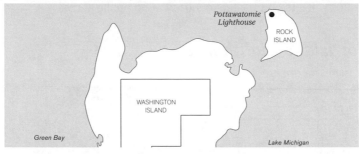

Built 1836; automated 1956. Rock Island features the county's oldest lighthouse with a tower height of 41'. After the completion of the Erie Canal in 1825, Great Lakes trade dramatically increased, making it necessary to build a lighthouse on Rock Island for safe passage to Green Bay. The first keeper, David E. Corbin, was a veteran of the War of 1812 and former member of the Fort Howard garrison who had worked for the American Fur Company—now that's a resumé! Corbin died at his post at the age of 57 and was buried in the small cemetery south of the light. The only way to get to the light is to charter a boat or take the ferry from Gills Rock to Washington Island, then hop another ferry to Rock Island. The lighthouse is a comfortable 2-mile hike from the landing point on Rock Island (Thordarson Viking Hall). Contact the park ranger for information about special tours.

Sherwood Point Lighthouse

Hwy 42 south from Sturgeon Bay, north on Idlewild Rd, which turns into County M. Continue north on County M about 7 miles and turn left on Sherwood Point Rd (gravel). This is an easy road to miss so look for a place on the corner called "Fishing Hole Bar." The lighthouse is at the end of the road.

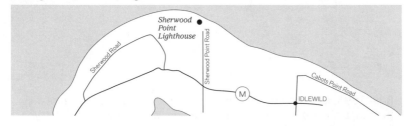

Built 1883; automated 1983. Sherwood Point Lighthouse is at the confluence of Green Bay and Sturgeon Bay and has a tower height of 37'. It carries the distinction of being the only Door County lighthouse built with red brick instead of the usual limestone or cream-colored brick.

Sherwood Point was also the last manned lighthouse on the Great Lakes and is still active. No tours except during the Door County Lighthouse Walk in May, because the Coast Guard uses the grounds as a vacation home for its personnel. However, you can drive to the lighthouse and get a picture, but stay behind the blockade.

Sturgeon Bay Canal Station

The station is located at the end of Canal Rd on the north side of the entrance to the Sturgeon Bay Ship Canal. (Drive north on Hwy 42/57 and turn east just past the Bay View Bridge onto Utah St. Turn right onto Cove Rd, then left on Canal Rd.) The Sturgeon Bay Canal Station North Pierhead (dwelling) is at the end of the breakwater on the north side of the canal entrance. Walk the pier from the Coast Guard Station at the foot of Utah St.

Built 1899; automated 1972. The first Sturgeon Bay lighthouse was built in 1881. It was a 29'-high open frame tower without a keeper's dwelling as funds had run out. The keeper, Rufus M. Wright, had to live on a dredge until the dwelling was completed five years later. In 1893, Congress authorized an additional light designed as a double-walled steel cylinder 8' in diameter and 78' high. The watch room on top of the tower was 12' in diameter and 7' high with an 18'-high cast iron lantern perched directly above. However, inadequate bracing caused severe wind vibration that affected light operation. The tower still swayed even after reinforcements were added. The problem was finally alleviated in 1903 by surrounding the tower with a steel skeletal frame as is seen today. The lights are still in operation and the grounds and pier are accessible. Tours are offered during the Door County Lighthouse Walk in May.

NOTE: To view the island lighthouses, book a charter cruise or rent a boat. Options include anything from sea kayaks to sailboats. See a list of boats in the Odds & Ends section of this chapter. For more information contact the Door County Chamber of Commerce.

Option: The **Door County Trolley, Inc.** has a tour of four lighthouses. The trip takes approximately 5 hours and includes lunch. The trolley leaves from Lautenbach's Orchard Country Winery on M, W & F, Jun–Sep. Fee charged; www.doorcountytrolley.com; 920-868-1100.

Museums

The museums of Door County range from posh and artsy to simple village streets. All provide a great opportunity for learning more about the county. The information centers have a useful handout listing historic buildings and sites with an abbreviated paragraph about each.

Door County Historical Museum

4th Ave and Michigan St, Sturgeon Bay 54235; 920-743-5809

The *Chicago Tribune* raves the Door County Historical Museum is "the best small museum in the Midwest." As with most museums, this one does a nice job bringing history alive through photographs, displays and videos, but it also has a really cool replica of an old-time firehouse with an 1869 horse-drawn water pumper and three other restored trucks. A very hands-on, kid-friendly place. Open daily May–Oct. Call for hours. Free admission.

> **Option** Buy homegrown produce and cut flowers at the **Farm Market** (across from museum) from end of Jun–Oct Sa mornings.

Door County Maritime Museum & Lighthouse Preservation Society

Two museums: 120 N Madison Ave, Sturgeon Bay; 920-743-5958; 12724 Wisconsin Bay Rd, Gills Rock; 920-854-1844; www.dcmm.org

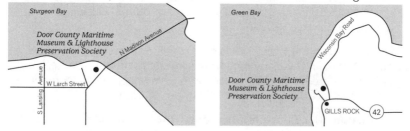

A group of commercial fisherman founded the Door County Maritime Museum in 1969 at Gills Rock. The museum is dedicated to the

preservation and public education of Door peninsula maritime life and features pictures of shipwrecks and stories of the fisherman who braved the stormy lakes. Explore the retired tug *Hope* and a replica of a net shed stuffed with fishing paraphernalia. Open daily. Call for hours. Admission charged.

What began in 1977 as a small museum in Sturgeon Bay is now a state-of-the-art 20,000-square-foot facility located along the waterfront at the foot of the downtown bridge. The museum's main focus is Sturgeon Bay shipbuilding, but other displays include lighthouse history, a working periscope and the entire pilothouse from a Great Lakes ore carrier. Open daily. Call for hours. Admission charged.

NOTE: The annual **Door County Lighthouse Walk** is the third weekend in May. The **Door County Classic & Wooden Boat Show** is the first weekend of Aug and held on the grounds of the Sturgeon Bay museum. Call for details.

Ephraim Moravian Church

9970 Moravia St, Ephraim; 920-854-2804

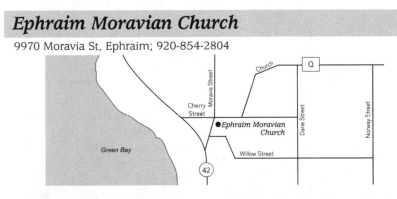

Built in 1857 out of cedar, the pretty little white church was the first in the county and is still in use today. Sunday services. Call for time.

Ephraim Walking Tour

3060 Anderson Ln, Ephraim; 920-854-9688; www.ephraim.org

The walking tour is four museums rolled into one history lesson. Once a general store, the 1858 **Anderson Store** is now a gift shop with old-fashioned candy and souvenirs. On display are some of the original store items as they were packaged, priced and sold over a century ago.

The **Anderson Barn** (ca. 1880) has an art collection, archives and an informative video documenting significant sites and happenings. The hands-on exhibits in the haymow is a big hit with kids.

Goodletson Cabin (ca. 1850), one of Door County's first log homes, is furnished to give a sense of what life was like for the early settlers.

The 1-room **Pioneer School** (ca. 1880) continued to hear the pitter-patter of little feet up until Dec 1948. Of special interest are the antique costumes on display. Open daily mid-Jun–Labor Day, weekends fall–Columbus Day. Call for hours. Admission charged; includes museums and walking tours.

NOTE: The guided walking tours begin at the Anderson Barn M, W, F & Sa. Call for time.

The Fairfield

Michigan St and Third Ave, Sturgeon Bay; 920-746-0001; www.fairfieldartmuseum.org

For a broad collection of contemporary art, head to Fairfield. You'll see black and white photos of Bob Dylan performing at Woodstock, political and humorous works of eighteenth-century British caricaturist James Gillray and a colorful display of paperweights. The permanent collection showcases Henry Moore's work. Open every day except Tu. Call for hours. Admission charged.

Historic Noble House

Hwy 42 and Main St, Fish Creek; 920-868-2091; www.doorcountycottage.com/noblehouse

The 1875 Noble House is Fish Creek's oldest existing building on the original site and contains most of the original furniture. The guided tour is an authentic look at what life was like for Fish Creek villagers more than a century ago. Open daily mid-Jun–mid-Oct, weekends mid-May–mid-Jun. Call for tour hours and evening Candlelight Tour schedule. Admission charged.

Miller Art Museum

107 S Fourth Ave, Door County Library, Sturgeon Bay; 920-746-0707

The gorgeous gallery features a permanent collection of works by Wisconsin artists from the 1900s to the present with a separate wing showcasing museum founder Gerhard Miller's paintings. Revolving exhibits, concerts, lectures, tours, gift shop and critiques of original works. Open M–Sa. Call for hours. Free admission. Handicapped-accessible.

Sister Bay's Corner of the Past

Hwy 57 at Country Ln and Fieldcrest Rd, Sister Bay; 920-854-7680

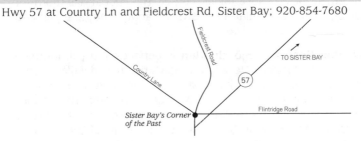

Sponsored by the Sister Bay Historical Society, five buildings were painstakingly moved to a common site to form a "yesteryear" village, with plans to add another three buildings. The most famous of the five is the **Old Anderson House** (1875). It was completely renovated right down to its period furnishings–a truly amazing feat when one compares the before and after photos. Changing events scheduled throughout the season include woodcarving, blacksmithing, an annual quilt show, gardening, etc. Call for a list of scheduled programs. Open weekends Jun–Sep. Call for hours. Free, but donations appreciated.

Romantic Door County

When the moon hits your eye like a big pizza pie, that's amoré—especially if you have your eyes on one of those dreamy Door County moons. Here are some more opportunities to romance the one you love.

The Bridal Church & Björklunden-Boynton Chapel

The Bridal Church, 901 Cherry St, Sturgeon Bay 54301; 920-432-8022; www.bridalchapel.com. Björklunden-Boynton Chapel, just 1 mile south of Baileys Harbor on Hwy 57; 920-839-2216; www.lawrence.edu/dept/bjork

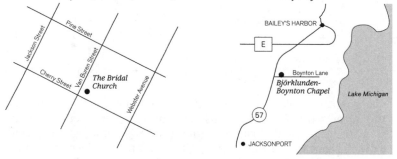

What could be more romantic than a wedding in Door County? Donna Streckenbach owns the charming 1888 country **Bridal Church** just outside Sturgeon Bay. She will help you design the wedding of your dreams. At the ceremony's conclusion, pull the bell as an announcement of your love for one other. The church has room for 100 guests, a decorated altar and pews, an antique pump organ and a non-denominational minister.

The **Boynton Chapel at Björklunden** is perfect for small, intimate gatherings. The historic Norwegian Stavkirke has detailed hand-carved woodwork and 41 hand-painted murals. It is part of a 425-acre estate on the shore of Lake Michigan. The property includes meadows, woods and more than a mile of waterfront. The 2-story lodge accommodates up to 54 guests. Guided tours of the property are given M & W mid-Jun–Aug. Call for hours. Admission charged.

Door County Trolley

EVENING UNDER THE STARS

Located at Lautenbach's Orchard Country Winery (½ mile south of Fish Creek on Hwy 42); 920-868-1100; www.doorcountytrolley.com

The romantic getaway is really a three-in-one package. It begins before sunset with an old-fashioned trolley ride to the Inn at Christopher's in Sister Bay. After an elegant, candlelit dinner, cuddle under the stars at an outdoor American Folklore Theatre Performance in Peninsula State Park. The trolley picks up passengers at M & Th

Jun–Oct at Lautenbach's Orchard Country Winery. Call for times. Fee charged. Make reservations in advance. See map page 73.

Ellison Bluff County Park

ELLISON BLUFF SUNSET WATCH

12050 Ellison Bluff Rd (Hwy 42 to Porcupine Bay Rd, then west, follow signs)
The overlook in Ellison Bluff County Park is the perfect romantic spot for watching the sun go down over the sparkling waters of Green Bay. Pick up a dessert wine from a local winery, grab a couple goblets and a blanket, then wrap up on a bench near the lookout to toast a dazzling sunset. The 174-acre county park has hiking trails, a picnic area and restrooms. See map page 43.

Mayberry's Carriage Rides

CLIP-CLOP CINDERELLA

Hwy 42, Ephraim's Olde Village Hall, Ephraim; 920-743-2352; www.mayberryscarriages.com

Green Bay

42

T

Plum Bottom Road

V

Mayberry's
Carriage Rides

You've had a wonderful day together cherry picking in the country, then relaxing on a sand beach. Dinner was great because you went to a **fish boil** and watched the boil master create the "boil over," but now what? You're with the one you love and there's no way you're going to waste that unbelievable sunset. **Mayberry's Carriage Rides** is the romantic answer to your dilemma. Standard tours of Ephraim and Egg Harbor are 10–30 minutes long. Evening rides begin in Ephraim. Call for times. Mayberry's offers winter sleigh rides Sa & Su at Lautenbach's Orchard Country Winery. The rides include wine and cider sampling.

NOTE: There are many different **fish boils** throughout Door County ranging in price from $13–$25. Some are on the beach, and some are all you can eat. The traditional boil includes whitefish steaks, baby red potatoes, sweet onions, coleslaw, lots of melted butter and lots of bones, so be careful. The dinner is always topped off with a slice of Door County's famous Cherry Pie. Try the **Old Post Office Restaurant** in Ephraim; 920-854-4034.

The Spa at Sacred Grounds

SWEDISH MASSAGE X 2

Hwy 42 and Townline Rd, PO Box 408, Ephraim 54211;
920-854-4733; www.sacredgroundsspa.com

As a couple, how would you like to experience 60 minutes of pure, scintillating pleasure? We're talking Swedish massage for two, but you knew that, right? The Spa at Sacred Grounds designed a room specifically for couples with twin tables and dual massage therapists. Groan and moan together as these experts ease the stress and fret from your body. The spa is open daily by appointment only. You must request "Couples Massage" when booking.

NOTE: The Spa offers many services including a Door County Cherry Hand and Foot Scrub to pamper and energize your hard-working extremities.

Sunset Concert Cruises

Departs from Gills Rock; 920-854-2986; www.concertcruises.com

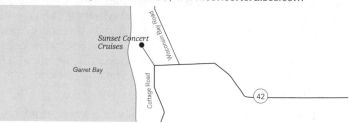

Board the *Island Clipper* at Gills Rock for a 3-hour tour of craggy shoreline bluffs and a spectacular sunset while enjoying a buffet supper of baked chicken and Swedish meatballs with all the trimmings. The Captain highlights many points of interest along the way, including lighthouses and nearby islands. Once the engines are cut, the band begins to play. And whether it's hot jazz, Dixieland, classical or folk, you're sure to pull your loved one close for a little cheek-to-cheek time. Intermission seems to come all too soon, but you won't mind because you'll be busy with a delicious Door County cherry crisp. Dress casual for lap-top dining. Iced tea, lemonade and coffee served or BYOB. Fee charged. Free parking at Gills Rock. Call for cruise departure times. Runs mid-June–Sep.

Wisconsin Water Wings   *UP, UP AND AWAY!*

PO Box 355, 9993 Hwy 42, Ephraim; 920-854-9000

Here's a thrill ride for you more adventurous couples. Go parasailing! See gorgeous Door County as few ever do—by water and air. It's easy and fun. You may have to take turns in the air, but absence makes the heart grow fonder. Toast your reunion with a nice bottle of champagne.

Theater

Door County has three professional summer theaters.

American Folklore Theatre

Located at Green Gables (north of Ephraim), PO Box 273, Fish Creek 54212; 920-854-6117

Performs under the stars at the Peninsula State Park Amphitheater mid-Jun–Aug, then hits the road for their Fall Town Hall series. It's original musical theater with a good deal of laughs and is appropriate for all ages; 920-854-6117; www.folkloretheatre.com

Door Shakespeare

PO Box 351, 8510 State Hwy 57, Baileys Harbor 54202; 920-839-1500

A zany, high-energy troupe that performs Shakespeare plays even the kids will like. Open Jul–Aug, W–M evenings. Hwy 57, south of Baileys Harbor (outdoors in the Björklunden Garden); 920-839-1500; www.doorshakespeare.com

Peninsula Players

W4351 Peninsula Players Rd, Fish Creek 54212; 920-868-3287

Performs the latest Broadway plays and musicals and have been crowd pleasers for 70 years. Get there early and walk the gorgeous gardens and trails. All-weather pavilion. Tu–Su evenings late Jun–mid-Oct. Reservations advised. Off Hwy 42 on Peninsula Players Rd south of Fish Creek; 920-868-3287; www.peninsulaplayers.com

Wineries

The Door County wineries seem barely a stone's throw from one another—in fact, one is named Stone's Throw Winery—but all are as different and delicious as the wines they produce.

Door Peninsula Winery

5806 Hwy 42, Sturgeon Bay 54235 (8 miles north of Sturgeon Bay); 800-551-5049 or 920-743-7431; www.dcwine.com

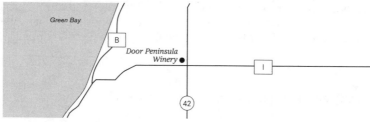

The 1868 historic schoolhouse-turned-winery is still in the business of educating—about wines, that is. Door Peninsula is the largest winery in Wisconsin. They specialize in fruit wines such as cherry, apple, cranberry and raspberry. A free guided tour explains wine fermentation and the aging process. Wine tasting in the Sunroom and the large gift shop is open daily. Call for hours. The winery's elegant **Vineyard Restaurant & Wine Bar** offers more than 140 different wines with appetizers and gourmet entrees. Reservations recommended; 920-743-9463.

> **Option:** For those folks along for the ride but not into wine, there's also a **Brew Pub & Restaurant** on the premises that is open daily throughout the summer. Call for hours. Their specialty is BBQ Memphis- and St. Louis-style ribs.

Lautenbach's Orchard Country Winery

9197 Hwy 42, Fish Creek 54212; 920-868-3479; www.wiswine.com or
www.doorcountyvacations.com

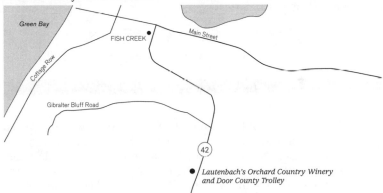

Lautenbach's Orchard Country Winery
and Door County Trolley

Lautenbach's started out as a dairy farm and fruit orchard. Owner Bob
Lautenbach's grandmother used to sell fruit from a wagon out by the
road—with an old cigar box serving as her cash register. The thriving
fruit business expanded in 1980 and now includes a winery in the renovated barn and 100 acres of Montmorency tart cherries. Recent
studies show that antioxidant compounds found in Montmorency tart
cherries have pain relieving properties. "I have many customers who
buy the cherry juice because they say it's great for their gout and
arthritis," says Bob Lautenbach. In addition to the more traditional
grape wines, Orchard Country has a wide variety of fruit vintages such
as Cherry Blossom, Swedish Lingonberry and Honey Crisp Apple. They
have free wine tasting, an observations window, family activities (such
as the Cherry Pit Spit!) and horse-drawn sleigh rides. The gift store sells
everything from fresh cherries and cherry juice to cherry salsa and
cherry mustard. Open daily year-round.

Option: For a 45-minute narrated history tour of the countryside
take a ride on the **Door County Trolley, Inc.** The tour includes
Millionaires Row (see how the "locals" live!) and an informative,
scenic ride through Peninsula State Park. Daily Jun–Oct. Admission
charged. Also offered is a 5-hour lighthouse tour M, W & F,
Jun–Sep, lunch is included in the fee. Catch the trolley at
Lautenbach's Orchard Country Winery; 920-868-1100; www.door-
countytrolley.com

Simon Creek Vineyard & Winery

5896 Bochek Rd, Sturgeon Bay 54235; (Hwy 42 north from Sturgeon Bay to Carlsville, turn east on Cty I, then north on Bochek Rd); 920-746-9307; www.simoncreekvineyard.com

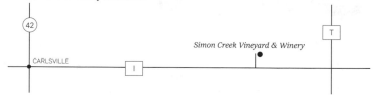

Located at the center of Door County, this wonderful winery opened in 2003 and is already an award winner! At 30 acres, it's the largest vineyard in Wisconsin. Free guided tours review the whole wine-making process from harvest through casing. The tour ends at the taste room overlooking the wine production area (free tastings of up to 4 varieties). If you'd like to enjoy a leisurely glass of wine, check out the lounge area with its cozy leather furniture and fireplace or the outdoor terrace overlooking the picturesque pond and vineyards. Open daily throughout the summer. Limited winter hours.

> **Option:** Watch the candlemaking process or dip your own at **Candleworks of Door County**. Open daily. Hwy 42, Carlsville; 920-746-2125; www.candleworks.com

Stone's Throw Winery

3382 Cty Rd E, Egg Harbor 54202; 877-706-3577 or 920-839-9660; www.stonesthrowwinery.com

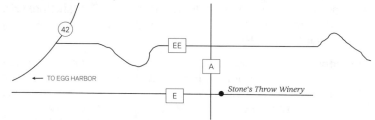

Stone's Throw Winery claims it's a mere 2,500 miles northeast of Napa Valley. You'll find them in a beautifully restored 80-year-old stone barn. Featured on The Food Network, Stone's Throw has wonderful, award-winning vintages to be sure, but their chocolate sauces made from their own wines absolutely make this winery a must on everyone's sightseeing list. Complimentary wine tasting with the purchase of a logo wine glass. Open daily during the summer, limited winter hours; picnic grounds, bocce ball. Call for hours.

Island Hopping: Washington Island

The passage between Washington Island and the peninsula is referred to as "Death's Door." In 1872, as many as 100 ships sank in these turbulent straights. Washington Island extends approximately 4½x5 miles, claims around 700 permanent residents and is the smallest school district in Wisconsin (125 pupils). However, if you're thinking about moving there you'd better be one tough hombre because it's the most wave-battered, wind-torn land in the whole of Door County. It's also one of the most laid-back vacation destinations, advertising as "North of the Tension Line."

Washington Island is easily accessible by a 20-minute ferry ride departing daily from Gills Rock (**Island Clipper** www.islandclipper.com; 920-854-2972; seasonal) or from Northport (**Washington Island Ferry Line** www.wisferry.com; 800-223-2094 or 920-847-2546; year-round). The island has 75 miles of scenic bike trails and more than two dozen places to stay including motels, cottages, resorts, B&Bs and camping. For more information, contact the **Washington Island Chamber of Commerce**; PO Box 222, Washington Island 54246; 920-847-2179; www.washingtonislandchamber.com

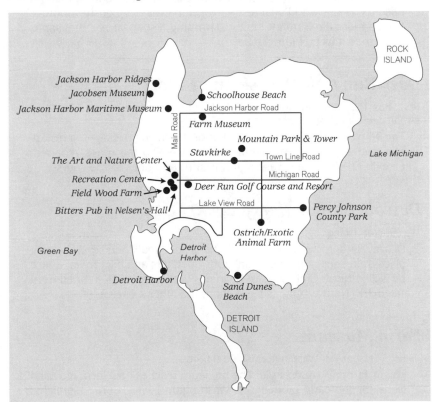

The Art and Nature Center

Main Rd, Washington Island 54246; 920-847-2025

Located in a 1904 schoolhouse, The Art and Nature Center showcases the works of local artists. The nature room has an observation beehive and naturalist-led hikes and classes. Take in one of the summer concerts. Open daily. Admission charged.

Bitters Pub in Nelsen's Hall

Main Rd, Washington Island 54246

The oldest continuously operating tavern in the nation, the pub was established in 1899 by Danish tavern owner Tom Nelsen. A firm believer in the medicinal power of bitters, Nelsen usually mixed a dash or two into every cocktail. A savvy business owner, Nelsen survived Prohibition by getting his pharmacist's license and dispensing his favorite "stomach tonic" to anyone who requested it. The custom survived and the pub is recorded in the Guinness Book of World Records as the world's largest single purveyor of Angostura bitters. You can join the Bitters Club by slamming a shot—it has thousands of members worldwide.

Deer Run Golf Course and Resort

Rt 1, Box 11D, Main and Michigan Rd, Washington Island 54246; 920-847-2017; e-mail deerrungolf4@hotmail.com

The 9-hole course features a pond, motel with golf packages, a restaurant and an 18-hole miniature golf course. No tee times required. Free shuttle from the Washington Island ferry dock to the course.

Detroit Harbor (ferry dock)

Washington Island

Detroit Harbor is your first look at the island. You'll find several eating places, gift shops, moped rental, tour operators and bike rental. Close by is Den Norsk Grenda—two buildings with grass roofs shipped from Telemark, Norway. One is a gift shop, the other a bookstore.

Farm Museum

Jackson Harbor Rd, Washington Island 54246

This is farming 1880s-style. The museum teaches how farm life used to be for the early pioneers of Washington Island. Some highlights include the old double log barn, blacksmith shop, farm animals, pioneer log home, sawmill, antique implements and ice cream-making.

They have weekly activities for the kids. Open mid-Jun–mid-Oct. Pack a picnic lunch and stay for the day. The museum is free, but donations are appreciated.

Field Wood Farm

W Harbor Rd, Washington Island 54246; 920-847-2490

Let's do something the kids want to do. How about horseback riding? Field Wood Farm conducts trail rides atop rare registered Icelandic horses. The horses are very gentle. Field Wood offers lessons, horse-drawn wagon rides and pony rides by appointment. Open May–mid-Oct.

Jackson Harbor Maritime Museum

Jackson Harbor Rd, Washington Island 54246; 920-847-2522

Jackson Harbor is known as "the last authentic, unadulterated fishing village on Lake Michigan." The whole village seems locked in a time warp where it's still possible to buy whitefish fresh off the boat. Housed in two former fishing shacks, the Jackson Harbor Maritime Museum takes a historical look at the local fishing industry. Besides artifacts, photographs and a video, you'll find the remains of a ship-wreck and the legendary Coast Guard vessel nicknamed *The Bull* for its remarkable feats as a tug and icebreaker. Open weekends Memorial Day–Jul 1, daily Jul 1–Labor Day, then weekends until Columbus Day. Admission charged. Call for hours.

Jackson Harbor Ridges

In Jackson Harbor Park, behind the Jackson Harbor Maritime Museum

The 100-acre nature reserve is a fragile mix of shore meadow, dune and boreal forest. While hiking the short trail keep an eye out for the rare Dune Thistle, Dwarf Lake Iris and arctic primrose.

Jacobsen Museum

End of Little Lake Rd, Washington Island 54246; 920-847-2213

Danish immigrant Jens Jacobsen decided to do things a little differently when he settled on the south shore of Little Lake. He built all of his buildings using vertical logs. Jens was an avid collector of artifacts, documents and assorted relics relating to island history. He built a museum to showcase his finds and several guest cottages so people wouldn't need to rush through the tour. Jens died in 1952, but his museum is the same cluttered, dusty, fascinating place he envisioned. Jens's log home is also open and restored to its original appearance. Open Memorial Day–mid-Oct. Call for hours. Admission charged.

Mountain Park & Tower

Mountain Rd in the center of Washington Island

Climb 184 steps up the 200' observation tower for a commanding view sure to take your breath away. The unique perspective of Washington Island, Rock and St. Martin Islands and Escanaba, MI, is well worth the heart attack.

Ostrich/Exotic Animal Farm

Michigan Rd, Washington Island 54246; 920-847-3202

See the world's largest egg. The farm offers narrated walking tours, a petting zoo and exotic animals such as Patagonian cavies. Open daily. Call for hours. Admission charged.

Percy Johnson County Park

640 Lake View Rd, Washington Island 54246

The 5 acres of beautiful sand beach is a paradise for sun worshipers. Swimming, picnic area and restroom.

Recreation Center

Main Rd, Washington Island 54246; 920-847-2226

Spend some time at the Recreation Center. It has a 32x60' indoor pool, whirlpool, exercise room, locker rooms, meeting/game room and two outdoor tennis courts. Daily passes and vacation passes.

Sand Dunes Beach

Southeast of Detroit Harbor along South Shore Dr, Washington Island

The beach is a crescent of gorgeous, fine white sand and perfect for soaking up some summer sun. Grills and picnic spots.

Schoolhouse Beach

Washington Harbor, on the northern coast

Did you know there are only five all-white limestone beaches in the world? Yep. And Schoolhouse Beach is one of them. Feel free to inspect these smooth white stones, but don't take them. They're preserved by law.

Stavkirke

Town Line Rd across from Trinity Lutheran Church, Washington Island

Stavkirke is a replica of the Norwegian stave church built by island residents. Its "stavs" or masts of vertically placed timbers recall old Viking ships as do the dragon heads at the peaks of its gabled roofs. Open daily.

Option: Take a peek at the **Trinity Lutheran Church** (across the street). Built in 1930, it was destroyed by fire then rebuilt at the same location in 1950. A ship model hangs from the ceiling as is customary in some Scandinavian churches.

Island Hopping: Rock Island

Rock Island is Wisconsin's most isolated state park and the easternmost point. It is unpopulated and accessible via the **Karfi Ferry** that departs daily from Jackson Harbor on Washington Island; 920-847-2252. Rock Island is for foot traffic only and, yes—that means *no bikes*.

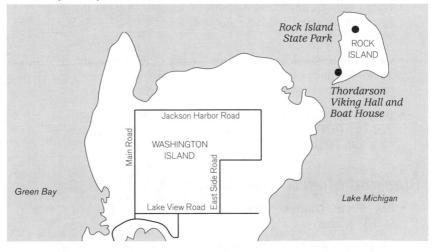

Rock Island State Park

Rt 1, Box 118A, Washington Island 54246-9728 (northcentral Rock Island); summer 920-847-2235; off-season 920-847-3156

Rock Island is 906 acres of breathtaking beauty with 10 miles of hiking trails and the state's oldest lighthouse. Built in 1836, the Pottawatomie tower is 41' tall. The lighthouse is a comfortable 2-mile hike from the landing point on Rock Island (Thordarson Viking Hall). The park has 35 primitive family campsites (all with awesome views!), 5 backpack campsites, fishing, sand swimming beach and a dock that allows private mooring for a fee.

Thordarson Viking Hall and Boathouse

Rock Island State Park, Rt 1, Box 118A, Washington Island, 54246-9728; 920-847-2235; fax 920-847-3105

Milwaukee inventor Chester H. Thordarson bought Rock Island in 1910 and for 55 years used it as his own private retreat. The limestone used for the massive Viking Hall and boathouse was cut by Icelandic artisans. The James Bondish-looking hall holds up to 120 people and has mullioned windows, hand-carved furniture and runic inscriptions.

Door County Odds & Ends

There are many things to see and do in Door County—fishing, horseback riding—all manner of ways to get from Point A to Point B and more. For more information call the **Door County Chamber of Commerce** at 800-52-RELAX.

Airplane Rides and Rental

- **Door County Cherryland Airport**, 3538 Park Dr (next to Potawatomi State Park), Sturgeon Bay 54235; 920-746-7131; www.codoor.wi.us

- **Orion Flight Services, Inc.**, Door County Cherryland Airport; 920-743-6952; daily flights on a first-come, first-served basis. Reservations recommended.

- **Door County Aviation, LLC.**, Door County Cherryland Airport; 920-743-7550; www.doorcountyaviation.com (aircraft maintenance and repair)

Bike and Moped

- **Bay Shore Outdoor Store**, 655 S Bay Shore Dr, Sister Bay; 920-854-7598

- **Boathouse**, Maple St, Fish Creek; 920-868-3745

- **D.C. Bikes**, 20 N 3rd Ave, Sturgeon Bay; 877-DC-BIKES or 920-743-4434 (also Potawatomi State Park Camp Store, open mid-May–Oct; 920-746-8663); www.dcbikes.com

- **Edge of Park Bike & Moped Rental**, PO Box 188 (main entrance to Peninsula State Park), Fish Creek; 920-868-3344; www.edgeofpark.com

- **Harbor Bike Rental**, Island Ferry Dock, Washington Island

- **Island Clipper Bike Rentals**, 12731 Hwy 42, Gills Rock; 920-854-2972

- **Latitude 45**, 20 N Third Ave, Sturgeon Bay; 920-743-4434

- **Nicolet Beach Rentals**, Peninsula State Park; 920-854-9220

- **Nor-Door Sport & Cyclery**, 4007 Hwy 42 (just north of main entrance to Peninsula State Park), Fish Creek; 920-868-2275; www.nordoorsports.com (cross-country skis, snowshoes, tubes)

- **Wagon Trail Marina**, 1041 Cty ZZ, Ellison Bay; 888-250-7666 or 920-854-2385; www.wagontrail.com (boat rental and charter fishing available)

Boat Charters and Rentals

- **Bay Shore Outdoor Store**, 655 Bay Shore Dr, Hwy 42, Sister Bay; 920-854-7598 (daily guided kayak tours, lessons, customized trips)

- **Bella Cruises**, Ephraim; 920-854-2628

- **Boat Door County**, Sturgeon Bay; 800-231-5767 or 920-743-2337; www.boatdoorcounty.com (three locations)

- **Door County Cruises**, Sturgeon Bay; 920-825-1112 or 920-495-6454; e-mail cruises@doorpi.net (retired Chicago Fireboat)

- **Ephraim Sailing Center**, South Shore Pier, Hwy 42, Ephraim; 920-854-4336; www.kayakdoorcounty.com (guided kayak tours)

- **Friendly Sailing Charters**, PO Box 874, Fish Creek; 920-868-3201; www.doorcountyvacations.com

- **Wisconsin Water Wings**, PO Box 355, 9993 Hwy 42, Ephraim; 920-854-9000 (parasail rides)

- **Captain Gerry Schwaller**, Fish Creek; 920-868-2949; e-mail gtschwaller@yahoo.com (antique/classic wooden boat)

- **Sail Door County**, Egg Harbor; 920-495-7245; e-mail pnelson@saildoorcounty.com

- **The Shoreline Charters**, 12747 Hwy 42, Gills Rock; 920-854-2606; www.theshorelineresort.com (specializing in lighthouse tours, scuba dive charter available)

- **Shorewood Beach Motel**, 3662 N Duluth, Sturgeon Bay 54235; 800-388-8055 or 920-743-3191; www.boatdoorcounty.com

- **Stiletto Catamaran Cruise**, South Shore Pier, 9993 Water St, Ephraim; 920-854-7245; www.stilettosailingcruises.com (cruise to Chambers Island)

- **Sunset Concert Cruises**, 10055 State Hwy 57, Sister Bay 54234; 920-854-2986; http://concertcruises.com; e-mail mail@concertcruises.com (buffet)

- **Wagon Trail Marina**, 1041 Cty ZZ, Ellison Bay; 888-250-7666 or 920-854-2385; www.wagontrail.com (bike rental)

Car Rental

- **Avis**, Door County Cherryland Airport; 800-331-1212 or 920-743-9250

Carriage Rides

- **Carriages of Door County**, Stone Harbor on 1st Ave and 3rd and Michigan St, Sturgeon Bay; 920-743-4343 (free/children ages 12 and under)

- **Mayberry's Carriage Rides**, Hwy 42, Ephraim's Old Village Hall; 920-743-2352; www.mayberryscarriages.com (sleigh rides)

Ferry

- **Island Clipper & Yankee Clipper**, 12731 Hwy 42, Gills Rock 54210; 920-854-2972; www.islandclipper.com

- **Washington Island Ferry Line**, PO Box 39, Washington Island 54246; 800-223-2094 or 920-847-2546; www.wisferry.com; e-mail wisferry@itol.com

- **Karfi Ferry**, Jackson Harbor, on Washington Island; 920-847-2252

Fishing—(24-Hour DC Fishing Hotline 920-743-7046)

- **Bousley's Sport Fishing Charters**, 150 W Larch St, Sturgeon Bay; 920-746-4560 or cell 920-495-4560; www.bousleyfishing.com

- **Elite Fishing Charters**, Quarter Deck Marina; 320-679-5995 or cell 218-390-4522; www.elitefishingcharters.com

- **First Choice Charter Fishing**, Baileys Harbor Town Marina; 920-839-1409; www.fishingdoorcounty.com

- **Fox 1 Charters**, 435 N Geneva Ave, Sturgeon Bay; 920-743-3092; www.fox1charters.com

- **Gary's Guide Service**, 711 Hickory St, Sturgeon Bay; 920-743-1100; www.doorcountyoutdoors.com

- **J-E Fishing Enterprises**, 1229 Georgia St, Sturgeon Bay; 920-743-7877; www.jefishing.com

- **Lynn's Charter Fishing**, Baileys Harbor; 920-854-5109

- **The Mariner**, 12747 Hwy 42, Gills Rock 54210; 920-854-2606 (shoreline resort)

- **May's Guide Service**, Sturgeon Bay; 920-856-6743 or cell 920-559-0069

- **Capt. Paul's Charter Fishing**, PO Box 254, Gills Rock 54210; 920-854-4614

- **Pharmasea Sport Fishing Charters**, 4105 Sand Bay Point Rd, Sturgeon Bay; 920-746-5257 or cell 920-493-7733; www.pharmaseacharters.com

- **Reel Action Sportfishing Charters**, 1802 Morning View Rd, Brussels 54204; 920-360-2136; www.reelactioncharters.com

- **Reel Addiction Charters**, Wagon Trail Resort & Marina, Rowleys Bay; 888-873-REEL; www.reeladdictioncharters.com

- **Refuge Fishing Charter**, 520 E Vine Ct, Sturgeon Bay; 920-746-9442; www.refugecharters.com

- **Salmon Depot Charter Fishing**, Baileys Harbor Yacht Club Resort; 800-345-6701 or 920-839-2272; www.salmondepot.com

- **Silver Strike Charter Fishing**, Baileys Harbor Marina; 920-839-2808

- **Stone Wing Charter Fishing**, PO Box 37, Ellison Bay; 920-854-4718

- **Wacky Walleye Guide Service**, Sand Bay Beach Resort, Sturgeon Bay; 920-743-5731; www.sandbaybeachresort.com

Horseback Riding

- **Ahnapee Ranch**, 6875 Tagge Rd, Sturgeon Bay 54235; 920-743-2715

- **Carole's Corral**, Hwy 57 S, Sister Bay; 920-854-2525

- **Herb's Horses**, Hemlock Hills Farm, 6926 Division Rd, Egg Harbor; 920-868-3304

- **Kurtz Corral**, Cty I, Egg Harbor; 800-444-0469 or 920-743-6742; www.kurtzcorral.com

- **Field Wood Farm**, W Harbor Rd, Washington Island 54246; 920-847-2490 (open late May–mid-Oct)

Kennel

- **Door County Kennels, Inc.**, 4860 Court Rd, Egg Harbor 54209; 920-868-3804; www.dckennels.biz

Motorcoach & Shuttle

- **Lamers**, Corporate Office, 2407 S Point Rd, Green Bay 54313; 800-236-1240

- **Door County Green Bay Shuttle**, 7412 Elms Rd, Sturgeon Bay 54235; 920-746-0500

Taxi

- **Service Taxi Cab Company**, Sturgeon Bay; 920-743-3443

Train Tours

- **Cherry Train**, RR1 Box 205, Washington Island 54246; 920-847-2039; e-mail cherrytraintours@itol.com

- **Viking Train**, 12731 Hwy 42, Gills Rock 54210; 920-854-2972; www.islandclipper.com

NOTE: Both tours are for Washington Island; not actually trains, but vehicles pulling carts. Arrangements are usually made through the ferry lines.

Trolley

- **Door County Trolley, Inc.**, 1113 Cove Rd, Sturgeon Bay 54235; 920-868-1100; www.doorcountytrolley.com

Wisconsin isn't all farmland. A lot of the terrain is rough, rugged and untamed—thanks, in part, to what the glaciers didn't do. These wild and beautiful landscapes present ample opportunities for some extreme adventures. This chapter is for you daredevils who need more bang for the buck than a garden tour provides. These trips are guaranteed to elevate the adrenaline and keep it pumping.

Extreme Adventures

Great Lakes Sport Fishing

If it's trophy fish you're after, there's no place like Algoma for Great Lakes sport fishing. Lake Trout, Coho Salmon, Chinook (King Salmon), Steelhead (Rainbow Trout), Brown Trout—they're all here in record weight and numbers, and so are the charter fleet. The port of Algoma has the largest and most experienced charter fleet on the lakeshore. Many of the captains have been featured in magazines and on TV. There are tons of fishing packages available; most include plush waterfront condos with fireplaces. The crew takes care of everything including the gear, license, refreshments and the handling of your catch. You need to bring a cooler, camera with plenty of film, soft-soled shoes and clothes for the weather because the boats leave rain or shine. The cost depends on the time of year and the number of people in your party, but it usually averages about $270–$370/person for two 8-hour charters and two nights lodging. Mid-Apr–mid-Jun offers nearly 100 percent success on limit catches with trophy-sized Lake Trout in May. Jun 1–mid-Oct is excellent for all types and sizes, but the target is Chinook and Steelhead with expected weights in the 10–30 pound range. For a full list of charters call the Algoma Area Chamber; 920-487-2041; www.algoma.org

- **Fishin' Magician Charters**; 920-660-2887; www.fishinmagiciancharters.com

- **Haasch Guide Service**; 888-966-FISH; www.fishalgoma.com

- **Howard Kinn's Sport Fishing Enterprises**; 800-446-8605; www.kinnskatch.com

- **Jimmie D Charters**; 715-572-FISH; www.jimmiedcharters.com

- **RV Charters**; 800-487-0022 or 920-487-5158; www.rvcharters.com

- **Sandpiper Sport Fishing**; 920-304-2200 or 715-384-9398; www.sandpiperfishing.com

- **Trik Sea II Charters**; 920-465-8727; www.trikseacharters.com

Shoreline Charters

12747 Hwy 42, Gills Rock; 920-854-2606; www.theshorelineresort.com

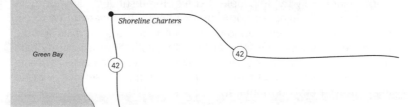

If you like poking around underwater in dark, creepy (haunted?) places, then you'll so love the coastal waters surrounding the Door of the Dead, or Door County as it's now known. To your morbid delight, you'll find more than 200 steamers, schooners and bulk carriers to dive on. Most date back to the mid-1800s. The cold water preserves the shipwrecks, so viewing is excellent. Call Shoreline Charters for a lift to the wrecks. If you'd like more information about individual shipwrecks, log onto www.maritimetrails.org

NOTE: Need scuba lessons or dive gear? There are nearly two dozen scuba businesses in the state that can hook you up. A couple are close to Door County in Green Bay; **Aqua Center**, 628 Bellevue St; 920-468-8080; **Green Bay Scuba**, 1901 Velp Ave; 920-498-8499; www.gbscuba.com

Sky Knights

East Troy Airport (30 miles from Milwaukee); 800-ET-CHUTE or 414-642-9494; www.skydiveskyknights.com

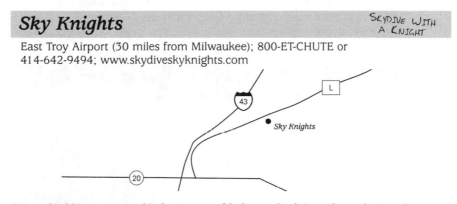

"I watched him strap on his harness and helmet, climb into the cockpit and, minutes later, a black dot falls off the wing 2,000' above our field. At almost the same instant, a white streak behind him flowered out into the delicate wavering muslin of a parachute—a few gossamer yards grasping onto air and suspending below them, with invisible threads, a human life, and man who by stitches, cloth and cord, had made himself a god of the sky for those immortal moments."

- Charles A. Lindbergh

Charles Lindbergh, America's most famous pilots, made his first jump a few days after watching someone else. And like most people, Lindbergh wrestled within to name that strong desire he felt to jump from a plane. So why do people skydive? Interestingly, many jumpers have a fear of heights or some other phobia they want to conquer. Once mastered, a new confidence is born enabling them to handle other life situations. The folks at Sky Knights believe a jump "clears the head and sharpens the senses." Whatever your reason, skydiving is a full-body screaming rush and there's nothing else in the world like it. Have fun, you maniacs!

Established in 1965, Sky Knights is open year-round (weather permitting) noon–sunset, weekends 8am–sunset. To jump you must be at least 18 years old with a photo ID to prove it and weigh less than 230 pounds. Reservations for classes are required; call at least 1 week in advance. Wear comfortable tennis shoes and plan to spend the entire day; there's lodging and dining nearby. Freefall videos with still shots available for a fee. There are three jump options available to first-timers (call for prices):

• **Tandem**—freefall and parachute ride strapped to an instructor;

• **Static Line**—parachute opened by a line attached to the plane;

• **Accelerated Freefall**—freefall while held by two instructors, but you deploy your own parachute.

NOTE: Jump rates are less during the week. There are about 10 other skydive operators in Wisconsin. Check them out on the Web or call the tourism department.

Trek & Trail

KAYAK THE APOSTLE ISLANDS

7 Washington Ave, Bayfield 54814; 800-354-8735; www.Trek-Trail.com

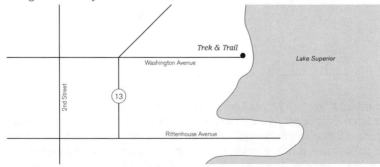

If you want an up-close and personal view of the Apostle Islands, the best way (and certainly the most adventurous) is by sea kayak. Trek & Trail has all kinds of options for exploring the islands. Sea kayak

rentals are for a half day or for three days with a price per day thereafter. Don't know how to kayak? Trek & Trail is a great place to learn. Their instructional courses run from beginners' basics to International BCU Coach II certification. Guided trips vary in length from overnighters to weekly campouts. Paddle along sea caves, hike wooded trails and abandoned quarries, explore lighthouses and historic villages. Call for prices.

NOTE: Trek & Trail rents **mountain bikes** (includes helmet) at an hourly or daily rate, **cabins** rented at a nightly rate and offers **dog sledding** trips.

Whitewater Rafting the Peshtigo

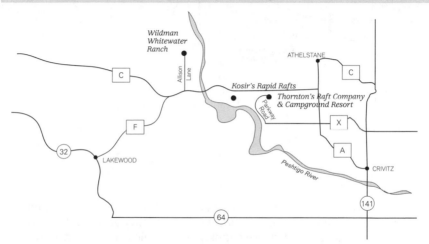

The Peshtigo River in Marinette County is the wildest, most exciting whitewater rafting in the state. Depending on the time of year, water flows range from 300 to 3,000 cubic feet per second, turning Class II rapids into Class V. To ride the roaring spring swells, book your trip for early Apr. First-time rafters looking for a milder ride should find the river plenty challenging all summer long. Trip prices vary—the earlier in the season, the more expensive the ride. Most outfitters include instructions and equipment, but ask to make sure. If you've never kayaked before but would like to try it, rent a Fan-Yak. These inflatable kayaks are much more stable and don't require experience. Spring and fall runs get pretty nippy, so wear layers and bring along a change of clothing. Oh, yeah—you will get wet.

- **Kosir's Rapid Rafts**; W14073 Hwy C, Athelstane 54104; 715-757-3431; www.kosirs.com (camping, cabins, bar, restaurant)

- **Thornton's Raft Co & Campground Resort**; W12882 Parkway Rd,

Athelstane 54104; 715-757-3311; www.thorntonsresort.com (camping, cabins, bar with music on weekends)

- **Wildman Whitewater Ranch**; N12080 Allison Ln, Athelstane 54104; 715-757-2938; www.wildmanranch.com (camping, cabins, ATV, biking, ropes course)

Wolfsong Adventures in Mushing   MUSH!

HC 64 Box 107, Bayfield 54814; 800-262-4176 or 715-779-5561; www.wolfsongadventures.com

John and Mary Thiel are the owners and guides of Wolfsong dog sledding trips. Their mushing crew includes some thirty gorgeous Siberian Huskies. The leader dogs have thousands of miles of experience over every kind of terrain. And whether you want to learn to drive a team or simply sit back and ride along, Wolfsong designs their trips to fulfill your adventure needs. Packages include equipment and meals. Stay warm by layering clothing. The Thiels recommend long underwear, snow pants, sweater and a parka or shell, hats, scarves, warm boots such as Sorels (hiking boots are not warm enough), knit gloves to handle the dogs, and larger mitts for the trail. Wolfsong Wear makes winter clothing that's available for sale or loan. The trips range from a day out learning to harness and drive the dogs (over $200/person) to three days of mushing and camping (over $800/person).

NOTE: Through the summer months the Thiels offer **Dreamcatcher Sailing Charters** from the City Dock. They'll teach you to sail and they have half- and full-day cruises or overnight packages.

Time spent with your children is priceless, but there are days when an offer of two cents for the little darlings would seem like buyer ripoff. When traveling with kids, it's especially important to find things they like to do. The trips in this chapter are easy-going and fun—even for the adults!

Family Day

A B&B for Kids

Green Bay Getaway

Madison Getaway

Play Day

Pothole Heaven

Visit a Real Farm

A B&B for Kids

Justin Trails Bed & Breakfast Resort

452 Kathryn Ave, Sparta 54656; 800-488-4521; 608-269-4522;
www.justintrails.com

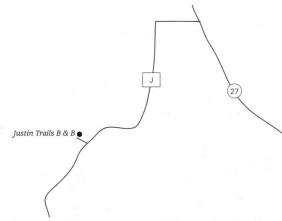

Justin Trails has it all—18-basket disc golf, the nearby Sparta-Elroy bike trail, 3 acres of gardens, a pond, stunning views and over 200 country acres on which the kids and dog can run wild. (Yes, they take pets and, yes, we do love them to death for it.) They can hook you up with just about anything your family desires—horseback riding, canoeing, kayaking, Amish tours, bird watching, massage (ahh, massage) and shopping. And as wonderful as all the summer activities sound, a winter trip is twice the fun. They have 10 miles of on-site Nordic skiing (short skis—lessons provided), two hills for snowtubing, skijoring (pulled on skis by a harnessed dog), dog sledding and snowshoe trails with equipment rentals. Hearty homemade breakfasts come with the deal. They have a restaurant license and will prepare meals if you desire. The cabins are equipped with fireplaces, 2-person whirlpools, plush robes and queen or king beds. Call for rates. Extra charge for pets.

NOTE: Justin Trails is open to the public, so if you don't want to stay the night (but why wouldn't you?) there is a minimal charge for the activities.

Green Bay Getaway

A Day in Packerland

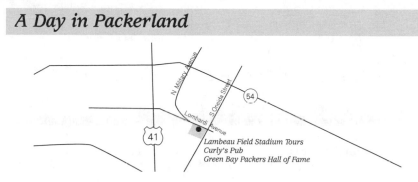

Green Bay Packers Hall of Fame, Lambeau Field Atrium, 1265 Lombardi Ave; 920-569-7512; www.packers.com

Founded in 1919, the Green Bay Packers have the longest standing team name in NFL history. They are the last remaining publicly owned pro sports team. Learn all about the Pack in the 25,000-square-foot Packers Hall of Fame. Movies and interactive videos take you through 80-plus years of team history and all the play-by-play highlights. On display are lockers of the 20 Packer Pro Football Hallers, the 3 Super Bowl trophies and rings, a recreation of Vince Lombardi's office (legendary coach and Packer god) and a life-size recreation of the Ice Bowl with famed quarterback Bart Starr. The kids' area is fabulous. They can do a Lambeau Leap into the stands, kick field goals, toss footballs or wear Brett Favre's shoes. Open daily. Admission charged. **NOTE:** Hall of Fame open to ticket holders only on home game days.

Lambeau Field Stadium Tours, Lambeau Field Atrium, 1265 Lombardi Ave; tour hotline 920-569-7513; www.packers.com

According to *Sports Illustrated Magazine*, Lambeau Field is the eighth best venue in the world to watch sports. Millions of Packer Fans would argue it's the number one place to watch football—the only true sport. Regardless of how you feel about football or the Packers, Lambeau Field is something to see. Newly renovated to accommodate 72,515 cheeseheads (every seat counts), the Packers have the most NFL titles (12) and the most fans. There are more than 63,500 names on the waiting list for season tickets—an incredible 30-year wait! The 1-hour tour treks through the team tunnel, private box and club seats, the Legends Club and onto the field to check out the new turf. Daily tours begin at Harlan Plaza at the statues of Curly Lambeau and Vince Lombardi. Admission charged. Call for hours. **NOTE:** No tours during home games.

Curly's Pub, Lambeau Field Atrium, 1265 Lombardi Ave; 920-965-6970

Curly's Pub overflows with Packer memorabilia and history. The servers talk nothing but PackerSpeak, regaling enthusiastic fans with all sorts of stories and facts from games of yesteryear. Curly's has 50 interactive games to play while you wait for your Super Bowl-sized food portions, so come linebacker hungry. There's also a kids' menu. The dining room is open to the public daily, but ticket holders only on home game days until after the game is over.

> **Option: The Packers' Experience** is your chance to run the team's actual obstacle course, snap, punt, kick, pass—essentially do everything the Pack does to gear up for another grueling season. Held during the training camp in late summer (Jul/Aug) at 1901 S Oneida St; 920-497-5664 or call the **Packer Country Regional Tourism Office** for dates and times; 888-867-3342 or 920-494-9507; www.packercountry.com

Bay Beach Amusement Park

1313 Bay Beach Rd, Green Bay; 920-448-3365; www.greenbay.com

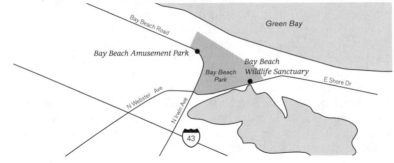

Kids of all ages love amusement parks, but it seems most rides are rather pricey these days. Without heading to the bank for a second mortgage, here's your chance to feel like Daddy Warbucks. The rides at Bay Beach cost as little as a dime per time. Concession stands and a picnic area add to the festivities. Open daily Memorial Day–Aug, weekends only May & Sep. Free admission. Call for hours.

Bay Beach Wildlife Sanctuary

1660 E Shore Dr, Green Bay (near Bay Beach Amusement Park); 920-391-3671; www.baybeachwildlife.com

Native Wisconsin animals live comfortably within the 700-acre refuge, including the ever popular timber wolves. Seven miles of nature trails pull double duty as cross-country ski trails. Nature center touts native plant and animal history. Open year-round. Call for hours. No fee. See map above.

Heritage Hill State Park

2640 S Webster Ave, Green Bay; 800-721-5150 or 920-448-5150; www.heritagehillgb.org

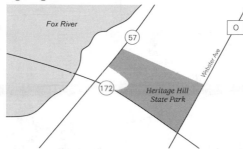

The 50-acre state park contains more than 25 historic buildings dating from 1672. Horse-drawn wagons haul you around four thematic areas—Pioneer, Military Life, Small Towns and Agricultural. Costumed guides demonstrate how people lived and worked and encourage participation. Wash clothes with lye soap on a washboard, learn to march like a soldier or help stir up a batch of cookies. Open Memorial Day–Labor Day, W–Su. Call for hours. Picnic area. Admission charged.

NOTE: Guided tours are M & Tu only.

National Railroad Museum

2285 S Broadway, Green Bay 54304; 920-437-7623; www.nationalrrmuseum.org

At nearly 133' long with a weight of 600 tons, the Union Pacific Big Boy is the world's largest steam locomotive. Sit in the Big Boy's cab, then inspect all 70-plus locomotives and railcars at the National Railroad Museum. The sheer size of the iron beasts is impressive, if not somewhat intimidating, but so is the view from the top of the 85' observation tower. Watch the video on railroad history, then hop onboard for a 1-mile ride on a narrow-gauge railroad. Open daily. Train rides May–Oct at scheduled times. Admission charged.

NEW Zoo

4378 Reforestation Rd (Cty IR), Green Bay; 920-434-7841

The zoo is divided into three animal areas—Prairie Grassland, Wisconsin native and International, as well as a children's area with interactive exhibits. They have animals from around the world—the newest residents are the Snow Leopards. Open year-round. Call for hours. Admission charged.

> **Option: Mountain Bay** is the state's longest multi-use railbed trail. At a whopping 89 miles long, it extends from Green Bay to Wausau. It's open to hiking, biking, horseback riding, cross-country skiing and snowmobiling; 305 E Walnut, Green Bay; 920-448-4466; www.mountain-baytrail.org

Madison Getaway

Geology Museum

Weeks Hall, 1215 W Dayton St, Madison; 608-262-2399; (for a group tour call 608-262-1412) www.geology.wisc.edu/ ~ museum/

Wisconsin's state mineral is lead sulfide (PbS), the state fossil is trilobite (a ribbed tubular glob related to lobsters) and the state rock is red granite. See all these cool things plus horn coral, dolomite, dinosaurs, a limestone cave, an ancient giant beaver, a 10,000-year-old mastodon skeleton and tons more. The museum is open for self-guided tours M–Sa. Call for hours. Free admission.

Henry Vilas Park Zoological Society

606 S Randall Ave, Madison; 608-258-9490; www.vilaszoo.org

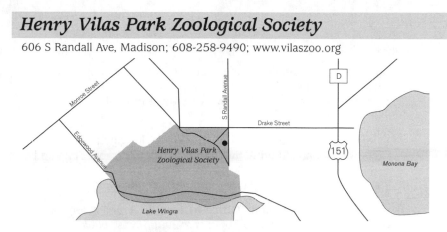

Do you want to see some animals? Great, because the Henry Vilas Zoo has around 700 of them! Penguins, primates, BIG cats, camels, giraffes, tarantulas, Tropical Rain Forest Aviary—well, you get the picture. But Henry Vilas has lots of other things, too. For instance, do you like bugs and crawly things? Then you're going to love the Discovery Center and Herpetarium. There are tons of hands-on activities such as looking at a snakeskin under a microscope or watching honeybees form a hive. The Children's Zoo is really a cool place. Animals such as miniature horses and prairie dogs are more kid-sized. Feed goats or say hello to a porcupine—but don't get too close! Picnic sites, concessions and gift shop. Open daily year-round. Children's Zoo is open Memorial Day–Labor Day. Admission is free.

Madison Children's Museum

100 State St, Madison; 608-256-6445; www.madisonchildrensmuseum.com

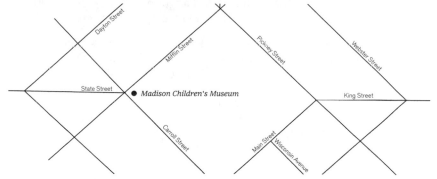

Geared for children from birth to age 12, the brightly colored Madison Children's Museum is educational and fun. Hands-on exhibits give tots the chance to work a crane, milk a cow and plant vegetables. Perennial

favorites are the music cave and shadow room. The museum is open year-round Tu–Su, open M Jun–Aug. Call for hours. Admission charged, free/everyone the first Su of every month.

Options: State Street is a picturesque stroll filled with great shopping and restaurants. Jugglers and street musicians give impromptu performances nearly every night throughout the summer months.

Several nights a week **Memorial Union** at 800 Langdon St (overlooks Lake Mendota) hosts **live bands on the Terrace**. Brats and hamburgers with a cold beer or pop are the usual fare. The building also houses a movie theater and games room.

Visit the **Outdoor Rentals Office** in Memorial Union for canoe and kayak rentals; 608-265-3000; www.union.wisc.edu/

For **glow-in-the-dark bowling**, head to **Union South** on 227 N Randall Ave; 608-263-2600.

The **Elvehjem Museum of Art** has three floors of galleries containing more than 17,000 works dating from 2300 B.C. They also have **Sunday afternoon concerts** Oct–May; 800 University Ave; 608-263-2246. Open Tu–Su. Call for hours. Free admission.

Madison has over **200 miles of bike trails**. For bike rental, call **Budget Bicycle Center**, 1230 Regent St; 608-251-8413.

The **Mad-City Ski Team** (water skiing) performs summer Su evenings on Lake Monona starting Memorial Day weekend. Watch from Law Park near the Monona Terrace Convention and Community Center.

For **UW-Madison campus** information and tours, contact the CIVC; Historic Red Gym, 716 Langdon St; 608-263-2400; www.civc.wisc.edu/; e-mail askbucky@redgym.wisc.edu

For more information about Madison, call the **Greater Madison Convention and Visitors Bureau**; 615 E Washington Ave, Madison; 800-373-6376 or 608-255-2537; www.visitmadison.com

Wisconsin State Capitol Tour

A CAPITOL IDEA

Capitol Square, 2 E Main St, Madison (downtown); 608-266-0382;
www.wisconsin.gov/state/core/wisconsin state capitol tour.html

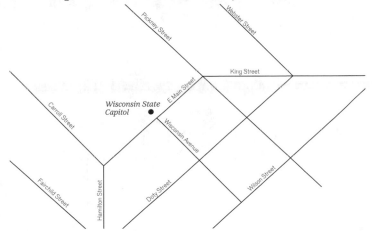

Madison has a population of around 200,000 and has been the state capital since 1848. And a magnificent capitol it is! Built from 1906-17 at a cost of $7.25 million, the building towers more than 200' high, with the statue Wisconsin (a gilded bronzed woman) atop its domed pinnacle. The Madison Capitol is the only state capitol built on an isthmus and boasts the only granite dome in the country. The building rivals the federal capitol in beauty and grandeur. The massive interiors contains 40 different kinds of stone from around the globe including a rare marble. It has hand-carved furniture, exquisite glass mosaics, murals and stenciling. Daily tours year-round. Call for times. The sixth floor museum and observation deck are open during summer months. Free admission.

Camden Playground

Palmer Park off Hwy 11, Janesville; 608-755-3030

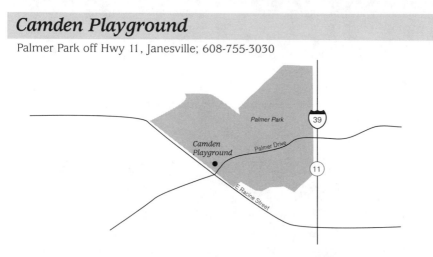

Located within Palmer Park, Camden is the world's biggest handi-capped-accessible playground. The size of a football field, Camden's main attraction is the gigantic castle with a life-size alligator and sea turtle swimming in the moat. Children's performers take the stage at noon during the summer months. In addition to Camden Playground, Palmer Park has a wading pool, sand court volleyball, tennis courts and softball fields.

> **Option:** Visit **"Miracle," a white female buffalo** born on the Heider farm in 1994. She's a true rarity, and many Native Americans consider the buffalo sacred. Fulfilling a prophecy told to the Heiders, the calf turned black, red and yellow before turning back to white, representing the four colors of man. The Heider farm is at 2739 S River Rd (take I-90 to Avalon Rd, Exit 177, drive west 4 miles to the Rock River, then turn right and go ¼ mile; parking is north of the farm); 608-741-9632. Admission is free, but call ahead for visiting hours. For your own safety, stay behind the electric fence and absolutely do not touch the animals.

Pothole Heaven

Interstate State Park

Hwy 35, St. Croix Falls 54024; 715-483-3747

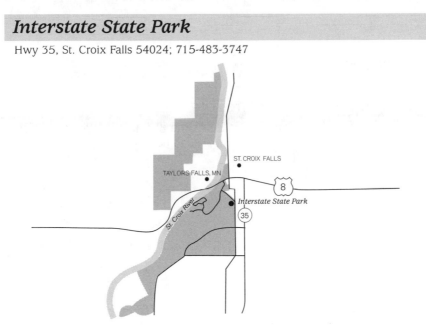

Interstate is Wisconsin's oldest state park and something of a twin; a second Interstate Park is directly across the river in Minnesota. The 1,300-acre park contains basalt rock over a billion years old. As the glaciers melted, torrents of water mixed with silt and spun perfectly round craters (potholes) into the basalt. The craggy cliffs looks like some giant drill went berserk and created pothole Swiss cheese. Some of the potholes are 26' in width, making them the largest in the world. When you're not looking down, look up and around. The gorge is spectacular. The 200' palisades are a major draw with rock climbers, but Bald Eagles are just as plentiful. Interstate has about 12 miles of hiking and cross-country ski trails. The nature center offers naturalist programs throughout the summer. Interstate is at the end of the Ice Age National Scenic Trail in Wisconsin. Camp, canoe, fish, swim—enjoy this park!

Option: Take the kids on an **authentic paddleboat cruise** on the St. Croix River. The narrated tours are informative without getting too windy. The guide points out different rock formations along the way, which is always interesting...but sometimes you have to squint just right to see what they see. **Scenic Boat Tours on the St. Croix River** (at the bridge in Taylors Falls, MN) is open May–mid-Oct. There are a couple different trip choices—the 3-mile (30 minute); the 7-mile (1½ hours). The 2-hour picnic cruise departs W evenings Jun–Aug. Call for prices and departure times; 800-447-4958 or 651-465-6315; www.wildmountain.com

NOTE: See the Romantic Getaways chapter (Osceola trip) for more options.

Visit a Real Farm

Hinchley's Dairy Farm Tour

2844 Hwy 73, Cambridge (west of Cambridge; from Madison take Hwy 12/18 east to Hwy 73 S, first farm on the east side of the road); 608-764-5090; www.hinchleydairyfarmtours.com

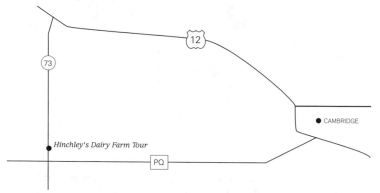

The kids will love exploring and learning about modern rural life at Hinchley's. The family-owned farm has 200 registered Holstein cows and operates about 1,800 acres of cropland. Although not a huge setup by today's standards, Hinchley's is an accurate portrayal of a mid-size Wisconsin farm (minus the tours and haunts). Take an antique tractor hayride out to the fields and watch huge machinery during spring planting and fall harvesting. The educational farm tour lasts anywhere from 1–3 hours and takes in the entire dairy setup from the cows and their four stomachs to the bulk tank in the milk house (ask for a drink of fresh raw milk!). There is lots to do here. Feed the goats and sheep, gather eggs from squawking hens, milk a cow or simply pet the kittens. If you're visiting during the fall season, you're in for a special treat. Hinchley's has a 6-acre corn maze turned scavenger hunt with all kinds of cool corn and farm facts. The maze costs extra, but includes a hayride and pumpkin. Two other farm attractions are the Haunted Hayride conducted in the dark on F and Sa nights in Oct (children under age 3 ride for free if on an adult's lap). Choose a pumpkin from thousands with weight ranges from 6 ounces to over 200 pounds. The Haunted Barn is a ghoulishly good time, but not for those faint of heart. The haunt is rated PG-13 and children under age 8 must be accompanied by an adult. Hinchley's Farm is open Apr–Nov harvest. Call for prices and times of farm tour. No tours during milking. Most attractions are separate from the tour and cost extra.

Nothing soothes the soul like a day spent puttering in a garden. Dirty fingers and aching backs result in peaceful minds and a good night's sleep. No wonder so many folks list gardening as a favorite hobby. This chapter features some of the state's most spectacular gardens. For you ambitious types, this is a great opportunity to glean interesting ideas for your own gardens.

✿ Garden Tours

Eastern Gardens

Madison Area Gardens

Western/Central Gardens

Eastern Gardens

Green Bay Botanical Garden

2600 Larsen Rd, Green Bay (take Exit 168 off Hwy 41 to Mason St, go west on Mason to Packerland Dr, turn north on Packerland to Larsen Rd, turn left); 920-490-9457; www.gbbg.org

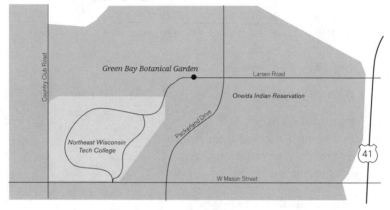

The focus of the 47-acre Green Bay Botanical Garden is on the four seasons. Fourteen display gardens, winding brooks and natural areas highlight and compliment the grandeur of each season. When all other gardens are long put to bed for the winter, Green Bay Botanical sets up an incredible holiday display featuring 150,000 lights designed in the shapes of flowers. Holiday display weekends Thanksgiving––Christmas. The Visitors' Center has a garden shop, library and children's library. Children's garden has a super cool tree house. Educational programs year-round. Call for hours. Admission charged.

John Michael Kohler Arts Center

608 New York Ave, Sheboygan (take Exit 126 off I-443 onto Hwy 23 E, which becomes Kohler Memorial Dr, then Erie Ave; continue east to Sixth St, turn right; follow Sixth St 4 blocks south to New York Ave); 920-458-6144; www.jmkac.org

The nine surrounding gardens support the Arts Center's design and vision. Every plant, tree, flower, grass and shrub has a sole purpose—

to visually enhance and integrate outdoor art with the remarkable Arts Center's visual and performing works of art within. The sensory result is nothing short of spectacular. Open daily. Call for hours. Free.

Options: The Kohler Company got its start in 1873 by producing cast iron and steel implements for farmers. Ten years later they created their first bathtub by applying a baked enamel coating to a horse trough. But if you're thinking Kohler only does bathrooms, think again. In addition to plumbing and bathroom/kitchen fixtures, the company of today produces quality furniture, engines and generators, cabinetry and tile. Their championship golf course is perhaps the best in the state. Kohler does everything well. A definite must-see is their fascinating 2½–hour **factory tour**. The tour is free and runs M–F. Call for time. Children must be at least 14 years of age, and a 24-hour advance reservation is required. **Kohler Design Center**, Highland Dr and Upper Rd; 920-457-3699; www.kohlerco.com. Open daily. Free admission. Oh, and about their bathrooms—they've been judged among the best in the nation. • **The American Club** on Highland Dr, Kohler; 920-457-8000 is the Midwest's only AAA rated Five Diamond resort hotel. Seven restaurants, two 18-hole Pete Dye-designed golf courses, water spa, health and racquet club, shopping and more.

Kemper Center & Anderson Arts Center

121 66th St, Kenosha (along the lakeside); 262-657-6005

The 18-acre grounds are a part of a gorgeous county park with an arboretum that showcases hundreds of roses and a herb garden designed for the blind. The **Kemper Center** is a Gothic Revival and Italianate antebellum hall that was once a school for girls run by nuns, now reportedly haunted. The **Anderson Arts Center** is a 9,000-square-foot mansion showcasing local and national artists with an area strictly devoted to students attending regional schools. Open Tu & Th–Su. Call for hours. Roam the gardens free dawn–dusk.

Memorial Park Arboretum & Gardens

1313 E Witzke Blvd, Appleton (from Hwy 41 on Appleton's north side, take Exit 144 to Ballard Rd, go south on Ballard to the park entrance); 920-993-1900; www.the-arb.org

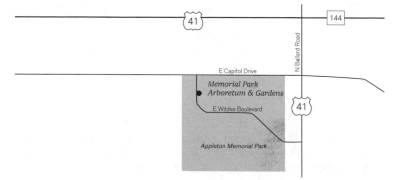

The 33-acre Arboretum is in a continual process of recreating the forests, prairies and wetlands native to the state. The goal is to represent all of the plants common to Wisconsin so future generations can study and enjoy these ecosystems. If you're debating about what shrubs and trees to plant in your yard, the Arboretum is a great place to check out the different types hardy to the climate. Make sure you check out the Learning Center as well. Frank Lloyd Wright's Taliesin architect group designed it. Open year-round. Admission is free.

Paine Art Center & Gardens

1410 Algoma Blvd, Oshkosh (take Exit 119 off Hwy 41 to Hwy 21, go east on Hwy 21 to Algoma Blvd, turn left on Algoma); 920-235-6903; www.paineartcenter.com/gardens

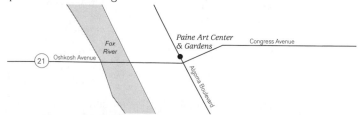

Regarded as one of "America's Castles," the Paine Art Center houses a world-class collection of American landscape paintings, period furnishings and oriental rugs. A tour of the 1920 Tudor Revival mansion is worth the admission price, but a walk through the 19 surrounding gardens cinches the deal. The rose garden features over 100 varieties. Open year-round Tu–Su. Admission charged. Call for hours.

Option: The **Oshkosh Public Museum** is right across the street from the Paine Art Center & Gardens. Built in 1908 for a local lumber baron, the mansion turned museum has elegant Tiffany stained glass windows and rich woodwork. Some of the permanent holdings include historical paintings and photographs, Native American Art and an Apostles Clock—an important piece of folk art (with music box and moving figurines) that dates to the late 1800s. The museum is at 1331 Algoma Blvd; 920-424-4731; www.publicmuseum.oshkosh.net. Open Tu–Su. Call for hours. Multimedia exhibits. Free admission.

West of the Lake Gardens

915 Memorial Dr, Manitowoc (from I-43, take Exit 152, go east on Hwy 10, which becomes Waldo Blvd, take Waldo all the way to Lake Michigan, then go north on Memorial Dr, watch for sign at the first stoplight); 920-684-6110

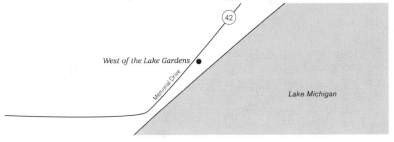

The gorgeous West of the Lake Gardens overlook beautiful Lake Michigan. Once the private residence of the late John and Ruth West, their modern-type 1930s home is now the headquarters for the foundation dedicated to keeping the gardens open for the public to enjoy. The six acres are divided into several themes such as the Japanese Garden, Rose Garden, Formal Garden, etc. Ruth's first attempt at gardening was a wheelbarrow path she designed to the lake. She planted 200 tulips along the path and with their blossoming success, Ruth was severely and forever bitten by the garden bug. Lucky for the rest of us who continue to admire her foresight and hard work. Open daily. Free admission.

Madison Area Gardens

Allen Centennial Gardens

University of Wisconsin-Madison, 620 Babcock Dr, Madison (from the east take University Ave, turn right on Charter, left on Observatory, right on Babcock); 608-262-1549; www.hort.wisc.edu/garden2001

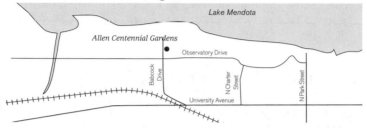

Referred to as the UW-Madison's largest outdoor classroom, the 2½-acre site features 23 amazing gardens wrapped around a Victorian Gothic home built for the first dean of the agricultural campus. Maintained by the university faculty, staff and students, the gardens represent gardening styles from around the world and provide valuable insight in horticulture, botany, entomology, plant pathology and art. But whether you're a master gardener or a novice, the Allen Centennial Gardens will more than inspire that green thumb of yours. Free, but donations welcome.

Longenecker Horticultural Gardens

University of Wisconsin Arboretum, 1207 Seminole Hwy, Madison (two entry points: north entry is at intersection of McCaffery Dr, N Wingra Dr and S Mills St; south entry is north of the W Beltline at intersection of McCaffery Dr and Seminole Hwy); 608-263-7888; http://wiscinfo.doit.wisc.edu/arboretum

There's never a bad time to visit the 1,260-acre arboretum, but spring has to be one of the most fragrant. Longenecker Horticultural

Gardens boasts one of the nation's largest collections of lilacs as well as the world's most up-to-date ornamental crabapple collection. More than 100 of the state's native woody plants are represented within the restored prairies, forests and wetlands. All plants are conveniently labeled which is a tremendous help for planning your own landscape. The annual spring garden tour is a huge hit with all fauna and flora lovers. The visitor center has changing exhibits. Open daily. Free admission.

Olbrich Botanical Gardens

3330 Atwood Ave, Madison (2½ miles east of downtown on the north shore of Lake Monona); 608-246-4550; www.olbrich.org

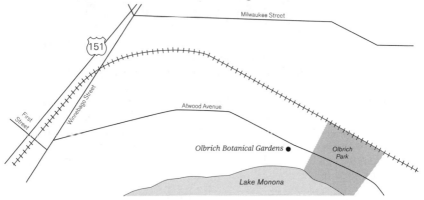

The word "glorious" doesn't do justice to the magnificence that is the Olbrich Botanical Gardens. Fourteen-acre displays include the Herb, Rock, Perennial and All-American Rose Gardens. An ornamental bridge ushers you across the serene reflecting pools that surround the intricately designed, gold leaf Thai Pavilion—a gift from the Thai government and the Thai Chapter of the Wisconsin Alumni Association. The Bolz Conservatory (a 50' high glass pyramid) is a tropical haven with showy orchids, chirping birds and a waterfall. Paradise rules here year-round, but the coolest thing about the conservatory is the summer presentation of the "Blooming Butterflies." From mid-Jul–mid-Aug live butterflies emerge daily from chrysalises and fly around in the building. How awesome is that? Olbrich has a wonderful horticulture library filled with all kinds of information from bugs to slugs and everything else. The gardens are free. Conservatory admission is minimal, free/everyone W & Sa mornings. Open daily. Call for hours.

Rotary Gardens

1455 Palmer Dr, Janesville (take I-90 to Exit 175A, east on Racine St to Palmer Dr, south on Palmer Dr ½ mile); 608-752-3885; www.rotarygardens.org

The 15 acres of gorgeous gardens are laid out in 18 international themes such as the English Cottage Garden, French Formal Garden, Scottish Garden and so on. The sculptures throughout the gardens inspire and awe. The crux of the Rotary Gardens is a three-part 20' bronze sculpture named "Dialogue: World Peace through Friendship." Another interesting sight is a Japanese Bridge made from recycled lamp posts. Rotary Gardens offer educational programs for 1st graders through the Master Gardener Certification. Open year-round. Free admission.

Western/Central Gardens

Foxfire Gardens

M220 Sugarbush Ln, Marshfield 54449 (3 miles north of town on Cty E); 715-387-3050; e-mail foxfire@foxfiregardens.com

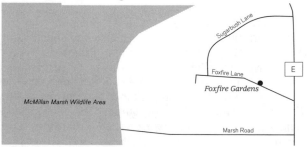

The oriental theme of the lovely Foxfire Gardens represents the souls of the gardeners, Dr. Tom and Linda Schulte. From the first willow tree planted in 1985 to the 3-acre pond and gurgling waterfalls, this

husband and wife team have lugged rock, laid mulch, fertilized, weeded, planted and nurtured their creation with precious little outside help. They do it because they love it. They have more than 500 varieties of hostas and many are for sale. Open daily Mother's Day weekend–Sep. Free admission. Call for hours.

Options: Right across the street are the mystical, magical iron swamp creatures of **JuRustic Park**. There are over 250 metal sculptures (including a 2-ton dragon) living in the peaceful environs of Nancy and Clyde Wynia's marsh Utopia. But keep a sharp eye out for their ferocious junkyard cat which is twice as mean as their junkyard dog—ha! The park is open spring–fall until 5pm. From Marshfield turn off Hwy 97 onto Cty W going north. Drive 3½ miles to Sugarbush Ln. The park is on the right side; www.jurustic.com
• Consistently named the best place to live in Wisconsin, Marshfield ranks third best in America. It is home to the top-notch Marshfield Clinic (Wisconsin's equivalent of the Mayo Clinic) and a leading dairy research center. A few sights worth seeing while here include **New Visions Gallery** in the Marshfield Clinic, 1000 N Oak Ave; 715-387-5562. Changing exhibits represent all media.
• **Upham Mansion** is an 1880 period house with gorgeous rose gardens; 212 W Third St; 715-387-3322; open Su & W. Call for hours. • The **Wildwood Zoo** covers 60 acres with more than 200 resident species of animal and bird; 1085 S Central Ave; 715-486-2056; mid-May–mid-Sep. Free admission to all attractions.

Rose and Lily Gardens

Corner of Jefferson and Bridgewater Ave, Chippewa Falls 54729 (next to the pool)

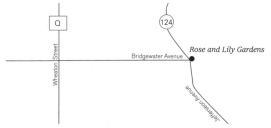

Time Magazine selected Chippewa Falls as a "Top Ten Small Town," and the National Trust For Historic Preservation agreed, naming it a national distinctive destination. The historic downtown has loads of charming shops and restaurants. It should come as no surprise that this lovely small town has an equally lovely public garden with over 500 rose bushes and 300 varieties of lilies.

Options: Built in 1836, the **Chippewa Spring House** is one of the oldest landmarks in the area. Find it at 600 Park Ave. • The **Cook**

117

Rutledge Mansion tour highlights the 1873 Victorian-Italianate home's five fireplaces, stained glass windows and embossed, hand-painted ceilings and walls; 505 W Grand Ave; 715-723-7181. Open Jun–Aug Th–Su. Call for tour times. Admission charged. • **Irvine Park** (Bridgewater Ave) features a zoo, the Glen Loch Dam and Overlook and a museum. During the holiday season the park turns into an illuminated Christmas Village; 715-723-3890 or 715-723-0051. • The **High Shores Supper Club** has a fun **champagne cruise on Lake Wissota** followed by a dinner at the club daily (summer only, weather permitting). To find the supper club from Chippewa Falls, take Hwy 29 east to Cty X. Reservations are required; 715-723-9854. • Take a **walking tour** of three dozen historic buildings in the downtown district. Free maps at the **Chippewa Area Visitors Center,** 10 S Bridge St; 888-723-0024 or 715-723-0331; www.chippewachamber.org. • The town of **Cadott** is only 15 miles east of Chippewa Falls on Hwy 29. Cadott is the **midway point between the Equator and the North Pole**—the marker is on Cty X. Notice the grey rock on the west side of the Cadott Falls Bridge on the Yellow River—they are 2½ billion years old.

Stockholm Gardens

Hwy 35, in the village of Stockholm along the Mississippi River; 715-442-3200

You're going to love this quaint little town of 89 folks. Besides being the oldest Swedish settlement in the state, it contains gardens from end to end. Many Europeans make a day of it here, finding the town reminds them of home. Fortunately, most of the century-old buildings haven't been gussied up too much. They've been put to use as antiques and specialty shops, cafes and bakeries. **Stockholm Gardens** is at the south edge of town (watch for the white picket fence). The display beds overflow with showy blooms and plants that are Wisconsin hardy. The gardens specialize in wildflowers and Hibiscus with dinner plate-sized blossoms. Open daily early spring–late fall. Call for a copy of their extensive wildflower catalogue.

NOTE: Many of the Stockholm shops shorten their hours after the Christmas holidays. Weekends are probably your best bet for finding them open through the winter months.

There's nowhere on earth like Wisconsin. Not one, but two Great Lakes and the Mississippi River helped carve the state's rugged and scenic borders. This is a land rich in Native American history and mining. Explore the caves, don a hard hat and take a mine tour or sign up for an archeological dig to learn about the incredible people who walked this great state thousands of years ago.

Geology, Archeology & Caves

Central

Rib Mountain State Park

4200 Park Rd, Wausau 54401; 715-842-2522

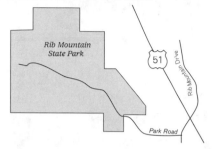

The park's focus is a quartzite-red granite hill billions of years in the making. Rib Mountain is one of the world's oldest geologic formations and at 1,940' above sea level, it was thought to be the highest point in Wisconsin, but no cigar—Timm's Hill grabs the honor (located 25 miles south of Phillips). The climb to the top is steep, but the view is worth the effort. And since you've gasped and scrambled this far, what's another 60' climb to the top of the observation tower? Feel the burn, baby. For all you winter enthusiasts, the downhill skiing at Rib Mountain can't be beat. It's the highest ski hill in the state and the Midwest's second longest vertical drop, 700'. Snowshoeing is another of the park's winter attractions and it has 8 miles of trails designed for the sport.

Options: The **Wausau River Walk** meanders through several parks, one of them is Whitewater. This challenging manmade kayak and canoe course was originally built in 1974 and is world famous for hosting international slalom competitions. This is a great place to cut your "whitewater rafting teeth." For more area attractions call the **Wausau/Central Wisconsin Convention & Visitors Bureau**; 888-WI-VISIT; www.visitwausau.com. • About 15 miles northwest of Wausau on Cty U you'll find the town of **Poniatowski**—microscopic when measured on the population scale, but humongous when it comes to a world attraction. On a spot in a cornfield at the edge of town, the **45th parallel crosses the principal meridian**, which makes Poniatowski exactly halfway between the North Pole and equator and one-quarter of the way around the world. There are only eight sites like this on earth; five are under oceans.

NOTE: Marathon County is the fourth-largest ginseng producer worldwide. With annual revenues exceeding 90 million, ginseng is Wisconsin's number one cash crop export.

Roche-A-Cri State Park

1767 Hwy 13, Friendship 53934; 608-339-6881

Hike the stairs to the top of the 300'-high outcropping. If you still have breath, you won't for long once you look at the view. The park has Native American petroglyphs, restored prairie, camping, a nature center with seasonal programs, fishing and 6 miles of hiking/cross-country ski trails.

Options: This whole area is a rock lover's dream. Many of the formations look like some giant kid stacked one rock on top of another in rows of neat columns. Some of the most interesting rock formations are **Ship Rock**, found on Hwy 21 east of Hwy 13; **Rabbit Rock**, on Hwy 13 north of Adams-Friendship; and **Rattlesnake Bluff** in the town of Quincy.

East

High Cliff State Park

N7630 State Park Rd, Sherwood 54169; 920-989-1106

Besides opportunities to do everything in this park from horseback riding to snowmobiling, there are the added attractions of effigy mounds (Indian burial sites) and a lime kiln and quarry. The limestone cliffs overlook Lake Winnebago, the state's largest inland lake. So book your camping trip at High Cliff because you can't *not* have a good time here.

North

The Apostle Islands

Bayfield Chamber of Commerce; 800-447-4094; www.bayfield.org

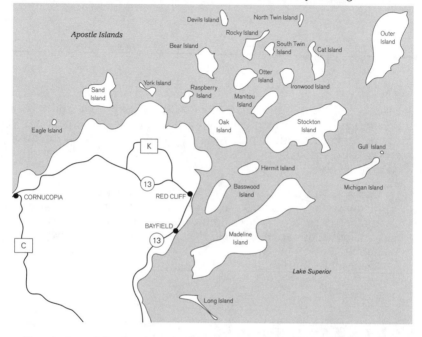

Twenty-two islands ring the northeast coast of Bayfield County. Known more for lighthouses than geology by the general public, the Apostle Islands are billions of years old. Several islands are the site of sandstone quarries used to rebuild Chicago after the fire. Hermit Island has a few quarried rocks strewn about the shore and the rusted remains of a loading pier, but you're going to have to find your own way there as it's a primitive locale with absolutely no amenities and perfect for those who want to get away from it all. For the kayaker in you dying for a little adventure, paddle your way around to the east side of Sand Island and explore the sea caves. The 3,000-acre island is worth a hike as well. Some of the highlights are the weather-eroded historic remains of a nineteenth-century village, an 1881 lighthouse and 250-year-old white pines. Primitive camping is available, but take precautions because you're not as alone as you might think. Black Bears can make nasty neighbors when searching for food. Still evident are the Basswood Island quarries. The largest island quarries, they supplied brownstone throughout the nation. Basswood has hiking trails and primitive campsites with and without water.

NOTE: Most of the Apostle Islands have natural areas designated for the protection of endangered wildlife and plant species. Watch for these areas as they are off-limits to the pitter-patter of anyone's feet. Two of the islands, **Eagle and North Twin**, are completely out of the tourist loop, with a 500' boater's buffer zone to boot. See more area attractions in the Romantic Getaways chapter (Bayfield).

South

Badger Mine & Museum

279 W Estey St, Shullsburg 53586; 608-965-4860

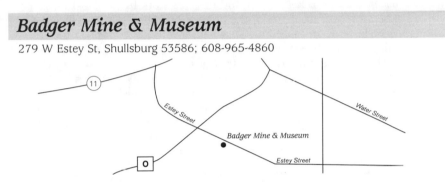

A guided tour of the hand-dug, 1827 lead mine travels 51 steps down, then ½ mile into the shafts beneath the city. The dark, narrow tunnels branch in all directions and inspire both empathy and amazement for the miners of the time. The museum does a nice job capturing the turn-of-the-century era through full-scale camp replicas such as a well-stocked general store, tobacco shop and 1900s kitchen. The artifacts on display are courtesy of the Shullsburg area residents. Open daily Memorial Day–Labor Day. Call for hours. Admission charged.

Bevans Lead and Mining Museum & Rollo Jamison Museum

405 E Main St, Platteville; 608-348-3301

A lead miner's wage in the 1800s was about $2 a day—not too shabby for the period. You weren't going to get rich, but you wouldn't starve either. It was lead miners who burrowed their homes into the

125

hillsides, giving Wisconsin the nickname "Badger State." Platteville is honeycombed with miles of underground mine shafts and it shows in its crazy street system. The guided tour at Bevans descends 90 steps into the mine and gives a good feel for the laborious mining process and perils faced by men and beast (donkeys helped with the excavations). Once topside, take the noisy but fun train ride in authentic ore cars that make a couple loops around the grounds. Afterward, head to the old schoolhouse for a self-guided tour of mining artifacts (such as the "candle-powered" hats) and Platteville history. The Roundtree Gallery is on the second floor and features work by local artists. The museum is sort of a two-for-the-price-of-one attraction and includes the Rollo Jamison Museum. Rollo had an obsessive passion for collecting southwestern Wisconsin history—junk by most people's standards at the time. The Jamison collection is the largest of any one person in the entire US. There are more than 20,000 items (not all on display as of this writing) from arrowheads, which were the first objects he collected, to farm implements. Of particular interest is the short video of Rollo reminiscing about his life and collection; he passed away in 1981 at the age of 82. Open daily May–Oct. Admission charged. Changing galleries open M–F Nov–Apr. Call for hours.

Options: A famous Platteville landmark is **the world's largest "M"** (symbolic for "mining"). Located east of town on Cty B, you can't miss the whopping 214x241' structure that pretty much takes over the entire Platteville Mound. Stairs to the top give a panoramic view of the area. • The **Chicago Bears** call the UW-Platteville campus "home" for a couple weeks during their summer training camp. The **Platteville Chamber of Commerce** has all the details; 608-348-8888; www.platteville.com. • Seven miles northeast of town (Cty Rd B and G) is the very short-lived home of **Wisconsin's first capitol**. Two buildings house historic exhibits. Open daily during the summer. Free. • The **St. John Mine** (the state's oldest lead mine) is south of Platteville along Hwy 133 in the town of Potosi. Don a hard hat for a tour of the mine and offices. Open daily 9–5 May–Oct; 608-763-2121. Take the hiking trail near the mine to see the remnants of an 1820 shelter where the "badgers" (miners) lived. • For a look at a historic smelting furnace, head 1 mile north of Potosi on Hwy 61, then drive east on Hippy Hollow Rd. The **British Hollow Smelter** boasts a 200' underground chimney and is the last one in the area.

Cave of the Mounds

2975 Cave of the Mounds Rd, Blue Mounds 53517; 608-437-3038;
www.caveofthemounds.com

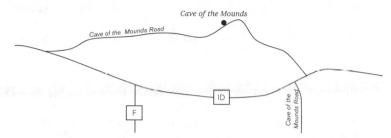

Discovered in 1939 by a quarry blast, the Cave of the Mounds literally drips with all the wonderful, millions-of-years-old rock formations, canyons and water pools. Another plus are the outdoor gardens and picnic areas. The 40-mile Military Ridge State Trail is nearby, so bring your bike. Tours offered daily mid-Mar–mid-Nov, weekends mid-Nov–mid-Mar, call for weekdays.

Option: Blue Mound State Park is almost within spitting distance of the cave and sits on the highest point in southern Wisconsin. It's an airplane view of thick woods and rolling cropland, punctuated with century farms and tiny hamlets—a must-see if you're in the area. The park has camping, mountain bike trails, a rustic cabin for people with disabilities and a swimming pool equipped with a lift. The address is 4350 Mounds Park Rd, Box 98, Blue Mounds 53517; 608-437-5711.

Effigy Mounds Grand Tour

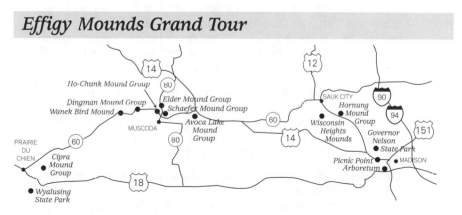

For history buffs and adventure seekers alike, this fabulous self-guided tour explores 14 different effigy sites along the Lower Wisconsin State Riverway. "Effigy" refers to the way the earthen mounds were built in the shapes of animals, spirit figures and humans. Constructed over 1,000 years ago by indigenous people, the mounds are roughly 3' high and range up to ¼ mile in length. Regarded as important archeological finds protected by law, some are human burial sites, but not all. Archeologists believe nearly 90 percent of these remarkable monuments have already been destroyed. The hike to some mounds is rugged, but all overlook sweeping vistas or amazing wooded lots. Traveling the state east (Madison) to west (Prairie du Chien), the sites are as follows:

- **Arboretum, Madison**—Interpretive signage present at this mound group, and restrooms are available. Detailed directions to the mounds are at the McKay Center at the University of Wisconsin Arboretum, 1207 Seminole Hwy, Madison; 608-263-7888.

- **Picnic Point, Madison**—Located on the south shore of Lake Mendota on Willow Dr, accessible by water. If you can't find it call 608-263-7888.

- **Governor Nelson State Park, Madison**—The mounds are found within the park at 5140 Cty M, near Waunakee along the northwest shore of Lake Mendota (north of Madison). It's water-accessible, restrooms are available and state park entrance fee is charged. Call if you have trouble finding it; 608-831-3005.

- **Hornung Mound Group, Sauk City**—From Sauk City, take Hwy 12 and cross the Wisconsin River (toward Madison). Turn left (east) on Cty Y. Go about ¼ mile and park at the Roxbury Shooting Club. Trail is directly west of the club driveway.

- **Wisconsin Heights Mounds, Sauk City**—This is a challenging hike. Wear comfortable shoes and clothing and lots of insect repellent. From Sauk City, cross the Wisconsin River via Hwy 12. Turn right on Hwy 78. Go about 2 miles (past Cty Y). Park in the turn out on your left (another parking lot is about 100 yards beyond). A trail leads to the mounds. Take the right fork.

- **Avoca Lake Mound Group, Muscoda**—Interpretive signage present, along with restrooms and water access. From Muscoda, drive east on Hwy 133 to Avoca. Watch for a sign near the east edge of the village pointing to Village Park and campground. The mounds are north and east of the ball field. 608-532-6831.

- **Elder (Shadewald) Mound Group, Muscoda**—From Muscoda, take Hwy 80 north across the Wisconsin River. Turn left (west) on Hwy 60. Drive 2 miles to Hwy 193, turn right (north). The mounds are on top of the high hill on the right (north of the first farmhouse). Park alongside the highway.

- **Schaefer Mound Group, Muscoda**—Water accessible. From

Muscoda, take Hwy 80 north across the Wisconsin River. Turn left (west) on Hwy 60. Cross Mill Creek bridge. The remaining mound is on your left (south) in a mowed grassy area. Parking is the first road to the left past the mound.

- **Ho-Chunk Mound Group, Muscoda**—Water accessible; restrooms available. From Muscoda, take Hwy 80 north across the Wisconsin River. Turn left (west) on Hwy 60. Drive 1½ miles towards the curve to the right (north). The drive to the Ho-Chunk National Farm is a dirt road. Park by the house. You must call ahead for a guide; 608-739-3360.

- **Dingman Mound Group, Muscoda**—This is a difficult hike. Dress appropriately. From Muscoda, take Hwy 80 north across the Wisconsin River. Turn left (west) on Hwy 60 for 4½ miles to Eagle Cave Rd, turn right. Turn left (south) on an unmarked road (by the sign to Eagle Cave Campground). Drive or hike to the gate. Enter and go south to the woods. Turn left (east) and follow the trail; watch for a fork to the right into the woods. The trail follows a deep ditch into the mound group.

- **Wanek Bird Mound, Muscoda**—Another rough and rugged hike for you adventurers! There's also a campground nearby. From Muscoda, take Hwy 80 north across the Wisconsin River. Turn left (west) on Hwy 60. Drive 1 mile west of Port Andrew, past the sand-pit and past the driveway to the Wanek homestead. A short distance farther west past Wanek Ln is an unmarked road on the left (south) through agricultural fields. If you get lost, call 221-3792 or 608-739-3188.

- **Cipra Mound Group**—From Prairie du Chien, take Hwy 18 and Hwy 35 south to Bridgeport. Take Hwy 60 east for approximately 5 miles. The mounds are in a wayside on the left.

- **Wyalusing State Park**—Interpretive signage and restrooms. From Prairie du Chien, take Hwy 18 and Hwy 35 to Bridgeport, cross the Wisconsin River. Almost immediately after the crossing, turn right (southwest) on Cty C which joins with Cty X. Follow the signs to **Wyalusing State Park**. Entrance fees charged. The park is one of state's oldest. Campsites are 560' above the confluence of the Wisconsin and Mississippi Rivers. Canoe rentals; 13081 State Park Ln, Bagley; 608-996-2261.

Effigy Mounds National Monument

151 Hwy 76, Harpers Ferry, Iowa (from Prairie du Chien, take Hwy 18 west across the river to Hwy 76 N, follow signs); 563-873-3491; www.nps.gov/efmo

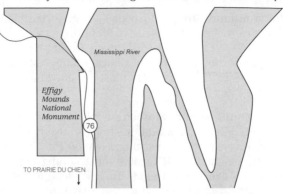

The 2,526-acre Effigy Mounds National Monument is the showpiece of the Effigy Mounds Grand Tour and contains 207 prehistoric mounds (some dating back 3,000 years), 31 effigies of bears and birds, and the Marching Bear group—one of the country's best examples of mound groups. You won't be disappointed in the hiking either—absolutely stunning views of the Mississippi River Valley. Visitor center is open daily. Summer entrance fee charged, free entrance Nov–Mar. For an Effigy Mounds site map, call the Wisconsin Department of Tourism; 800-432-8747; or write Cultural Landscape Legacies, Inc., PO Box 187, Muscoda 53573.

Gottschall Rock Art Site

Highland vicinity (address guarded); must call ahead or e-mail for directions

Another interesting tour is the Gottschall Rock Art Site, an internationally acclaimed cave with more than forty wall pictographs. Archeologists have unearthed pottery, symbolic imagery and sandstone carvings. Ongoing digs continue throughout the summer months. If you want to help with the work, they require a minimum week-long commitment. The cost to you is around $150, plus another $150 for food and sleeping quarters. The cave is east of Prairie du Chien near Highland. Guided tours offered Jun & Jul Su noon–2:30pm. You must e-mail salzerrj@beloit.edu or call ahead mid-May–Jul 608-532-6385; rest of year 608-362-8812.

Option: For even more prehistoric culture, visit the effigy mounds south of New Lisbon off Hwy 12/16. Also in the region are the rare **Twin Bluff petroglyphs**—ancient rock art/carvings by early Woodland tribes found in caves along Cty A (west).

Kickapoo Indian Caverns

54850 Rhein Hollow Rd, Wauzeka 53826 (15 miles southeast of Prairie du Chien, watch for signs); 608-875-7723; www.kickapooindiancaverns.com

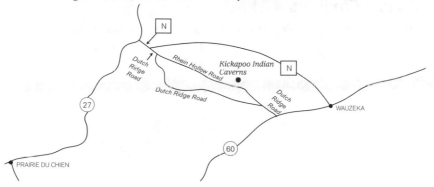

Once the shelter of the Kickapoo tribe, this is Wisconsin's largest underground cave. Besides the usual fascinating cave stalactites and crystals, tour highlights include large pools of water and a 60'-high cathedral room with an onyx ceiling. Open daily mid-May–Oct. Call for tour times. Admission charged.

Logan Museum of Anthropology

Memorial Hall, Beloit College (corner of College St and Bushnell), Beloit; 608-363-2677

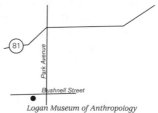

A recent $4-million renovation turned the museum into a world-class facility. It houses some of the world's oldest jewelry, pre-Columbian ceramics and thousands of Native American artifacts including stone axes and arrowheads. There are 22 Indian mounds on the campus. Open daily except M. Free admission. Call for hours.

NOTE: Not included in this chapter are two state parks of notable archeological and geological significance. Interstate State Park is Wisconsin's first state park and features the world's largest potholes. A more detailed description is in the Family Day chapter. Copper Culture State Park features an ancient Indian burial site with some of the first artifacts from the Copper era. See the Museums chapter for more information.

Merry Christmas Mine

Pendarvis State Historic Site, 114 Shake Rag St (east side of town), Mineral Point; 608-987-2122; www.wisconsinhistory.org/pendarvis

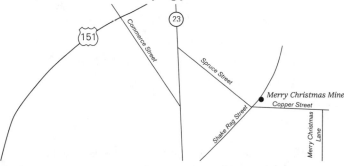

How does a miner's wife get the attention of her husband while he's working? No, lingerie is not involved. She stands in the doorway of her quaint stone home and shakes a rag, thus the birth of Shake Rag St. The Merry Christmas Mine opened on Christmas Day in 1905 and was the largest zinc mine in the area. Although you can't enter the mine, interpretive trails explain the mine's history. Follow costumed guides along stone paths through the manicured gardens of about a half-dozen miner's cottages. These were the state's first permanent homes. Open daily mid-May–Oct. Call for tour times. Tour admission charged. Self-guided interpretive trails are free.

West

Crystal Cave

W965 State Rd 29, Spring Valley; 800-236-CAVE; www.cavern.com/crystalcave

Open since 1942, Crystal Cave is Wisconsin's longest cave and features multiple levels filled with stalactites, stalagmites, drip stone, curtains, helectites, sodastraws and a few cuddly brown bats. Try your luck prospecting in their sluice trough or come for their home-made fudge—mmm, fudge... Daily 1-hour tours mid-May–Oct, weekends Apr & May. Call for hours. Admission charged.

Option: At 122' high and 1,800' long, the **Eau Galle Dam** is the largest earthen dam of its type in the Midwest. Completed in 1968, the project required over 2 million cubic yards of rock and fill. A scenic overlook provides a great view of the dam and Spring Valley below. Operated by the Army Corps of Engineers, Eau Galle Lake has picnicking, swimming, hiking, fishing, camping and nature programs. To find the park and overlook from Spring Valley, drive west on Hwy 29, turn right onto Van Buren Rd, drive 1 mile to Cty B, cross B, follow signs; 715-778-5562.

Stop at any of the big interstate information centers and ask the folks behind the counter this question: What do people want to know about? The top three responses are:

- Do you have any information on the Wisconsin Dells?

- What's there to do in Door County?

- Where are the best (scenic) roads for Harley riding?

So, Harley riders you've been heard, and this chapter is for you.

NOTE: Some of the areas in this chapter are covered in others throughout the book and not repeated here. Harley Trips highlights those attractions not featured elsewhere.

Harley Trips

Great River Road

The Great River Road parallels the mighty Mississippi River from its birthplace in Lake Itasca, Minnesota, all the way south to the Gulf of Mexico in New Orleans. For 235 miles the Great River Road (Hwy 35) traces Wisconsin's western border from Prescott to Kieler. On this trip expect to find friendly small towns, cafes and bars with honest, hard-working folks, incredible vistas, antiquing, dairy farms, riverboats, locks and dams, trains, Bald Eagles, Tundra and Trumpeter Swans, and a yearning to return again and again.

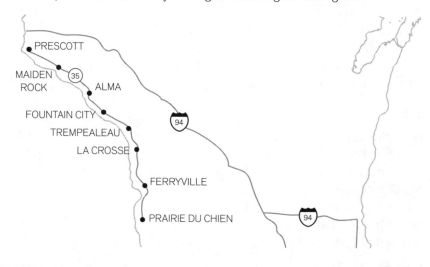

Prescott

Established in 1827 as a military land claim, Prescott is the **state's oldest river town** and one of its most romantic. Stop by the **Welcome & Heritage Center** (next to the bridge; 715-262-3284) for free maps of the Great River Road, then explore the 1923 Vertical-Lift Bridge Gearhouse. • A pre-Civil War era home sets the stage for the unique perennial display beds at **Funkie Gardens** off Hwy 10 E (turn right on Pearl St, go 5 blocks, gardens on the left); 715-262-5593. • The ambience at the **Steamboat Inn** couldn't be better as it overlooks the St. Croix River. They offer fine dining, dinner cruises and a piano bar (located next to the bridge); 800-262-8232; www.steamboatinn.com. • Heading south on Hwy 35 you'll see the sign for **Mercord Mill Park** (on the right side at the top of the hill). The overlook provides an excellent view of the Mississippi and St. Croix River confluence. • Continuing south on Hwy 35, notice the jagged limestone outcroppings of **Diamond Bluff**. Keep a sharp eye out for **Bald Eagles** scouting prey.

Maiden Rock

32 miles from Prescott

The actions of a distraught Native American maiden put Maiden Rock on the history map. As ancient lore tells it, the Indian maiden leapt from a nearby cliff, preferring death to a prearranged marriage. A **historic marker** relates the tale (south of town on the right side of Hwy 35). • **Ole's Bar & Grill** (715-448-9231) is in downtown Maiden Rock. The bar makes a big deal out of welcoming bikers, so it would be rude not to stop. Besides, they've got good food and a great outdoor deck with an artistic rendition of an old-time saloon scene. • The **Smiling Pelican Bakery** is 1 block north of Ole's and specializes in pastries and pies prepared from scratch. The grandma's-type kitchen in this old 1870s house smells wonderful, and the food does not disappoint. Open Th–Su spring–Christmas holidays. The Smiling Pelican has everything your sweet tooth craves; 715-448-3807. • Mosey across the road for a look through **Basil's**, an eclectic gift shop firmly planted inside a quaint nineteenth-century church. Open weekends spring–holidays; 715-448-3039.

Alma

29 miles from Maiden Rock

Before entering historic Alma, stop at the observation platform at **Rieck's Lake Park** for some bird watching (eagles, egrets, herons). Staffed with volunteers during the Tundra Swan fall migration, the place looks like a New York rush hour. • Once you get into town, head to the **Lock and Dam No. 4** observation deck and watch the barges glide through the locks. The open catwalk to the deck happens to be directly over the train tracks. It's an awesome thrill to stand on the catwalk as a train thunders beneath your feet. • Southwestern Wisconsin is known as part of the "driftless region," an area untouched by glaciers. A trip 500' straight up the bluffs to **Buena Vista Park** affords an amazing panoramic view of rolling hills and valleys, river bottoms and jagged bluffs. Watch for park signs at the southern edge of town.

Fountain City

17 miles from Alma

At 600', Eagle Bluff is the highest point on the Mississippi River, and **Elmer's Auto & Toy Museum** has a cozy perch on top of it. Elmer, a junk dealer/used car salesman, has the world's largest collection of pedal cars, pedal airplanes and pedal tractors—over 700 of them! At Elmer's you'll see 5 buildings full of antique, classic and muscle cars, antique tools, toys and a view of the river valley that doesn't end. Fee charged for self-guided tour. The grounds have concessions, a picnic area and umbrellas when needed. Open selected weekends May–Oct. Call for schedule; 608-687-7221. To get there, take Hwy 95 ½ mile out of Fountain City to Cty G for ¼ mile to Elmer's Rd. • Lock and Dam 5A is about 3½ miles south of Fountain City on Hwy 35. To your right (west, and before the lock) is the Dam Saloon—the only floating bar on the Mississippi River. Highlights include the view of the locks system, and an outdoor deck for fishing. They sell bait as well as bar food. Open summer months; 608-687-8386.

Options: For a really cool side trip, stay on Hwy 95 all the way to **Arcadia**. If you've never traveled Hwy 95 before, you should. The road rides a winding ridge for full, breathtaking vantage of the valleys below. Arcadia is home to **Ashley Furniture**. Ashley ranks fifth nationally in sales and is privately owned by a couple of farm boys from Winona, Minnesota. Besides furniture, the showroom has a great little **English pub** with soups, sandwiches and libations. Open daily year-round; 343 Detloff Dr; 608-323-2270. • **Memorial Park** is on the corner of Cty J and Gavney Rd. The 54-acre park is the nation's only memorial to veterans of all wars and conflicts. If you've got the kids along, the park has a children's playground and water park.

Trempealeau

20 miles from Fountain City

The marshy bogs and soaring cliffs of Trempealeau make it a wildlife paradise. The town itself is a bit of a one-horse show with the Trempealeau Hotel being the main attraction and well worth a stop. It's an unpretentious atmosphere with great food, cheap rooms and a river view along the main street; 608-534-6898; www.trempealeauhotel.com. • If you're a nature lover, the 6,200-acre Trempealeau National Wildlife Refuge is a wetland alive with Great Horned Owls, woodpeckers, river otters and wildflowers. Hiking and cross-country ski trails get you to the action. The refuge is off Hwy 35/54, then right on W Prairie Rd. • Perrot State Park is next door on Sullivan Rd and features burial mounds and over 1,200 pristine acres tucked between river bluffs. There's nothing here but prime fishing, camping, adventure hiking and incredible views that do not stop; 608-534-6409.

Options: For those of you not riding a Harley, but find yourselves perusing these pages, the **24-mile Great River State Bike Trail** runs through these scenic backwaters. For more information, call 608-534-6409. • The McGilvray Rd features five **nineteenth-century steel bowstring bridges**. Located east of Trempealeau in the Van Loon Wildlife Area, the rustic unpaved back road is one you'll be glad you found. For directions call the **Trempealeau Chamber**; 608-534-6780; www.trempealeau.net

La Crosse

24 miles from Trempealeau

As far as western Wisconsin river towns go size-wise, La Crosse is the granddaddy with a population over 51,000. It's the homeport for the **Julia Belle Swain**, one of five remaining authentic paddleboats on the Mississippi (see the Odds & Ends chapter for boat trips). La Crosse has its share of interesting museums and historic houses, parks, a small zoo, Lock & Dam No. 7, **downtown trolley rides for 25 cents**, downhill skiing, eateries, shopping, a university and **brewery**, but the attraction to see is the view at **Grandad Bluff**. The 540' bluff has a 40-mile radius overlooking the city and three states—Wisconsin, Minnesota and Iowa. To find the overlook, take Main St east, which becomes Bliss Rd. At the top of the bluff, turn right on Grandad Bluff Rd. For more information, call the **La Crosse Area Convention and Visitor's Bureau**; 800-658-9424; www.explorelacrosse.com

NOTE: **Vernon County** is south of La Crosse on the Great River Road. It has the nation's highest concentration of **round barns**. See the Odds & Ends chapter for barn locations.

Ferryville

35 miles from La Crosse

Ferryville bills itself as having the longest main street, without an intersection, of any town with only one street. (Huh?) Regardless, it is a long street and since you're here you might as well see the sights. Tip back a cold one at the **Swing Inn** on Main St. The bar has a rattlesnake skin tacked to the wall and a ghost on the stairway. • The **Ferryville Cheese Retail Outlet** sells more than 100 varieties of cheese. Pick up a brick or wheel for the ride home.

Prairie du Chien

23 miles from Ferryville

Prairie du Chien is the **state's second oldest settlement** (Green Bay is the oldest). Seafood is the main restaurant fare, catfish in particular, but it's good so give it a try while you're here. A couple of other things you don't want to miss while in town—the historic **Villa Louis mansion on St. Feriole Island** was the home of the state's first millionaire, and **Wyalusing State Park** in nearby Bagley has effigy mounds and one of the best overlooks on the river. Stop by the **Information Center** along Hwy 18 (by the bridge in Prairie du Chien) for maps and information. Open daily. Call for hours; 608-996-2261.

NOTE: See the Museums chapter for more area attractions.

Option: The 9-vehicle **Cassville Car Ferry** is one of the remaining two on the Mississippi River. Depending on river conditions, it runs daily from Cassville to Turkey Creek in Iowa. The ferry is in Riverside Park. Take Hwy 81 west to the river. One-way fares charged per person, motorcycle, car; www.cassville.org

The Northwoods

Depending on who you talk to, the Northwoods encompasses the whole northern third of the state, but this Harley Trip slices it down to the extremely picturesque north central region of Oneida and Vilas Counties. Almost half of the area is lakes upon lakes upon lakes; the rest is the Northern Highland American Legion State Forest, especially gorgeous during fall. Take this trip if you love winding roads, lots of peaceful solitude, fishing resorts, unbelievable fall color and tiny towns few and far between.

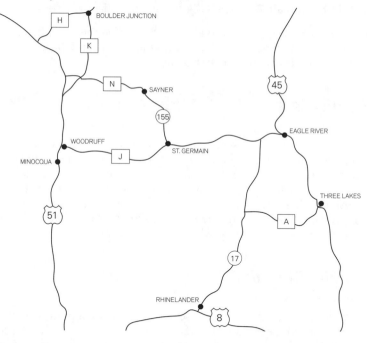

Rhinelander

Beautiful Rhinelander is at the intersection of Hwy 8 and 17. This is Musky country with top tournament prizes worth upwards of twenty grand. Rhinelander is the Oneida County seat and with a population around 4,500, it is by far the largest town in this neck of the woods. The **century-old courthouse has a Tiffany glass dome** and is especially striking lit up at night. Located on Oneida Ave. Open M–F. • **Free**

summer concerts take place every Th evening outside the Riverwalk Centre along the Wisconsin River. • The **Logging Museum Complex** maintains it's the most complete one of its kind in the state. The museum grounds are host to the CCC Museum, a blacksmith shop, 1-room schoolhouse, Soo Line depot, train engine and 1913 caboose. Located in Pioneer Park off Hwy 8, the museum is open daily Memorial Day–Labor Day. Free admission. • Not everything in Rhinelander is all scenery and resorts; there's a monster lurking in its past—the **Hodag**. The mythological green and white beast is now a favorite town trademark and you'll see it everywhere. For more information, see the **Rhinelander Chamber of Commerce**; 450 W Kemp St; 800-236-4FUN; www.rhinelanderchamber.com.

Three Lakes

22 miles from Rhinelander

The Three Lakes claim to fame is the **world's largest inland chain of lakes**, twenty-eight in all. Fishing is wildly popular but so is snowmobiling and cross-country skiing, with more than 120 miles of groomed trails. • **Three Lakes Winery** is the original cranberry wine maker. They have free tastings and tours year-round; 6971 Gogebic St; 800-944-5434; www.fruitwine.com. • The **wild rice harvest** begins about the middle of Aug near the Spur Lake area off S Hwy 45. Visitors are welcome to watch. And if you're around during the **cranberry harvest** in mid-Sep, you're more than welcome to watch that, too. There are about a half-dozen marshes in the area, most along Cty A or S Hwy 45. • The **Three Lakes Aqua Devils water ski team** performs every W and Su from mid-Jun–mid-Aug. An entertaining show with trick jumping, pyramids, barefooting and ballet. Admission is free; concessions on-site. Take Hwy 32 east from Three Lakes and watch for signs by the golf course. For more information, call **Three Lakes Information Bureau**; 800-972-6103.

Eagle River

10 miles from Three Lakes

No, you are not out of Musky country yet, nor will you ever be while on this trip. Lest you forget, reeling in the monster fish and snowmobiling are the prime reasons for a Northwoods holiday, but there's always shopping and a lot of other interesting things to see and do. Case in point is **Carl's Wood Art Adventure**, 2 blocks west of McDonald's at 1230 Sundstein Rd; 715-479-1883. You'll know you're in the right place when you see the parade of wooden folks outside the front entrance. Chainsaw carving demonstrations, Paul Bunyan oversized furniture and hands-on exhibits make this a fun place to stop. The museum is open daily Memorial Day–mid-Oct. Admission charged;

www.carlswoodart.com. • The **Trees For Tomorrow Education Center** is an accredited specialty school with a focus on natural resources. Established in 1944 by the paper and electric companies for the purpose of reforestation, the center offers free guided nature hikes through a demonstration forest. The grounds are open year-round. Tours Tu Jun–Aug. Call for hours and tour times. For more area information, call the **Eagle River Chamber of Commerce**, 201 N Railroad St; 800-359-6315; www.eagleriver.org

St. Germain

13 miles from Eagle River

St. Germain, proclaimed the "Birthplace of Colorama" by the Wisconsin Secretary of State, is home to the **International Snowmobile Racing Hall of Fame** at 6035 Hwy 70 W; 715-542-4488; www.snowmobilehalloffame.com. You'll see some of the first racing sleds, videos of famous races and uniforms worn by the inductees. They're open year-round M–F & most every Sa, but call ahead. Free admission. • For prime Bald Eagle and Osprey watching, head south of town to **Rainbow Flowage Lake** along Cty J. For more area information, call the **St. Germain Chamber of Commerce**; 800-727-7203; www.st-germain.com

Sayner

7 miles from St. Germain

Since you're in Sayner, you may as well learn about the local history and see the **world's first snowmobile**. Invented in 1924, the weird-looking contraption is basically an outboard motor attached to skis. It's at the **Vilas County Historical Society Museum** on Hwy 55 (1 block from Cty N); 715-542-3388. Open daily Memorial Day–mid-Oct. Free admission, but a donation is suggested.

Boulder Junction

15 miles from Sayner

In amongst the blaze orange and camouflage fatigues of the Northwoods is the downright enchanting town of Boulder Junction. The cutest cafes, bakeries and specialty shops line a main street one wishes would trail on much longer. It's touristy in the traditional sense with flower boxes and old-fashioned lampposts. Many Windy City dwellers migrate to Boulder Junction for long, leisurely weekends. Huge flea markets run through the summer, but that's not to say the town doesn't have its roots firmly embedded in fishing. Proudly known as the Musky Capital of the World, Boulder Junction boasts nearly 200 lakes within a 9-mile radius. Hike, bike, go berry picking, ski or snowmobile. Call the Boulder Junction Chamber for more information; 800-GO-MUSKY; www.boulderjct.org

Options: **Manitowish Waters** is northwest of Boulder Junction. It has over 600 acres of cranberry bogs. **Free tours of the marshes** run mid-Jul–mid-Oct and begin with a short video and food sampling. Call the **Manitowish Waters Chamber of Commerce** for more information: 715-543-8488. • In 1934 **John Dillinger and Baby Face Nelson** took refuge from the FBI in **Little Bohemia**, but they weren't very good hiders. Once found, a fierce shootout took place riddling the lodge walls with bullet spray. The gangsters got away, but 70 years later the bullet holes remain. Little Bohemia is still in business as a lodge and restaurant. Open mid-Apr–mid-Jan for lunch and dinner; 715-543-8433; www.littlebohemia.net

Minocqua/Woodruff

19 miles from Boulder Junction

After a jaunt through Northern Highland American Legion State Forest where scarcely a vehicle is seen, the traffic in the twin towns of Minocqua and Woodruff feels like hustle and bustle. Although it may be a faster world here, the pace is decidedly Northwoods leisure. Some cool things to see include a tour of the **Art Oehmcke Fish Hatchery** on Cty J in Woodruff; 715-356-5211. The hatchery raises Walleye, Musky and Northern Pike. The entrance display room has lots of interesting trivia about fish and the ecosystem. Open Memorial Day–Labor Day M–F. Tours available at scheduled times. • Tame deer roam freely throughout **Peck's Wildwood Wildlife Park** located 2 miles west of Minocqua on Hwy 70; 715-356-5588. Pet a baby skunk or woodchuck, feed a Black Bear, go fishing, see zebras, the big cats, kangaroos, a stingray lagoon and 500 other animals. Open daily May–mid-Oct. Admission fee; www.peckswildwood.com. • The incredibly popular **Scheer's Lumberjack Shows** at Hwy 51 and 47 entertain with logrolling, pole climbing, cross-cut sawing, axe throwing and just about every other impressive lumberjack skill with the exception of flapjack eating. Shows daily except M Memorial Day–Labor Day. Call for show times; 715-634-6923; www.scheerslumberjackshow.com. • To see a large concentration of Bald Eagles and Osprey, take the 2-hour sightseeing cruise offered by **Wilderness Cruises** on Willow Dam Rd in Hazelhurst. Fee charged. Call for a schedule and list of other cruise options; 800-472-1516; www.wildernesscruises.com. • For family-style grub, try **Paul Bunyan's Cook Shanty** on Hwy 51; 715-356-6270. Log camp decor. Open daily 7am–9pm. • The **Minocqua Brewing Company** proudly serves their hand-crafted ales, along with the usual bar drinks and tasty burgers. On Hwy 51 at Lake Minocqua next to Torpy Park; 715-358-3040. For more area attractions, contact the **Minocqua/Arbor Vitae/Woodruff Chamber**, Hwy 51; 800-446-6784; www.minocqua.org

Yellowstone Trail

With the invention of the automobile came the need for roads. In 1912, the Yellowstone Trail became the nation's first transcontinental highway from Plymouth Rock to Yellowstone Park and eventually Puget Sound. But back in the day, road signs marking the route did not exist, so yellow paint got slapped on anything that didn't move such as fence posts, big rocks and trees. The markers were called "hoodoos." The roadway began as a rough mud path. It was later covered with gravel and ultimately paved. Early travel logs detailed road conditions, area businesses, hotel and dining options and even community temperament. Today, yellow and black signs mark the Wisconsin route as it travels from Hudson to Kenosha. For more about the Yellowstone Trail, log onto www.yellowstonetrailwi.com

Withee

How fun would it be to go to a produce auction? Come on, you know you want to. Well, you can at the **Wisconsin Produce Auction** on Cty O in Withee; 715-229-4838. Up for bids are produce, bedding plants, crafts and shrubbery. Auctioneers pound the gavel at 10am F May–Oct; other week dates added as needed.

Colby

17 miles from Withee

The town of Colby is the birthplace of its namesake cheese, so it seems only right to stop at the **Colby Cheese House** and buy a pound or two. You'll find them on Hwy 13; 715-223-2610. • Many **Mennonite and Amish families** live in the Colby area. They sell quilts, baked goods and wood furniture from their farms. Watch for signs indicating they're open for business. There's also an organized **Mennonite Countryside Tour** that travels the region and stops at about a half-dozen "country supermarkets." For more information about the tours, call the **Clark County Economic Development & Tourism**; 212 S Main St, Greenwood; 715-267-3205; www.clark-cty-wi.org

Marshfield

20 miles from Colby

The Central Wisconsin Fair Park is home to the **world's biggest round barn** and it's a whopper at 150' in diameter and 70' high. Conceived and designed by the Central Wisconsin Holstein Breeders Association as a show and sales barn, it seats 1,000 with additional space for 250 head of cattle. Find it at 513 E 17th St, Marshfield; 715-387-1261; www.centralwisconsinstatefair.com. • Since you're in the area, you may as well ride on over to the awesome (and hilarious) **JuRustic Park**. There are over 250 iron swamp sculptures (including a 2-ton dragon) living in the peaceful environs of Nancy and Clyde Wynia's marsh Utopia. Watch out for their killer junkyard dog—ha! The park is open spring–fall until 5pm. From Marshfield turn off Hwy 97 onto Cty W N, drive 3½ miles to Sugarbush Ln, JuRustic is on the right side; www.jurustic.com

Stevens Point

34 miles from Marshfield

Stevens Point is roughly the halfway mark on the Yellowstone Trail. It's a beautiful river town of stately mansions, pristine parks and a historic downtown with great shops and eateries. One attraction you shouldn't miss while here is the **Stevens Point Brewery** at 2617 Water St, Stevens Point 54481 (take Hwy 10 east to Stevens Point, turn right at the first stoplight after crossing the bridge, follow Water St 1 mile to the brewery); 800-369-4911; www.pointbeer.com. Founded in 1857, the brewing company supplied beer to the Civil War troops. The tour marches through the brewhouse, aging cellars, packaging and the warehouse. Beer sampling follows in the Hospitality Room. The gift shop is open year-round M–Sa. Tours given at scheduled times. Admission charged.

Plover

5 miles from Stevens Point

For a real feel for the Yellowstone Trail, head south to Plover for a gander at an **authentic log cabin** that was once a rental on the route. In the 1800s an overnight stay in these prestigious lodgings set you back $1.50. The cabin and several other period buildings are open Memorial Day–Labor Day weekends. Located in **Heritage Park** on the corner of Washington and Willow Dr; 715-311-2238.

Appleton

66 miles from Plover

Appleton has a population of about 66,000, with the largest shopping mall north of Milwaukee and some of the best parks and museums (see the Museums chapter). Ringed by Hwy 41 and 441, the Fox River cuts straight through. There's tons to do in Appleton, but a couple tours not covered in other chapters that are worth your while include **Vande Walle's Candies** on 400 Mall Dr. They have self-guided tours of their bakery and candy factory M–F. The store is open daily; 920-738-7799. • Take a trip to **Lamer's Dairy** and watch the whole milk producing process through a huge observation window. In business since 1913, Lamer's sells glass bottled organic milk along with other dairy products. They're off Hwy 441 on N410 Speel School Rd; 866-830-0980. Open M–Sa. Call for best viewing times.

Oshkosh

20 miles from Appleton

Another taste of the old days is at **Ardy & Ed's Drive-In** at 2413 S Main St; 920-231-5455. The 1950s burger joint has the best root beer floats in town. They're served in frosty mugs by roller-skating carhops, rocking to a '50s beat. Ardy & Ed's has an old-fashioned soda fountain and they're open daily. From Appleton, take Hwy 45 south into Oshkosh, go through downtown, cross the bridge and travel 1 mile farther to the drive-in.

NOTE: Since you're riding a Hog you're probably wondering how you're going to get your food? The carhops bee-bop out to the restaurant picnic tables as well.

Fond du Lac

25 miles from Oshkosh

Fond du Lac sits on the southern tip of **Lake Winnebago—the state's largest inland lake**. The 80' Columbia Park Tower affords a stunning view; found 10 miles north of town on Hwy 151. • Brochures mapping an 88-mile drive around the lake are at the **tourist center** on 171 S Pioneer Rd; 800-937-9123. • Another great way to see the area is from a plane. Half-hour rides offered daily at **Fond du Lac Skyport Airplane Rides**, Rolling Meadows Dr (between Hwy 151 and 23). Fee charged; 920-922-6000. • **Free outdoor concerts** M & W 7pm Jun–Aug in **Buttermilk Creek Park** on S Park Ave. • **Lakeside Park** is the charming hostess with the mostest—panoramic lake view from the historic lighthouse deck, train rides, an old-fashioned carousel, bumper boats, aqua bikes, canoes, gardens, concessions and picnic areas. Found at the end of N Main St and N Park Ave; 920-929-2950. • The famous 32,000-acre **Horicon Marsh** is about 16 miles south of town on Hwy 49. It is the largest freshwater cattail marsh in the US and habitat for over 260 bird species. Explore nature trails and an observation tower. The wildlife art gallery is open daily May–mid-Nov. Admission charged; 920-386-2182. Guided pontoon boat tours of the marsh and naturalist programs are offered 30 miles south of town on Hwy 33. For more information, call 920-485-4663 or 920-387-2658; www.horiconmarsh.com. • For a juicy buffalo burger, ice cream or cappuccino, visit **Glacier Ridge Animal Farm and Restaurant**. A $5 hayride tour of the farm drives past bison, camels, goats and deer. They're located at N9458 Ridge Rd, Van Dyne (east of Hwy 41 between Cty N and Hwy 26); 920-688-3488.

Theresa

22 miles from Fond du Lac

Widmer's Cheese Cellars at 214 Henni St in downtown Theresa is an 80-year-old, third-generation cheese factory with over 50 cheese and sausage varieties for sale. View the cheesemaking process through the observation window. Guided tours are available if you call ahead. Open Jun–Oct 5–5 M–Sa, 10–4 Su; 888-878-1107; www.widmerscheese.com

Allenton

8 miles from Theresa

The Addison House, 6373 Hwy 175, Allenton, has worn many hats. It opened in 1840 as a saloon, then became a brewery turned brothel and is now a respectable B&B. During the brewery years, caves chiseled into the hillside kept the beer cold. The cost of an overnight stay in the Addison House includes cave tours and a big Wisconsin breakfast of bacon and eggs. Call for prices; 262-629-9993.

Slinger

8 miles from Allenton

Age and speed don't usually go together, but at nearly six decades old the **Slinger Speedway** is the world's fastest ¼-mile oval. Dale Earnhardt, Mark Martin, Matt Kenseth and Rusty Wallace all won races here before moving on to NASCAR. Cars race on Su late Apr–mid-Sep. Admission is $12. The track is off Hwy 41 at Hwy 144 and Cty AA, Slinger, 262-644-5921; www.slingersuperspeedway.com

> **Options:** To shop the state's largest antique mall, head west of Slinger on Hwy 60 to the town of Columbus. The **Columbus Antique Mall and Museum** on 239 Whitney St features 180 dealers with more than 540 booths. Open daily 8–4; 920-623-1992; www.columbusantiquemall.com. • A person can't help feeling like novelist Clive Cussler's adventure hero Dirk Pitt when admiring the rare Reos and Pierce-Arrows at the **Wisconsin Automotive Museum**—the state's largest auto museum. Over 100 rare classic and vintage motorcycles, farm implements and cars including. The museum is at 147 N Rural St, Hartford (west of Slinger on Hwy 60). Open daily May–Sep. Closed M & Tu Oct–Apr. Admission charged.

Germantown

14 miles from Slinger

Do you have ringing in the ears? You may after a visit to the **Sila Lydia Bast Bell Museum** at Six-way Crossroads, Holy Hill Rd (in the Dheinsville Settlement). The museum features a 1,000-pound bell made for the historic silo tower as well as another 5,000 bells on display in the 1870 restored barn. Open Apr–Oct Tu–Su; 262-628-3170. Admission charged.

Racine

51 miles from Germantown

Ahh, Racine. Put your nose skyward and breathe deeply, because you are in kringle heaven. For those of you not familiar with the mouth-watering treat, a kringle is a cross between a Danish and a coffee cake. There are at least a half-dozen bakeries in town that make a fabulous kringle, but **Bendtsen's Bakery** on 3200 Washington Ave (Hwy 20) got the Racine people's vote as numero uno; 262-633-0365.

NOTE: For more on Racine, see the Lighthouses chapter Lake Michigan section.

Throughout the ages lighthouses and the lives of those who manned them have been romanticized in novels, poems and songs. Remote and far from romantic, a lighthouse tour of duty meant hard work, long days and endless lonely stretches where the only other two-legged creature seen was the sea gull. One can't help admire the stalwart dedication and resourcefulness of the keepers and their families, and yet... There's just something so captivating about the lighthouse.

NOTE: The Door County chapter features Door County lighthouses. For information about Apostle Island's lighthouses, see the Romantic Getaways chapter, Bayfield section.

Lighthouses

Lake Michigan

Lake Superior

Lake Winnebago

Lake Michigan

Algoma/Pierhead Lighthouse

End of North Pier, Algoma harbor; 414-747-7188; www.algoma.org/views

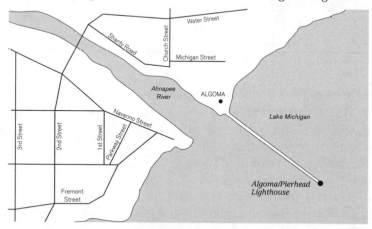

The Algoma Lighthouse was built in 1893 and rebuilt in 1932. The beautiful century-old red lighthouse is fully operational, but no tours are offered. Walk to the end of the pier to feed the gulls and get some great photos.

Options: The entire lakeshore drive along Hwy 42 is exceptionally beautiful and abundantly sprinkled with picturesque harbor towns. Known as the "Salmon and Trout Capital of the Midwest," **charter fishing** is an industry staple in Algoma. See the Extreme Adventures chapter for charter information. • The **von Stiehl Winery** is the oldest in Wisconsin. It's located at 115 Navarino St and a guided tour costs $3; 800-955-2508. • Before the construction of the lighthouse, sailors used the church steeple of **Saint Agnes-By-The-Lake** for navigational guidance. **Richard Upjohn**, founder of the American Institute of Architects and designer of Wall Street's Trinity Church, drafted the original 1877 building. After a devastating fire in 1884, the church was rebuilt as an exact replica. It's located at 806 4th St (along the lake).• Algoma's impressive **sand beach and boardwalk** follows the coastline from the marina to the **Algoma Visitor Center** at the end of town. Plan to spend a few hours here soaking up the sun and scenery; 920-487-2041.

Kenosha Pierhead Lighthouse &
Kenosha Southport Lighthouse

The Kenosha Pierhead Lighthouse is located at the end of the Kenosha Pier and the Southport Lighthouse is on Simmons Island adjacent to the park, 50th and Lighthouse Dr (Fourth Ave), Kenosha; 262-654-5770

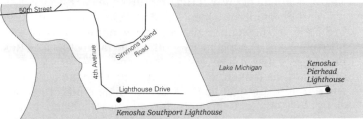

Built in 1906, the Pierhead tower is 50' tall. No tours. The Southport Lighthouse was built in 1866. The 10-sided lantern room has a tower 55' tall. The adjacent keeper's cottage is currently under restoration, so no tours offered as of this writing.

Options: Ninety percent of the **Kenosha lakefront** is parks, gardens, hiking trails, beaches, open-air market and fishing piers—so head to the lakefront! For 25 cents, hop on an **authentic electric streetcar** for a ride through Harborpark and the historic downtown. Runs M–Sa, call for hours; 262-653-4000. • See the bones of a 12,500-year-old woolly mammoth at the **Kenosha Public Museum**. Interactive exhibits, natural history, Native American artifacts, fossils, priceless art (Picasso, Renoir, Chagall) and fabulous lifelike dioramas make this museum a must on the tour list. It's located at 5500 First Ave; 262-653-4140. Open daily. Call for hours. Free admission. • For more information about the area, call the **Kenosha Area Convention & Visitors Bureau**; 812 56th St; 800-654-7309; www.kenoshacvb.com

Kewaunee Pier Lighthouse

On the harbor's breakwater pier, Kewaunee; 414-747-7188

Built in 1889, then rebuilt in 1931, the Kewaunee Pier Lighthouse was automated in 1981. The tower is 45' tall. It is fully operational year-round with both main light and fog signal. No tours.

153

Options: Besides the lighthouse, the main attraction in town is the **Kewaunee County Historical Museum**. The primary draw is the dismal 1876 cell block. The 5x6' dungeons are the last of their kind in the US. Museum is in the former Sheriff's office/residence; 613 Dodge St, Court House Square; 920-388-7176 or 920-388-3858. Open Memorial Day–Labor Day, noon–4. Admission $2. • Take a tour of an old **WW II tug** that served in the D-Day invasion. It's on the waterfront. Open Jun–Sep. Admission charged; 920-388-5000. • The state's only **rooftop windmill** is southwest of Kewaunee and a couple miles south of the town of Krok. • **Rustic Road 7** is a few miles west of the windmill. The scenic route drives past the remains of a crumbling lime kiln, an old flour mill and a historic German home. • Drive 1 mile north of Kewaunee along Hwy 42 to Geppetto's Top of the Hill Shop (Svoboda Industries) and check out the **world's biggest grandfather clock**—35'. Open daily; 800-678-9996. Call the **Kewaunee Visitor Center** for more information; 800-666-8214.

Long Tail Point Lighthouse

In Long Tail Point State Wildlife Area, on an island in the bay of Green Bay; 920-832-1804

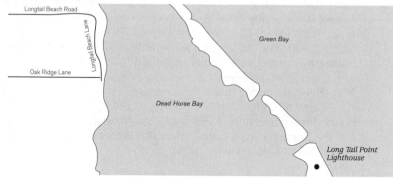

Sadly, this lighthouse is nothing more than a ruin and accessible by boat only. No tours and the structure is not safe for climbing.

NOTE: For more Green Bay attractions, see the Family Day and Museums chapters.

Manitowoc Breakwater Lighthouse

On the Manitowoc breakwater pier; 800-627-4896 or 920-683-4388

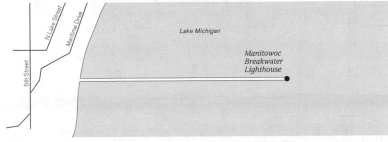

The original lighthouse was built in 1895, rebuilt in 1918 and automated in 1971. The lighthouse itself is not open, but the walk to it is.

Options: Manitowoc is the state's **Maritime Capitol**, and for good reason. It's home to the **Wisconsin Maritime Museum** (the largest of its kind on the Great Lakes) and the **WW II Submarine USS COBIA**. The museum is 60,000 square feet of maritime history, shipbuilding displays, interactive exhibits, multimedia theater and a children's area. For a cool adventure, book an overnight stay on the USS COBIA. Learn what it was like to prowl the waters aboard a real war patrol sub. The cost includes a meal. The museum is open daily. Admission charged; 75 Maritime Dr; 866-724-2356 or 920-684-0218; www.wisconsinmaritime.org. • It takes about 4 hours to cross Lake Michigan by ferry and there really isn't a better way to go than by the **Lake Michigan Carferry Service**, 900 S Lakeview Dr, Manitowoc 54220; 800-841-4243 or 920-684-0888; www.ssbadger.com. They have onboard dining, a gift shop, live entertainment lounge, family movies, children's play areas, sundeck and private berths. Open mid-May–mid-Oct. One-way fares from Manitowoc to Ludington, MI. • The gorgeous 6-acre **West of the Lake Gardens** is free and located along Hwy 42. See the Garden Tours chapter for details. • Take a free bakery tour at **Natural Ovens Bakery**, 4300 Cty CR; 800-558-3535; www.naturalovens.com. The breads are preservative-free, made from whole grains. Tours run M, W, Th & F. Call for times. Natural Ovens Bakery has a self-guided tour of the **Farm & Food Museum** with antique farm equipment, beautiful flower gardens and a farm animal petting zoo. For more area attractions (and there are tons of them) call the **Manitowoc/Two Rivers Area Chamber of Commerce**; 800-262-7892; www.manitowocchamber.com

North Point Lighthouse

East end of North Ave (north on Wahl Ave), Milwaukee; 414-747-7188

Built in 1855, the lighthouse was rebuilt in 1888, then raised in 1912. No longer operational, the tower is 74' tall. No tours given. See the Milwaukee chapter for a mega list of area attractions.

Peshtigo Reef Lighthouse

Located approximately 10 miles southeast of Peshtigo and 3 miles offshore of Peshtigo Point; 920-743-3367

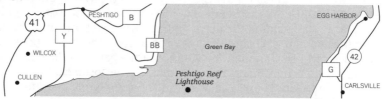

Built in 1934 and accessible only by boat, the lighthouse tower is 72' tall. No tours. See the Museums chapter for more area attractions.

Port Washington Lighthouse & Lightstation Museum

Port Washington; 262-284-7240; www.portlightstation.org.

Lucky Port Washington has both a lighthouse and a lightstation. Built in 1935, the city's art deco lighthouse is located at the end of the harbor breakwater, but is not open for tours. The 1860 lightstation's 14' tower was donated and built in 2002 by the Duchy of Luxembourg to the original specifications. Ongoing restoration work continues. The keeper's residence serves as a museum. Open Apr–Oct Sa & Su. Call for hours.

Options: Located 30 miles north of Milwaukee, Port Washington is known for its charter fishing, but also boasts **the most pre-Civil War buildings in the state** and the **first manmade harbor in North America**. Pick up a walking tour at the **visitor center** located in the historic **Pebble House** (a home painstakingly constructed using stones collected from Lake Michigan beaches); 126 E Grand Ave; www.portwashingtonchamber.com; 800-719-4881. • On June 14, 1885, a 1-room schoolhouse in nearby Fredonia birthed the national event called **Flag Day**. The beautiful little **Stony Hill School** is at 5595 Cty I. • Since you're in the area, go see the **Ozaukee County Pioneer Village** located a few miles south of Stony Hill at 4880 Cty I (Hawthorne Hills County Park). Take a self-guided tour of over 20 restored buildings showcasing various methods of construction used by the immigrants. Costumed interpreters are on hand to answer any questions. Open Sa & Su Memorial Day–mid-Oct. Admission charged. Call for hours; 262-377-4510.

Rawley Point Lighthouse & Two Rivers Lighthouse

Two Rivers; 414-747-7188

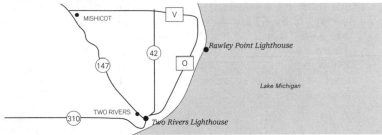

Built in 1853 and rebuilt in 1894, the Rawley Point Lighthouse tower is 113' high. It's the tallest octagonal skeletal light tower and the only one of its kind on the Great Lakes. Manually operated until 1979, the present light system was installed in 1987. No tours here as the dwelling is the caretaker's private residence. The lighthouse is at the north end of Point Beach State Park (drive 7 miles north on Hwy 42, then take Cty O). A walking trail leads to it; 920-793-5905.

The 1886 Two Rivers Lighthouse is one of the few authentic wooden structures left on the Great Lakes. You'll find it on the banks of the East Twin River in the historic Rogers Street Fishing Village, itself a notable stop on the tourist trail. Besides the lighthouse, the fishing village museum details the history of commercial fishing and the shipwrecks off Rawley Point. Open daily Memorial Day–mid-Oct. Admission charged.

Options: Two Rivers is the **birthplace of the ice cream sundae** and the whole world is grateful for that. That's right folks, Ed Berner of Two Rivers invented the ice cream sundae in 1881. You can still choose from 18 different flavors in a replica of Ed's soda fountain in the **Washington House**. Once an immigrant hotel, the Washington House is a maze of rooms packed with period furnishings and artifacts. Of special note is the elegant grand ballroom on the top floor with its rare hand-painted Americana murals. In this room one can almost hear the rustle of full skirts and the fiddler's waltz. The old hotel also houses the **Two Rivers Visitor Center**. The address is 1622 Jefferson St (on the corner of 17th and Jefferson, 1 block east of Washington St); 888-857-3529; www.two-rivers.org. Free admission. • Across the street from the Washington House is the **Hamilton Woodtype and Printing Museum**—another one-of-a-kind invention from the mind of yet another Two Rivers genius. James Hamilton invented the veneer wood type in 1850 and revolutionized the industry. Displays feature original machinery and patterns for wood type. Open daily, free admission; 920-794-6272; www.woodtype.org. • Seven miles of **beautiful sand beach** (with concessions) along Lake Michigan is reason enough to visit Two Rivers, but another is the **parks**; they are incredible. Excellent **hiking and biking trails** traverse from Manitowoc to Point Beach State Forest. Forgot your bike? No problem. Here are a couple rental places: **The Fitness Store**, 1611 Washington St; 920-794-2245; **Village Inn**, 3310 Memorial Dr; 920-794-8818. • The town of Mishicot is a few miles northwest of Two Rivers and worth a stop at the **Old Rock Mill** on Cty R. The 1848 mill has a working waterwheel built over a series of beautiful waterfalls. Guided tours leave hourly during the summer Tu–Su. Call for hours; 920-863-2812.

Sheboygan Breakwater Lighthouse

Off Deland Park (the light is on the harbor's north break wall), Sheboygan; 414-747-7188

Built in 1915, the light tower is 55' tall. It has a working foghorn, but no tours. Reach the lighthouse via the concrete breakwater.

Options: Sheboygan owns the rights to several Midwest bests—the best surfing, the best brats and the best golfing (the 2004 PGA

Championship was held at Whistling Straights). The **Riverfront Boardwalk** on Riverfront Drive meanders past the **Fish Shanty Village** with scores of weather-beaten fishing shacks converted into fun bars, restaurants, antiques and specialty shops. • The big name in Sheboygan is **Kohler**, as in the John Michael Kohler Arts Center, John Michael Kohler-Terry Andrae State Park (sand dunes and boardwalk hikes), The American Club, Artspace, Kohler Design Center and free Factory Tours, Waelderhaus (free daily tours of an Alpine house barn; 920-452-4079) and the Shops at Woodlake (see the Garden Tours chapter for details). • The **Indian Mound Park** at 5000 S 9th St (located at the far south side of town) has 18 effigy burial sites in animal and geometric shapes dating from AD 500–1000. The Open Mound exhibit showcases Woodland Indian artifacts. Free admission; 920-459-3444. • By the time you read this, the **Blue Harbor Resort** will have opened. This posh nautical-themed vacationland is on the shores of Lake Michigan. It has a 40,000-square-foot water park, several restaurants and bars, a spa, fitness center and conference center; 725 Blue Harbor Dr; 866-701-2583; www.blueharborresort.com.• For more information on area attractions, call the **Sheboygan County Chamber of Commerce**; www.sheboygan.org; 920-457-9491.

Wind Point Lighthouse

Lighthouse Dr on Wind Point, Racine; 262-639-5432

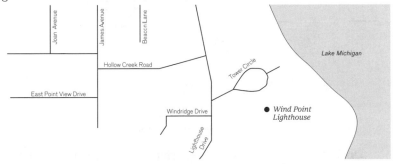

Built in 1880, the 112' light is the **oldest and tallest lighthouse still operating on the Great Lakes**. Automated in 1964, the grounds are always open but lighthouse tours only happen twice a year.

Options: Racine is the **national leading manufacturer of farm equipment** along with about a dozen other industries including glass and rubber. At over 100 acres, it has the **largest marina on Lake Michigan**. The Racine bakeries are world famous for their Danish sweet bread/coffeecake called **"kringle."** It is also home to Frank Lloyd Wright's **SC Johnson Administration Building &**

Golden Rondelle Theater (see the Odds & Ends chapter for information).• For a fun day that's free visit the cool **Racine Zoological Gardens** at 2131 N Main St; 262-636-9189. There are over 200 animals including the wildly popular rare white tiger, wolves and a petting zoo. Summer evening jazz concerts are a big hit midweek on W. Open daily.• The **Spinning Top Museum** is located at 533 Milwaukee Ave in nearby Burlington. You not only see over 2,000 tops, yo-yos and gyroscopes, you get to show off your own skills on about three dozen prototypes. Call ahead for a tour and yo-yo twirling demonstration. Admission charged; 262-763-3946. • Racine has numerous art and historical museums. Of note is the recently opened, architectural award-winning **Racine Art Museum** (downtown; www.ramart.org). It features collections of ceramics, glass, fiber, metal and wood. For more information about the area attractions, contact the **Racine County Convention & Visitors Bureau;** 800-272-2463; www.racine.org

Lake Superior

Ashland Breakwater Lighthouse

End of Ashland Breakwater in Chequamegon Bay; 218-720-5412

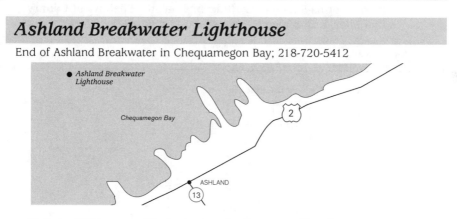

Built in 1913; accessible by boat only. No tours offered.

Options: If you want to know Ashland's history, a stop at the **Great Lakes Interpretive Center** is a must. Located on Cty G, the interpretive center's displays and videos focus on the industries that shaped the region, mainly shipping, lumber, mining and brownstone quarrying. It's a dynamite visitor center full of travel information and a 100-seat theater. Climb or ride the elevator to the top of the 5-story observation tower for a fantastic view of Lake Superior and the Apostle Islands. Stretch the legs with a stroll on the boardwalk through wetlands that wrap the center. Open daily 9–5, longer summer hours; 715-685-9983; www.northerngreatlakescenter.org. • Explore the giant 1,800-foot-long ore dock (the world's largest). To find it, head north toward the Chequamegon Bay. • For a walking tour map of Ashland's famous historical murals found on buildings throughout the city, stop in at the **Ashland Area Chamber of Commerce**, 805 Lake Shore Dr W; 800-284-9484; www.visitashland.com. • As gorgeous as the Ashland area is in the summer, it may be doubly so in the winter. Miles and miles of scenic cross-country ski trails plow through frosted forests and icy sea caves. For up-to-the-minute **cross-country trail conditions** call 800-234-6635; www.norwiski.com

Wisconsin Point Lighthouse

West pierhead entrance to Superior harbor (from Superior, take E 2nd St to Moccasin Mike Rd, turn north onto Wisconsin Point Rd); 218-720-5412

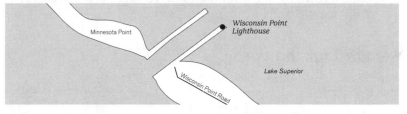

Built in 1913, the lighthouse is accessible by a concrete walkway, but is not open for tours. Two keeper residences are nearby. With its miles of sand beach, Wisconsin Point is the **world's largest breakwater**. It's also a great place to hunt for agates.

NOTE: See Museums and Waterfalls chapters for other area attractions.

Lake Winnebago

Fond du Lac Lighthouse

Lakeside Park, Fond du Lac; 800-937-9123

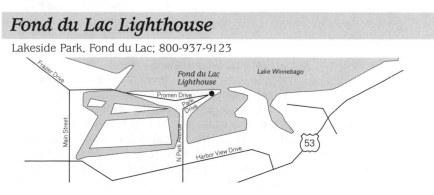

Built in 1933, the lighthouse is an eight-sided, wooden Cape Cod structure that's 40' tall. Open daily (weather permitting) mid-Apr–mid-Oct, climb the working lighthouse for a bird's-eye view of

the 400-acre park and Lake Winnebago (the state's largest inland lake and the second largest in the US).

Options: The charming **Lakeside Park** is a perfect place to spend the day with the family. Besides the historic lighthouse, the park has an antique carousel, miniature train, bumper boats and a deer park. Find it at the north end of Main St, open daily. Rides and rentals are Memorial Day–Labor Day. Fee charged for rides.
• The **Galloway House and Village** is a step back in time to the mid-1800s. Tour over 20 historic buildings including the famous 30-room Victorian Galloway House. The village is at 336 Old Pioneer Rd (south of town and midway between Hwy 175 and 45); 920-922-6390. Open daily 10–4 Memorial Day–Labor Day & Sep weekends. Admission charged. For more information, call the **Fond du Lac Area Convention and Visitors Bureau**; 800-937-9123; www.fdl.com

Neenah Lighthouse

Kimberly Point Park on Lakeshore Ave, Neenah; 920-751-4614

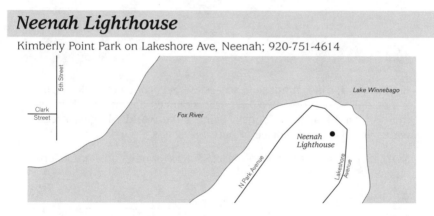

Built in 1945, the lighthouse is not open for tours, but you can fish from the deck which is kind of cool. The park has restrooms and picnic facilities.

Option: The **Bergstrom-Mahler Museum**, once a home (neverending palace) to a businessman, now houses one of the world's most spectacular **paperweight collections**. More than 2,100 eye-popping orbs sparkle and amaze. Other displays include paintings, photography and sculpture. The museum is at 165 N Park Ave, Neenah; www.paperweightmuseum.com; 920-751-4658. It's open Tu–Su. Call for hours. Admission is free. For more **information about Neenah** and the surrounding area, call 800-236-6673; www.foxcities.org

Rockwell Lighthouse

6 Lake St, Oshkosh; 920-236-5205

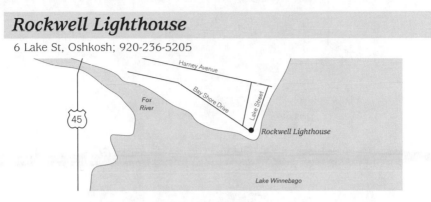

Built in 1909, the lighthouse is privately owned and not open for tours.

Options: Oshkosh has a lot to be proud of. This city of 160,000 people is rich with beautiful gardens, important (yet still interesting!) museums, opera and symphony, dinner cruises, fabulous restaurants and accommodations, **Timber Rattlers baseball**, tons of water activities and, yes, **Oshkosh B'Gosh** pinstriped jeans (no tours, but a huge retail outlet). One of the biggie tourist attractions is the **EAA AirVenture and Pioneer Airport**. The vintage aircraft museum offers daily flights (weather permitting) in old open cockpit planes. See the Museums chapter. • There are over **900 nativity sets** fashioned from everything imaginable on display at Algoma Blvd United Methodist Church, 1174 Algoma Blvd; 920-231-2800. • For more information on area attractions, contact the **Oshkosh Convention & Visitors Bureau**; www.oshkoshcvb.org; 877-303-9200.

Over 1½ million people from all walks of life live in Milwaukee, Wisconsin's largest city. These folks are Midwest friendly in a city with an easy road system and plenty of parking.

Known as the City of Festivals, Milwaukee celebrates its diversity with a summer-long series of parties. Their Irish Festival is second in size to Ireland's. The 11-day Summerfest in late June is the world's largest music festival with 13 stages of nonstop entertainment from noon until midnight. The festival features local and big-name talent such as Paul Simon, Bonnie Raitt, BB King and Sting. Perhaps this will ring your doorbell—Milwaukee is the birthplace of the Harley-Davidson motorcycle, the Milwaukee Brewers and the Miller Brewing Company. It has more than 140 parks and the world's largest four-faced clock. Once the city's oldest center of commerce, the Historic Third Ward is now one of the nation's top ten thriving theater and arts districts. Old World Third Street is strong in German heritage with cobblestone streets and specialty shops. For the finest restaurants you can't beat historic Brady Street; it links the lakefront with downtown.

Milwaukee

Churches

Family Day

Gardens

Museums & the Arts

Churches

Milwaukee churches score a perfect 10 in architecture and aesthetics. Steeped in tradition and grounded in history, a tour through their revered halls is an opportunity to better understand the people who founded this amazing city.

Annunciation Greek Orthodox Church

9400 W Congress St, Milwaukee; 414-461-9400

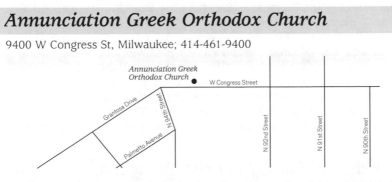

The Annunciation Greek Orthodox Church was Frank Lloyd Wright's last major commission. Unfortunately, he died in 1959 before the ground breaking. At first glance, the church has a sort of flying saucer look to it. It's been reported that when Wright met with the congregation to discuss his plans, he placed a saucer over a teacup and said, "There's your church." The shallow, blue-tiled concrete dome is 106' in diameter, set on top of a floor plan in the shape of a Greek Cross. The cross/circle pattern repeats many times—even the air conditioning vents are hidden within this motif. Opened in 1961, Wright called this building "his little jewel." Tours Tu & F. Call for times. Admission charged. Tour and Greek cross viewing additional charge.

Basilica of Saint Josaphat

2333 S Sixth St, Milwaukee; 414-645-5623; www.thebasilica.org

The Basilica of Saint Josaphat is proof positive that sometimes good things happen when church and state commingle. The massive stone building is patterned after Saint Peter's in Rome, but most of the materials used to create the magnificent structure came from Chicago government buildings slated for demolition. The six imposing granite columns gracing the front entrance were part of the old Chicago Courthouse. In ancient times a basilica was a typical indoor shopping mall and not connected to religion in any form. Basilica architecture simply related to the style of the building. Christianity became popular during the Roman Empire and it was then that the populous took over the massive buildings as centers of faith. The Basilica of Saint Josaphat is jaw-dropping beautiful. Painted ornamental plasterwork finished in gold leaf decorate the frieze and faux marble columns. The interiors include stencil work, trompe l'oiel paintings, a 214'-high dome and stained glass windows. The amazing murals are the work of an Italian artist commissioned from the Vatican. Weekly tours are offered after the 10am Sunday mass. Call to make arrangements for group tours. The visitor's center has an elevator and handicap entrance to the Basilica. The gift shop is across the street. Open Tu–Sa & the first Su of every month. Call for times.

Cathedral of Saint John the Evangelist

812 N Jackson (corner of N Jackson and Wells), Milwaukee; 414-276-9814; www.stjohncathedral.org

```
                        Kilbourn Street

                        Cathedral
                        of Saint
                        John the
                        Evangelist
                              ●           (18)

        Broadway    Milwaukee   Jefferson  Jackson  Van Buren   Cass      Marshall
        Street      Street      Street     Street   Street      Street    Street

                        Mason Street
```

The definition of cathedral is chair or throne. The cathedral is the Catholic bishop's chair. Built in 1847, the Cathedral of Saint John the Evangelist is the seat of the Archdiocese of Milwaukee. For years the clock in the magnificent tower was the official timepiece of Milwaukee. Bronze eagles decorate the cornice line and are 5' 6" tall and weigh 950 pounds each. The gated courtyard garden is a beautiful place to sit and meditate. Inside the cathedral a 14' "crown of thorns" sculpture hangs 28' directly above the central white marble altar. The hauntingly beautiful commissioned piece is the work of Italian sculptor Giuseppe Maraniello. Portraits of all the Milwaukee archbishops are above the stained glass windows. Self-guided tours daily. For group tours call 414-276-9814 ext 3202.

Option: There's a **free jazz concert** Th evenings Jun–mid-Sep at Cathedral Park Square, directly across from the cathedral; 414-271-1416; www.easttown.com

Holy Hill National Shrine of Mary

1525 Carmel Rd, Hubertus 53033-9407 (30 miles northwest of Milwaukee);
262-628-1838; www.holyhill.com

Built in 1863, Holy Hill's twin spires rise 1,350' above sea level, making this site one of the highest points in Wisconsin. For a small
donation, climb the observation tower's 178 steps and you'll feel as
if you're halfway to heaven—or at least on top of the world. What a
view! Holy Hill receives around 500,000 visitors a year, many seeking healings. The interior decor is quite simple and blends nicely with
the farm country surroundings. A small chapel wing juts off to the
side, displaying a nineteenth-century statue of Mary with the child
Jesus; crutches and canes flank the entrance. Directly beneath the
main body of the church is (surprise!) another church of equal size
and simplicity. Outdoors, ½-mile hiking trail reveals 14 groups of
life-size sculptures depicting the Passion of Jesus. Cafe and gourmet
bake shop serves up soup and sandwiches along with 15 kinds of
pies, breads, pastries, cookies and muffins (holy moly, why isn't
everyone around here roly-poly?). Gift shop. Grotto. Reserve in
advance for guest rooms and group retreats. Maps for self-guided
tours. Open year-round; observation tower closed in winter.
Wheelchair accessible.

Saint Joan of Arc Chapel

Marquette University, 1442 W Wisconsin Ave, Milwaukee; 414-288-6873;
www.marquette.edu/stjoan

No one seems to know the exact age of the little French Chapel, but
artifacts and historical records date it at more than five centuries old.
Steeped in legend and lore, it's said that part of the sanctuary floor is

the tomb of a famous French knight. Another story reveals that Joan of Arc (1412–31 AD) prayed in the church before a statue of Mary. She kissed the stone beneath the statue and ever since that stone has been colder than the surrounding ones. In 1926, the daughter of James J. Hill (the American railroad magnate) bought the historic chapel and shipped it from France to Long Island where it was rebuilt stone by stone. Heirs to the estate donated the chapel to Marquette University in 1964 where it now resides as the only medieval structure in the western hemisphere that remains true to its original purpose—daily worship. Gorgeous stained glass and fifteenth-century artifacts including a crucifix, candlesticks, torcheres, lectern and vestments. Open daily. Free tours. Call for hours.

Family Day

What's there to do? Will other kids be there? These are familiar questions you've heard time and again from your kids, right? Luckily, Milwaukee has a ton of things for families to do together. And, yes, other kids will be there.

Apple Holler

An Apple A Day

5006 S Sylvania Ave, Sturtevant; 800-238-3629 or 262-884-7100; www.appleholler.com

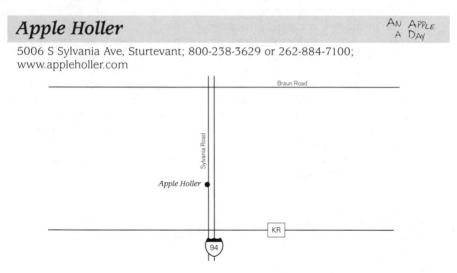

Want the kids to sleep good tonight? Take them to Apple Holler—a farm that also happens to be an apple orchard, pumpkin patch, corn maze, petting zoo and dinner theater. Open year-round, there are hay rides and sleigh rides, pony rides and Pygmy goats. Lots of games for the kids, including a special kids barn where the tots put on musical plays. Ride the wooden train or roast marshmallows over a bonfire. The restaurant is home-style cooking and open for breakfast, lunch and dinner. Gift shop, bake shop, farm market. No general admission, but charges for some activities.

Betty Brinn Children's Museum   LET'S PLAY

929 E Wisconsin Ave, Milwaukee (O'Donnell Park); 414-390-KIDS;
www.bbcmkids.org

Rated in the top 10 for best museum for families by *Parents* magazine, Betty Brinn is Milwaukee's only museum just for kids ages 10 and under (parents are welcome, too!). Three Milwaukee women held a vision that there be a place for children to develop fundamental skills, self-esteem and the ability to work with others through hands-on learning. They labored six years until the Betty Brinn Children's Museum became a reality in 1995. And no, none of them were Betty Brinn. The museum's namesake was a successful Milwaukee businesswoman who lived most of her childhood in foster homes and orphanages. Ms. Brinn spent her adult life helping women and children secure health care. The museum is a super fun place where the kids can crawl through a giant human heart, give a kid-sized car a tune up, play a musical instrument, broadcast the news or run a real TV camera. Special events and programs, museum store and take-home craft projects. All exhibits are extremely interactive. Just make sure *you* aren't the one holding up the line! Open Tu–Su. Admission charged.

Cool Waters Aquatic Park   SPLISH-SPLASH

2028 S 124 St, Milwaukee (Greenfield Park); 414-321-7530.

Cool off at a couple of aquatic centers right in Milwaukee's county parks. Cool Waters in Greenfield Park has a beach-entry heated pool with a giant tube and waterslides, sand volleyball courts and small tots waterslides and playground. Cafe. Open daily Memorial Day–Labor Day. Admission charged.

Option: If you happen to be in town in Aug, take in **River Flicks**

free outdoor movies every F at Pere Marquette Park. Activities for the kids begin at 7pm, movies start at dusk; 900 N Plankinton Ave; 414-276-6696; www.westown.org

East Troy Electric Railroad

2002 Church St, East Troy (take Hwy 20 1 mile south of East Troy to Cty ES, turn north on Church St); 262-642-3263; www.easttroyrr.org

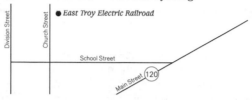

Take the kids on a *real* trolley ride—one that runs on rails, not tires. The brightly colored red and yellow vintage cars date from the late 1800s. There are several tours to choose from; the most popular is a 10-mile round-trip ride. The museum is full of train memorabilia. Open weekends May–Oct. Rides depart at scheduled times; mid-Jun–Sep also open W–F. Admission charged. For lunch, take the kids to the **Elegant Farmer** in nearby Mukwonago. The big white barn's smiling face gives a welcoming, homey feel to the place. The specialty is an apple pie baked in a paper bag. Open year-round 8–6; 262-363-6770; www.elegantfarmer.com

> **Options:** For you romantics, there's a special 2-hour **"dining by rail"** aboard an elegant Art Deco train. A 3-course meal is served; reservations are required. • Another option for kids is the **Green Meadows Petting Farm** located 6 miles east of East Troy on Hwy 20. More than 300 farm animals—pigs, goats, sheep, chickens. Milk a cow, ride a pony or go on a hayride. Open mid-May–mid-Aug Tu–Sa; opens again Labor Day–Oct. Call for hours. Admission charged; www.greenmeadowsfarmwi.com; 262-534-2891.

Harley-Davidson

HOG TOURS

11700 W Capitol Dr, Wauwatosa; 877-883-1450 or 414-535-3666; www.harley-davidson.com

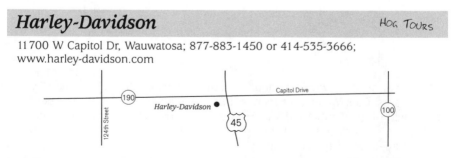

Got some teenagers you want to impress? Take them to the Harley-

Davidson engine plant. Harley farms out the actual motorcycle assembly, but you can still watch them put the vroom in their engines and transmissions. Free hour-long tours M–F. No children under 12 and the schedule is subject to change depending on demand, so call ahead.

Humphrey IMAX Dome Theater

MOVIE MAGIC

800 W Wells St, Milwaukee (inside Milwaukee Museum Center); 414-319-4629; www.mpm.edu/imax/imax.html

Wisconsin's only IMAX theater, the 7-story dome screen always thrills no matter the age. Open daily. Call for movie schedule. Admission charged See page 182 for map and information on the Milwaukee Museum Center.

Miller Park

TAKE ME OUT TO THE BALLGAME

One Brewers Way, Milwaukee; 800-933-7890 or 414-902-4005; ballgame tickets 414-933-9000; www.millerpark.com

How do you go to Milwaukee and not go to a Brewer's game? It's just not done. Milwaukee is ultra-famous for its pre-game tailgate parties and grilled bratwursts. Those two things alone are worth the trip, but there's more. Whether you're a baseball fan or not, you need to see the $400 million retractable dome stadium. It's not a world wonder, but it is pretty remarkable. Guided tours highlight the dugout, clubhouse, press box, luxury suites and Bob Uecker's broadcast booth. If you actually get to a game you'll witness an event you won't anywhere else—the Klement's Sausage Race. Four ground crew members don sausage costumes and "race" for home plate. It's hilarious. Stadium tours daily. Call the ticket office for costs, stadium tour times, game schedule and tickets.

NOTE: No tours on days the Brewers play afternoon games.

Milwaukee County Zoo   *ZOO-PERB!*

10001 W Blue Mound Rd, Milwaukee; 414-771-5500; www.milwaukeezoo.org

Hidden moats separate predator from prey at the Milwaukee County Zoo, adding another fascinating dimension to an already awesome place. Polar bears, red pandas, lions, zebras, snakes, monkeys, wolves, giraffes—over 2,500 animals, birds, fish and reptiles from around the world live here. What more could you want? How about a petting zoo, dairy setup, children's rides and animal shows? Consider it done. Hop aboard a zoomobile to tour the grounds. Open daily. Call for hours. Admission charged; additional parking fee. All rides and activities are extra. Wheelchair accessible. Cross-country ski trails; rentals available.

Oak Leaf Recreational Trail   *BIKE THE PARKS*

Milwaukee County Parks

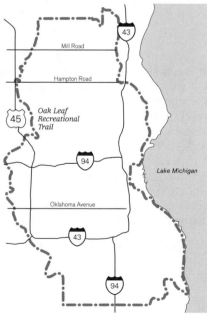

This is the mega trail of bike trails with over 100 miles of multiple

loops through all the major parkways and parks in the extensive Milwaukee County system. Paved trails lead through some of the best nature and bird watching in the county. For a free trail map, call 414-257-6100. Birding maps available at Wehr Nature Center, Whitnall Park; 414-425-8550. See the Odds & Ends section of this chapter for bike rental.

Pelican Cove Aquatic Park

SPLISH-SPLASH

2201 S 7th St, Milwaukee (Kosciuszko Park); 414-384-9498

Pelican Cove in Kosciuszko Park is brand new (summer 2004). Beach-entry heated pool, two giant body-waterslides and a tots area with interactive toys and waterslides. Concessions stand. Open daily. Call for hours. Admission charged. See map page 171.

Pier Wisconsin

SET SAIL, MATEY

500 N Harbor Dr, Milwaukee 53202; 414-276-7700; www.pierwisconsin.org

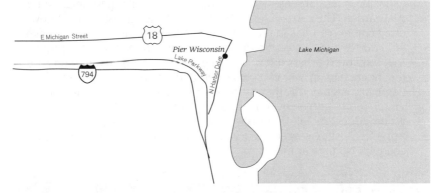

This is not a mere day trip, this is an adventure! Pier Wisconsin owns and operates Wisconsin's flagship, the *Denis Sullivan*. The ship is a 137', 3-masted vessel that looks like a nineteenth-century Great Lakes schooner. Volunteers spent over 900,000 hours building her. It serves as a floating classroom, dedicated to marine ecology. There are a number of good programs to choose from including a 12-day "Science Under Sail" for high school and college students, but the best thing about the *Denis Sullivan* is you get to help the crew sail her! A hands-on, 2½-hour day sail or sunset cruise. Call for fees.

Gardens

Colorful, fragrant, alive. Milwaukee gardens run the gamut between untamed native to symmetrical hybrid.

Boerner Botanical Gardens

9400 Boerner Dr, Hales Corners (within the 600-acre Whitnall Park); 414-525-5600; www.countyparks.com/horticulture

An amazing 40 acres of formal "garden rooms" showcase plant collections such as the peony, daylily and rose (over 3,000 bushes!). Other Boerner gardens include shrub, herb, annual, perennial and a trial garden. The surrounding arboretum has the largest stand of flowering crabapple trees in the country. The statuary and wood carvings are courtesy of the Works Project Administration, a federal project that employed artists during the Depression. The actual gardens are the brainchild of Alfred L. Boerner and Charles B. Whitnall—the nationally regarded Father of the Parkway System. Get a map at the visitor center and enjoy! Gift shop, cafe, horticulture library and glass atrium. Concerts Jul–Labor Day Th evenings. Gardens open daily late Apr–Oct. Visitor center open year-round. Call for hours. Admission charged. No pets or bikes.

Forest Home Cemetery

2405 W Forest Home Ave, Milwaukee; 414-645-2632; www.foresthomecemetery.com

Um, not sure if Forest Home belongs in the Garden Tours chapter or Museums & the Arts section of this chapter, but either way it's 200 acres of amazing gardens and magnificent mausoleums reminiscent of Washington DC monuments. Start the tour at the climate controlled mausoleum that doubles as the Halls of History—a community education center with exhibits and handy self-guided tour maps pointing to the final resting places of Milwaukee's famous. Of course, the Brewmasters are here, but so are lawyers, restaurant owners, politicians and the wholesale florist who originated the FTD service. Open most days.

Mitchell Park Conservatory (The Domes)

524 S Layton Blvd, Milwaukee; 414-649-9830;
www.countyparks.com/horticulture

Billed as the "only structure of its kind in the world," the conservatory is three separate 7-story glass domes that look like NASA designed them. The domes total 15,000 square feet, each with its own habitat. The Tropical Dome sees its share of wedding couples, thanks, in part, to the lush foliage, showy orchids and picturesque 35' waterfall. In stark contrast to the muggy, having-a-bad-hair-day-rainforest, the Arid Dome is a collection of desert cacti and succulents. It's bright and dry and a world far removed from Wisconsin. The Show Dome changes garden themes five times a year, ending the season with a brilliant display of vibrant poinsettias. The Learning Center gives an interesting view of what life looks like through a bug's eyes. Self-guided tours. Open daily. Admission charged. Gift shop. Wheelchair accessible.

Seven Bridges Trail

Grant Park, Milwaukee (enter at S Lake Dr and Park Ave; parking and trail entrance are on the left, ⅛ mile east)

This may not be a garden in the traditional sense, but it's definitely a hike not to be missed. The main entrance is through the Covered

Bridge. Unpaved paths, staircases and footbridges wind through a gorgeous wooded ravine and along the Lake Michigan shoreline.

Wehr Nature Center

9701 W College Ave, Franklin (within Whitnall Park); 414-425-8550; www.countyparks.com/horticulture

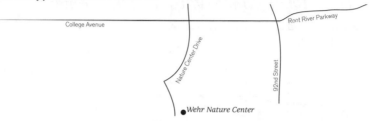

Primarily conceived as a place to learn more about the environment, the Wehr Nature Center maintains a controlled wildness about its gardens and trails. Hike around a 20-acre lake through woodlands, wetlands, oak savanna and prairie. The center has wildlife exhibits, cross-country ski trails, field trips and a gift store. Wehr is also the major hub on the **Oak Leaf Birding Trail**, part of the **Great Wisconsin Birding Trail**. More than 100 bird species live in the Milwaukee area and another 150 other species pass through during migration. The Oak Leaf Birding Trail identifies 35 prime birding locations in county parks and parkways. There's a map with a checklist at the nature center, along with binoculars for rent. Wehr is open year-round. Free admission. Parking fee. Wheelchair accessible.

Museums & the Arts

Prepare yourself to be amazed. Milwaukee is a colossal culture center for design, art and history. If you do nothing more than visit the museums, you're looking at a week's stay. Here are a few to get you started.

America's Black Holocaust Museum

2233 N 4th St, Milwaukee; 414-264-2500; www.blackholocaustmuseum.org

Founded by America's only known survivor of a lynching, the museum serves as a memorial to those who suffered five centuries of slavery as well as an education center aimed at understanding the forces behind racial injustice. Open M–Sa. Guided tours. Fee charged.

Charles Allis Art Museum

1801 N Prospect Ave, Milwaukee; 414-278-8295; www.cavtmuseums.org

The first president of Allis-Chalmers tractors amassed an incredible worldwide collection of art and wrapped it all up in an elegant 1911 Tudor mansion built solely for the public's delight. The museum includes original and antique furnishings, along with galleries featuring Wisconsin artists. Beautiful English gardens surround the mansion. Galleries feature Wisconsin artists. Open W–Su. Su guided tours. Fee charged.

Clown Hall of Fame

161 W Wisconsin Ave, Ste LL700, Milwaukee (lower level of the Grand Ave Mall); 414-319-0848; www.theclownmuseum.org

You'll find lots of funny business here. The museum houses clown exhibits and memorabilia, including costumes from some of the world's most famous jesters. Videos and summer performances. Open M–F. Admission charged, clown show additional charge.

Eisner Museum of Advertising and Design

208 N Water St, Milwaukee (Third Ward); 414-847-3290; www.eisnermuseum.org

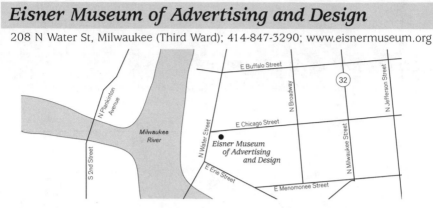

The Eisner has tons of advertising exhibits in all media forms. Two of the most popular displays are the Television Gallery and the Radio Studio. The Television Gallery is nonstop viewing of commercials from the "olden days" as well as more recent award-winning international ads. The Radio Studio allows you the opportunity to record your own radio commercial, but it's not as easy as you think. The studio tests timing and interpretive skills, giving you a taste of what a real commercial shoot is like. Open W–Su. Call for hours. Admission charged.

Haggerty Museum of Art

Marquette College, 530 N 13th St, Milwaukee; 414-288-1669;
www.marquette.edu/haggerty

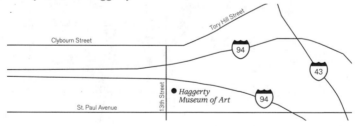

From the masters to contemporary, there are over 4,000 pieces in a permanent collection at the Haggerty Museum of Art. You'll see everything here—sculpture, pottery, paint, paper. Free admission and free parking.

Historic Trimborn Farm

8881 W Grange Ave, Milwaukee; 414-529-7744 or the Historical Society
414-273-7744; www.milwaukeecountyhistosoc.org

A limestone quarry and kilns helped grow this historic (1851) 10-acre
farm to 650 acres, becoming the regions largest employer at the time.
Take a self-guided tour through farm buildings spring–fall. Also on the
Trimborn grounds and worth a look is the **Jeremiah Curtin House**, a
first-of-its-kind stone house built in 1846. The **Kilbourntown House**
is an 1844 Greek Revival and one of Milwaukee's original settlements. Free admission.

Milwaukee Art Museum

700 N Art Museum Dr, Milwaukee; 414-224-3200; www.mam.org

Named the "best design of 2001" by *Time Magazine*, the Milwaukee
Art Museum building resembles Jean-Luc Picard's spaceship
Enterprise. Giant skeletal "wings" raise and lower to suit lighting
needs. It's truly a spectacular feat of architecture. Inside are the works
of *the* masters—Monet, Picasso and Renoir—and the more contemporary O'Keeffe, Johns and Warhol. Permanent collections include
nearly 20,000 pieces as well as changing exhibits throughout the year.
Open year-round. Admission charged. Wheelchair accessible.

> **Option:** The Milwaukee Art Museum is part of the **Milwaukee
> County War Memorial Center**. Exhibits pay tribute to the
> veterans who served their country; 750 N Lincoln Memorial Dr,
> Rm 315, Milwaukee; 414-273-5533.

Milwaukee Museum Center

Milwaukee Public Museum, 800 W Wells St, Milwaukee; 414-278-2700; www.mpm.edu; **Discovery World,** 815 N James Lovell (7th St); 414-765-9966; www.discoveryworld.org; **Humphrey IMAX Dome Theater,** 800 W Wells St; 414-319-4629; www.mpm.edu/imax/imax.html

The Milwaukee Museum Center houses three unique attractions under one roof—Milwaukee Public Museum, Discovery World and the Humphrey IMAX Dome Theater. The 15,000-square-foot **Milwaukee Public Museum** contains everything from strangler trees to the world's largest dinosaur skull to an interactive live butterfly garden. Three floors of mazes lead through the Streets of Old Milwaukee, Asia and Africa, the Pacific Islands, Latin America, the Arctic and the Pre-Columbian era. Hunt down a buffalo with Native Americans, identify bird calls, come face to face with wildlife, find out what's at the bottom of the ocean, catch a butterfly—you'll do it all and more. Interactive displays, gift shop, motion simulator ride, cafe and special exhibits throughout the year. Open daily. Admission charged.

Discovery World has three floors of totally interactive learning adventures. Live theater shows and 150 hands-on exhibits roll science, technology and entrepreneurship into one word—fun! Control robots, see in the dark with an infra-red camera, predict the weather, test pilot a plane, produce your own TV show or design your own invention. It's all possible at Discovery World. Special events and programs, including overnight science sleep-ins. Open daily. Admission charged.

Humphrey IMAX Dome Theater is Wisconsin's only IMAX theater. The 7-story dome screen always thrills no matter the age. Open daily. Call for movie schedule. Admission charged.

Mitchell Gallery of Flight

Mitchell International Airport, 5300 S Howell Ave, Milwaukee (upper level of the airport); 414-747-4503; www.mitchellgallery.org

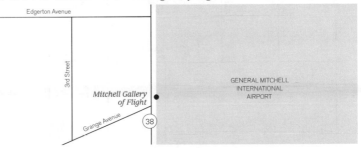

The museum houses several old aircraft—Graf Zepplin, Lawson Airliner, 1911 Curtis Pusher—and commercial air memorabilia. Hear about military aviation pioneer Billy Mitchell. Open daily. Free admission.

Old World Wisconsin

S103 W37890 Hwy 67, Eagle (35 miles southwest of Milwaukee); 262-594-6300; www.oldworldwisconsin.org

Old World Wisconsin is the Midwest's largest outdoor museum of living history. See costumed "pioneers" hard at work tilling the land with horse and oxen-drawn equipment, hand-stitching quilts and cooking on wood stoves. The village has over 65 relocated historic Wisconsin buildings and all the necessities of the 1870s. Help knead bread or weave baskets; clean wool for spinning. Take a hike on one of the trails—there are 600 acres to explore. Talk with the villagers and find out what life was like in the nineteenth century. Gift shop. The barn restaurant serves cafeteria-style. Open daily May–Oct. Admission charged (includes tram rides).

Pabst Mansion

2000 W Wisconsin Ave, Milwaukee; 414-931-0808; www.pabstmansion.com

The 1892 grand mansion was the home of Captain Frederick Pabst, the founder of the brewery empire that bears his name. Pabst was also an accomplished sea captain, real estate developer, philanthropist and patron of the arts. The mansion, with its 37 rooms and 12 baths, is a mere 20,000 square feet—cozy, don't you think? It displays original furnishings and the finest in wall coverings, ironwork, stained glass, woodwork and well, everything. Open daily, closed M mid-Jan–Feb. Admission charged.

Riverwalk

Riverwalk encompasses 6 blocks between Highland Ave to Clybourn St on both sides of the Milwaukee River.

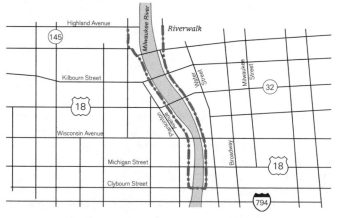

There are brewpubs and restaurants galore along this 6-block stretch, but also some fascinating sculptures that range from humorous to hmm?

Villa Terrace Decorative Arts Museum & Gardens

2220 N Terrace Ave, Milwaukee; 414-271-3656; www.cavtmuseums.org

In close proximity to the Charles Allis Art Museum, the 1923 Italian Renaissance villa presents art from the fifteenth through the twentieth centuries. The real showstoppers, however, are the priceless wrought iron masterpieces by Cyril Colnik. Formal gardens and a stunning view of Lake Michigan rank this museum a must-see. Open W–Su, tours Su. Admission charged.

Wisconsin Automotive Museum

147 N Rural St, Hartford; 262-673-7999; www.wisconsinautomuseum.com

The museum houses 100 vintage automobiles such as Pierce-Arrows, Studebakers, Reos and the rare Kissel luxury automobiles. Manufactured right in good old Hartford from 1906 until the depression, only 200 of the original 2,500 Kissels are known to exist. Amelia Earhart owned one of the speedsters. For the gearhead in you, there are all kinds of automobile memorabilia on display such as spark plugs, oil cans, signs, industrial engines and a 250-ton locomotive. Admission charged.

> **Option:** This isn't a museum or actual "art" per se, but it is the world's largest four-faced clock. Built in 1962, the **Allen-Bradley clock tower** soars 333'4". The clock faces are over 40' wide and weigh more than 12 tons, with minute hands 20' long; that's twice the size of Big Ben's clocks! Imagine the fun the clock-changing technicians have during Daylight Savings. The Allen-Bradley is at 1201 S Second St.

Wine & Beer Tours

Before Wisconsin was even a territory, it had breweries. Lots of them. By the late 1890s nearly every community had at least one operating brewery—Milwaukee had more than 80! Milwaukee has always been known as Beer City, but it has its share of superb, award-winning wineries as well.

Cedar Creek Winery

N70 W6340 Bridge Rd, Cedarburg (17 miles north of downtown Milwaukee); 800-827-8020 or 262-377-8020; www.cedarcreekwinery.com

As charming as it is historic, the folks of Cedarburg had the foresight to preserve over 100 of their original limestone buildings. Once restored, the buildings reopened as antiques shops, galleries, restaurants and quaint bed and breakfasts. The Cedar Creek Winery took up residence in a former 1850s woolen mill. Daily guided tours of the wine cellars are available year-round. Free tastings.

> **Option:** **Wisconsin's last covered bridge** (1876) is about 3 miles north of town. Take Hwy 143/60 junction on Washington Ave. For more information, contact the **Cedarburg Chamber of Commerce**; 800-CDR-BURG; www.cedarburg.org.

Lakefront Brewery

1872 N Commerce St, Milwaukee; 414-372-8800; www.lakefrontbrewery.com

What do you get when two brothers mess around in a kitchen? A wildly successful brewery that's not afraid to produce pumpkin beer as well as the traditional brews. For the purists, Lakefront pours an organic beer (one of the few certified worldwide). Tours and tastings are M–Sa. Call for times. Admission charged.

Mason Creek Winery

6 W Main St, Delafield; 262-646-5766; www.masoncreekwinery.com

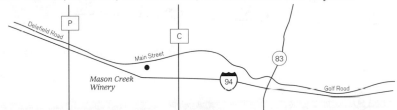

Mason Creek Winery was a hobby that became an obsession and now a profession for owners Max and Bobbi Gomon. With backgrounds in engineering and business marketing, they started the winery with a desire to "produce the highest quality wines and offer extreme customer service." They make approximately 23,000 bottles on the premises, hand labeled and corked. Max delivers the wine in his blue 1947 Ford pickup. They feature many of the standard favorites such as Riesling and red zinfandel, but they also sell a special cranberry wine made from 100 percent Wisconsin cranberries. Open daily except M. Tour fee charged.

Miller Brewing Co.

4251 W State St, Milwaukee; 414-931-BEER; www.millerbrewing.com

It's Miller time! Founder Frederick Miller's brewery produced 300 barrels of beer its opening year in 1855. The Miller Brewing Co. now produces 500,000 cases of beer per day and is the second largest brewery in the US. Displays at the entrance highlight Miller's history and the brewing process. The free 1-hour guided walking tour starts with a movie, then moves to the packaging center, shipping center, brew house (56 steps) and Caves Museum. A good share of it takes place outside as you traipse from building to building, so dress for the weather. Open Memorial Day–Labor Day M–Sa. Sampling is in the outdoor beer garden and the Inn. Call for hours and tour times.

Milwaukee Ale House

233 N Water St, Milwaukee; 414-226-2337; www.ale-house.com

Established in 1997, the Ale House is one of the largest brewpubs in the state. They have good food, live music four nights a week and specialty beers to wet the whistle. No organized tours, but you may find a chatty bartender to show you the ropes. Open daily.

Riverwalk Boat Tours

414-283-9999; www.riverwalkboats.com

Why take a cab when you can take a boat to your favorite brewpubs? Riverwalk Boat Tours may be America's only brewery tour by boat. The 3½-4-hour, round-trip tour starts at your choice of the Lakefront Brewery, Rock Bottom Restaurant & Brewery or the Milwaukee Ale House and stops at each of these three breweries (see maps in this section). The tour is offered on weekends during the summer months. It's unlimited sampling for one fee. Reservations are required. Call for times and fees.

Rock Bottom Restaurant & Brewery

740 N Plankinton Ave, Milwaukee; 414-276-3030

Rock Bottom serves only their own beers, but no worries. They have numerous choices with a wide selection on tap. Get this, they make a honey beer that contains no honey. For the proper traditionalist, they have two beers placed on cask and served from British hand pumps. No organized tour here either, but after slamming a Raccoon Red quickly followed by a Brown Bear Brown, you may not care.

Sprecher Brewing Company

701 W Glendale Ave, Glendale; 414-964-2739; www.sprecherbrewery.com

Founded in 1985 by a former brewery supervisor for Pabst Brewing, Sprecher's is Milwaukee's original microbrewery, producing craft beers and gourmet sodas such as Ravin' Red, a yummy cherry/cranberry concoction. Take the tour, it's a good one. It begins at the Rathskellar Museum and moves through the brewhouse, bottling line and warehouse. The lager cellar has fabulous Bavarian murals. The beer garden is a festive indoor tent with polka music and plenty of beer and soda for sampling. You'll leave with a smile on your face and a complimentary tasting glass in your hand. Gift shop. Open year-round. Scheduled tour times on F & Sa. Admission charged. Call for reservations.

Water Street Brewery

1101 N Water St, Milwaukee; 414-272-1195; www.waterstreetbrewery.com

The Water Street Brewery is Milwaukee's oldest brewpub. They have a gigantic beer memorabilia collection and full menu of tasty food from salads to dinners. Tours by appointment only. Open daily. Their second location is 3191 Golf Rd, Delafield; 262-646-7878.

Option: Okay, so this isn't a brewery or winery tour, but you can get both libations at the **Safe House** along with a lot of other Spy's demise concoctions—shaken, not stirred, of course. The restaurant is cloak- and-dagger hijinks starting with the secret password at the red door entrance. Don't know the password? Oh-oh? The place is a plethora of spy games, mine fields, secret hallways and photos of famous people who've eaten there. The food isn't fancy—burgers and the like—but good. Make sure you pay your tab, because finding your way out of the place ain't easy. Here's the 411 on the Safe House, but don't tell them you read it here! Open daily. Behind International Exports, Ltd., 779 N Front St, Milwaukee; 414-271-2**007**; www.safe-house.com

Milwaukee Odds & Ends

As you can tell, there's lots to do in Milwaukee. Here's a list of some other things you might find helpful. Contact the **Milwaukee Visitor Information Center** at 414-908-6205 for more information.

Bike Rental

- **Veterans Park**, 1010 N Lincoln Memorial Dr, Milwaukee; 414-257-6100; www.countyparks.com (in-line skates and bikes)

- **Milwaukee Bike and Skate Rental**; 414-273-1343 or 262-510-3439

Boat Excursions & Rentals

- **Iroquois**, 445 W Oklahoma Ave, Milwaukee 53207; 414-294-9450

- **Juneau Park Paddleboats**, Veterans Park lagoon; 414-466-7235 (paddleboats, hydro bikes, remote-controlled sailboats)

- **Lake Geneva Cruise Line**, 812 Wrigley Dr; PO Box 68 Riviera Docks, Lake Geneva 53147; 800-558-5911; www.cruiselakegeneva.com

- **McKinley's Pebble Beach**; 414-630-5387; www.jetski-milwaukee.com (jet ski, kayak)

- **Pier Wisconsin**, 500 N Harbor Dr, Milwaukee 53202; 414-276-7700; www.pierwisconsin.org

- **Performance Yacht Services**, 520 S Water St, Milwaukee 53204; 414-788-0990; e-mail gforce@execpc.com

- **Riverwalk Boat Tours & Rentals**, 1137 N Old World Third St, Milwaukee 53203; 414-283-9999; www.riverwalkboats.com

- **Sea Dog Sailing**, 3134 S Pine Ave, Milwaukee 53207; 414-687-3203; www.seadogsailingmilwaukee.com

Bus

- **Milwaukee County Transit System**, 1942 N 17th St, Milwaukee; 414-344-6711; www.ridemcts.com

Car Ferry

- **Lake Express**, Milwaukee Terminal, 2330 S Lincoln Memorial Dr; 866-914-1010 or 414-291-9000; www.lake-express.com (2½-hour trip across Lake Michigan to Muskegon, MI; 3 departure times daily)

Carriage Rides

- **Milwaukee Coach & Carriage**; 414-272-6873 (year-round)

Dog Park

- **Granville Dog Park**, 11718 W Good Hope Rd, Milwaukee; www.pipdogpark.com (the only Milwaukee County park where dogs are leash-free)

Downhill Skiing

- **The Mountain Top Ski Hill**, Grand Geneva Resort, 7036 Grand Geneva Way, Lake Geneva 53147; 800-558-3417; www.grandgeneva.com (15 runs)

- **Olde Highlander Golf & Ski Hill**, Olympia Resort & Conference Center, 1350 Royale Mile Rd, Oconomowoc 53066; 262-567-6048; www.olympiaresort.com (6 runs)

- **Alpine Valley Resort**, East Troy (south and east along County D); 800-227-9395 or 262-642-7374 (12 runs)

Fishing Charters

- **Blue Max Charters**, 414-828-1094; www.bluemaxcharters.com

- **Wishin "N" Fishin**, 1246 S 34th St, Milwaukee 53215; 414-305-9196; e-mail captnjoe777@hotmail.com

Ice Skating

- **Pettit National Ice Center**, 500 S 84th St, Milwaukee 53214; 414-266-0100; www.thepettit.com (official US Olympic Training Facility, open daily to public)

- **POWERade Iceport**, 3565 E Barnard Ave, Cudahy 53110; 414-744-5026; www.poweradeiceport.com (opened summer 2004, one of the only places in the country to house five ice rinks under one roof)

- **Wilson Park Recreation Center & Ice Arena**, 4001 S 20th St, Milwaukee; 414-281-6289; public skating 24-hour hotline for hours 414-281-4610

Motorcycles

- **Harley-Davidson**, 6221 W Layton Ave, Milwaukee; 877-518-4643 or 414-282-2211; www.houseofharley.com (closed Su; must be 21, motorcycle license required)

- **Milwaukee Iron Motorcycle Tours**; 800-964-1257 or 262-628-9421 (fully chauffeured tour on a Harley Hog)

Sports

- **Elkhart Lake's Road America**, N7390 Hwy 67 (60 miles north of Milwaukee), PO Box P, Elkhart Lake 53020; 800-365-7223; www.roadamerica.com (North America's only permanent 4-mile road racing circuit, vintage cars, motorcycles, on-site driving/racing school)

- **Milwaukee Admirals Hockey Club**, 1001 N 4th St, Milwaukee 53203; 414-902-4400; www.milwaukeeadmirals.com

- **Milwaukee Brewers Baseball Club**, Miller Park, One Brewers Way, Milwaukee 53214; 414-902-4400; www.milwaukeebrewers.com

- **Milwaukee Bucks**, 1001 N Fourth St, Milwaukee 53203-1312; 414-227-0500; www.bucks.com

- **Milwaukee Mile**, 7722 W Greenfield Ave, West Allis 53214; 414-453-5761; tickets 414-453-8277; www.milwaukeemile.com (state fairgrounds; high-speed auto racing)

- **Milwaukee Wave Professional Soccer**, 510 W Kilbourn Ave, Ste B, Milwaukee 53203; 414-224-WAVE; www.milwaukeewave.com

Taxicabs

- **American United Taxicab Service**, 646 S 2nd St, Milwaukee; 414-220-2010

- **Yellow Cab Co-Op**, 1840 N Martin Luther King Dr, Milwaukee; 414-271-1800

Theater Companies

- **Apple Holler**, 5006 S Sylvania Ave, Sturtevant; 800-238-3629 or 262-884-7100; www.appleholler.com (musical comedy dinner theater and murder mysteries in a converted cow barn)

- **Chamber Theatre**, Broadway Theatre Center, 158 N Broadway,

Milwaukee; 414-276-8842; www.chamber-theatre.com (primarily Wisconsin artists, classic and contemporary plays)

- **First Stage Children's Theater**, 929 N Water St, Milwaukee; 414-273-2314; www.firststage.org (classic and contemporary plays for families)

- **M & W Productions**, PO Box 511821, Milwaukee; www.mandwproductions.com (family theater at The Cooley Auditorium, downtown)

- **Milwaukee Repertory Theater**, 108 E Wells St, Milwaukee; 414-224-1761; www.milwaukeerep.com (drama, classics, comedy, cabaret—downtown theater district)

- **Next Act Theater**, 342 N Water St, Milwaukee; 414-278-7780 or 414-278-0765 box office; www.nextact.org (critically acclaimed, off-Broadway and contemporary located in Milwaukee's newest theater, the Off-Broadway Theatre)

- **Renaissance Theaterworks**, 342 N Water St, Ste 400, Milwaukee; 414-273-0800; www.r-t-w.com (classical and staged productions)

- **Skylight Opera Theatre**, 158 N Broadway, Milwaukee; 414-291-7811; www.skylightopera.com (opera, operetta, Broadway musicals, musical reviews in the Cabot Theatre)

Trains

- **Amtrak**, 800-USA-RAIL; www.amtrak.com; Milwaukee stations: 433 W St. Paul Ave 53203 or General Mitchell International Airport, 5601 S 6th St 53221.

Trolley

- **East Troy Electric Railroad**, PO Box 943, 2002 Church St, East Troy (take Hwy 20 1 mile south of East Troy to Cty ES, turn north on Church St); 262-642-3263; www.easttroyrr.org (museum, tours and dining)

- **Milwaukee County Transit System Trolley**, year-round daily River Route and Lake Route; Downtown Trolley operates May–Oct with stops at Third Ward, Brady St and Old World Third St. Admission charged. Guided tours in summer; 414-344-6711.

T here are hundreds of museums and historic sites in Wisconsin, and all of them provide valuable insight and information about the state and local communities. However, if one were to detail each of these wonderful places, you'd be using this book as a booster for a small child rather than the use for which it was intended. So for brevity's sake and ease, this chapter breaks into several regions and attempts to highlight one-of-a-kind attractions or those that underscore agriculture, business, history, and people unique to the state.

Museums, Historic Sites & the Arts

Central

East

North

South

Museums, Historic Sites & the Arts. . .

West

Central

Dells Mill

E18855 Cty Rd V, Augusta 54722; 715-286-2714

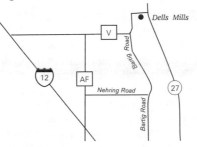

The 1864 Dells Mill operated for over a century using water as its only source of power. The Clark family bought the mill in 1894 and still owns it. No longer a mill (although grinding is done on special occasions), the building was converted into a museum in 1968. A guided tour hikes up and down 5 stories of groaning steps, past 3,000' of belts and 175 pulleys—all powered by a picturesque waterfall within an arm's-length of the building. It's an awe-inspired moment when the guide gets the whole shebang moving and grinding as it did in bygone years. Another eye-popping feature is that the entire mill is built from hand-hewed timbers and wooden pegs. Open daily May–Oct. Call for hours. Admission charged.

High Ground Veterans Memorial Park

W7031 Ridge Rd, Neillsville 54456 (4 miles west of town on Hwy 10); 715-743-4224; www.thehighground.org

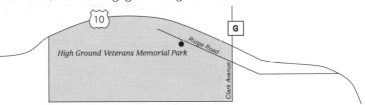

The 140-acre park pays homage to war veterans and their families for their services and sacrifices. Its root beginnings stem from a promise made by Tom Miller on a Vietnam battlefield. As Miller held his mortally wounded friend, he vowed his friend's death would not be forgotten. After securing a site for the park in 1986, a 60' Flag Pole, flag and lights became the first symbolic monument. Wartime statues dot the acreage, but one of the most moving is the **Vietnam**

197

Veterans Tribute. It is the first in the nation to include a woman in the statuary. Beneath her flowing poncho are hundreds of "wind chimes" constructed from bronze rods inscribed with the names of every Wisconsin veteran killed in Vietnam. It is at once both appalling and compelling. Other monuments include the **Earthen Dove Effigy Mound**. Built from soil collected from every county within the state, the Effigy Mound has a wingspan of 140' and is a living memorial to all POWs and MIAs. Trees and bushes form a **5-point Gold Star sculpture** honoring all families who have lost loved ones due to war. The families used the soil from their gardens and yards to plant the bushes. The **National Native American Vietnam Veterans Memorial** is the first national memorial at High Ground. It depicts an Native American soldier grasping a rifle in one hand and an Eagle Feather Staff in the other. Names of all Native Americans who died in the war are carved on a black granite base beneath the statue. The park has walking trails and a Timber Frame information center. Amazingly, High Ground runs without federal or state funding, but continues to expand trails and make plans for future monuments. It's open 24/7 and is free to the public.

Options: On Hwy 10, **Neillsville** is one of those unexpected delightful places that pops up out of nowhere. Hanging baskets, Victorian mansions, flower gardens, a manicured golf course—it's Bedford Falls with a lot more class. • The **1897 Neillsville Jail Museum** is a interesting place to visit, but you certainly wouldn't want to stay there. During its day it was an impenetrable fortress. Tours tramp through the sheriff's quarters and cell block. Open Memorial Day–Sep Su; 215 E State St; 715-743-6444. Call for hours. Admission charged.

Paul Bunyan Logging Camp

1110 Carson Park Dr (inside Carson Park), Eau Claire 54702; 715-835-6200 or 715-834-7871; www.paulbunyancamp.org

You're probably wondering what Paul and his sidekick Babe the Blue Ox are doing so far from Brainerd, Minnesota, but in truth, Eau Claire's only what? Five or six steps away for the giant lumberjack?

Anyway, here he is at a replica 1890s logging camp. Begin the self-guided tour with a short video at the Interpretive Center, then stroll through the log bunkhouse, cook shanty, blacksmith shop and equipment shed. Costumed interpreters demonstrate on antique equipment and answer questions. Open daily Apr–Sep. Call for hours. Admission charged.

Options: The **Chippewa Valley Museum** is also inside Carson Park; 715-834-7871; www.cvmuseum.com. The award-winning museum is always expanding its exhibits with a creative view on the changing world. One of the newest displays is the 1,000-square-foot FULL REFLECTION, which ponders the question why we wear the clothing we do. You'll see a century's worth of apparel including maternity wear. The museum is very hands-on. The 1920s town exhibit teaches children how to build a city and earn a living. A malted milk at the old-fashioned ice cream parlor is always a hit. Open daily in summer. Open Tu–Su in the winter. Call for hours. Admission charged. • Take ½-mile train ride through Carson Park on the **Chippewa Valley Railroad**, Memorial Day–Labor Day Su. Small fee. • Elegant **Fanny Hill** is a Victorian inn, dinner theater and restaurant. Every season is a celebration, but none more so than autumn. Local college students carve more than 5,000 pumpkins for the Halloween display. The pink and cream house looks like a fancy birthday cake overlooking 8 acres of gardens and the Chippewa River. Call waaaaay in advance for reservations; 3919 Crescent Ave, Eau Claire; 800-292-8026; www.fannyhill.com. • One of the prettiest theaters in the state is the **Mabel Tainter** in downtown Menomonie. A wealthy lumber baron dedicated the building to the community in 1889 after his daughter's death. Sandstone exterior, solid oak doors, hand stenciling, marble staircase, Tiffany stained glass windows, gilded opulence, a rare Steere & Turner tracker pipe organ and talented performers make the Tainter a must-see; 205 Main St; 800-236-7675; www.mabeltainter.com. Guided tours daily unless in use. Call for tour schedule; 715-235-0001. • As long as you're in Menomonie you may as well pop in at the **Russell J. Rassbach Heritage Museum** at 820 Wakanda St (inside Wakanda Park); 715-232-8685. Besides the tons of historic county displays and artifacts, they have a cool interactive bank robbery exhibit and a full-scale replica of the **Caddie Woodlawn kitchen**. Caddie was the grandmother of Carol Ryrie Brink, the author of the classic children's book, *Caddie Woodlawn*. Open W–Su May–Sep, F–Su Oct–Apr. Call for hours. Admission charged. NOTE: Wakanda Park has a small zoo with buffalo, deer and water park. • The 1857 **Caddie Woodlawn home site** is 8 miles south of town in a wayside on Hwy 25. The house, smokehouse and cemetery are open spring–fall. Free admission.

Wisconsin Cranberry Discovery Center

204 Main St, Warrens 54666 (1 mile off I-94); 608-378-4878;
www.discovercranberries.com

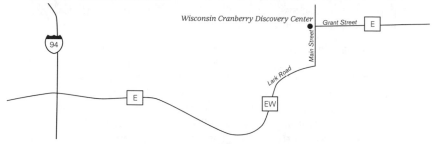

Warrens is the "Cranberry Capital of Wisconsin." A state native, the tart red berry is Wisconsin's number one fruit crop, claiming more than 40 percent of the nation's total production. The Warrens marshes yield around 40 million pounds of cranberries. The annual 3-day festival in late Sep draws a crowd of more than 100,000 to the village with a population of 340. The Discovery Center gives an in-depth overview of the cranberry industry with tours of the bogs available. Sample cranberry ice cream and many other cranberry products in the Taste Test Kitchen. The Discovery Center is open Apr–Oct. Call for hours. Admission charged. Free entrance to the Taste Test Kitchen, Old Fashioned Ice Cream Parlor and gift shop.

Options: Take a self-guided (bike or drive) **23-mile wetland tour** featuring bogs, bogs and more bogs. Most of these are red oceans of cranberries, but there is a huge sphagnum moss drying bed in the mix as well. The moss, also native to the area, is harvested once every five years. It's considered a florist industry staple because it retains more water than Anna Nicole Smith on a Frito-Lay diet. Pick up a bogs tour map almost anywhere in Warrens. • **Ocean Spray** offers free tours of their Wisconsin Rapids cranberry processing plant mid-Sep–early Oct. Call for times and dates; 414-421-5949. • You're closer to Pittsville than you think, and that's not some slang expression for a depressing day of mishaps. The town of Pittsville happens to be the **geographic center of the state**. The proof is written on the marker at Cty Rd E just off Hwy 80 (a few miles northwest of Wisconsin Rapids). • **South Wood County Historical Society Museum** exhibits expand on cranberry agriculture, but include an antique children's toy room, schoolroom, general store and the usual kitchen appliances of the era. The beautiful 1907 mansion is open Su, Tu & Th Memorial Day–Labor Day; 540 Third St S, Wisconsin Rapids; 715-423-1580. Free admission. Call for hours. • **Burnstad's European Village & Café** is part indoor Swiss Alps village with oodles of specialty shops and part lace and schnitzel dining with a dessert tray you'll dream about years after the chocolate-raspberry-mousse-cheese-cake-pie-no-calories-at-all-confectionary is past the lips and on the hips. They're at 701 E Clifton St (Hwy 12 and 16 E), Tomah; 608-372-5355. Open daily year-round. • Cashton is in the heart of Amish Country. Educational tours are offered through **Down A Country Road Tour Service & Gift Shop** (2 miles east of town on Hwy 33; 608-654-5314) or pick up a map from area businesses for a do-it-yourselfer.

East

Birthplace of the Republican Party

Little White Schoolhouse, Blackburn St (Hwy 23), Ripon; 920-748-6764; www.ripon-wi.com

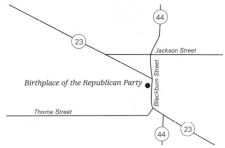

On March 20, 1854, fifty men, three women and one child met in the hallowed halls of the Little White Schoolhouse in Ripon and declared themselves "republicans" after dismantling the local political organizations that were in favor of expanding slavery. They garnered support from an influential editor of the *New York Tribune* and in 1860 elected their first president—Abraham Lincoln. The schoolhouse contains pictures and artifacts from the era. Open May–Sept. Admission free. Donations welcome.

And in case you didn't already know, Ripon is also called **"CookieTown USA."** In 1996, they baked the World's Biggest Cookie and a quick thumb through the *Guinness Book of Records* proves it.

Option: **Larson's Famous Clydesdales** are a few miles south of Ripon. There are over a dozen gentle giants to pet and pose with until your heart is content. Afterward, one of the horses performs a variety of tricks while hitched to a cart. Open May–Oct M–Sa; 90-minute guided tours and show at scheduled time. Call for ticket information. Larson's is at W12654 Reeds Corner Rd, Ripon (take Hwy 49 S, turn east on Reeds Corner Rd); 920-748-5466; www.larsonsclydesdales.com

EAA AirVenture Museum

3000 Poberezny Rd, Oshkosh 54902; 920-426-4818; www.airventuremuseum.org

Held annually, the Experimental Aircraft Association (EAA) Museum hosts the world's biggest airshow convention. Over 800,000 spectators marvel at more than 12,000 airplanes of every shape, size and vintage. The museum's permanent collection features more than 250 airplanes and over 20,000 historic aviation objects. Five theaters and interactive displays bring history alive and explain the nuts and bolts of flying. Take the short tram ride to Pioneer Airport, a recreated 1920s airport complete with grass runway and 50 vintage airplanes inside seven period hangars. The kid's play area has swings and pedal planes, but the absolutely coolest thing about the place is you can actually fly in one of the vintage open cockpit aircraft. Sweet! The museum is open daily. Call for hours. Admission charged. It includes access to the museum, all theaters and the Pioneer Airport, which is open May–Oct. Vintage plane rides for an additional charge. No reservations required. Flights go daily, weather permitting. Call the Pioneer office for flight updates; 920-426-4867.

NOTE: See more Oshkosh museums in the Garden Tours chapter, Eastern Gardens section.

Hazelwood Historic Home

1008 S Monroe Ave, Green Bay; 920-437-1840; www.browncohistoricalsoc.org

The 1837 Hazelwood is one of Wisconsin's oldest buildings located in the **state's oldest settlement—Green Bay**. The Greek-revival home was the residence of the president of the state's second Constitutional

Congress. Meticulously refurbished, the home retains many of the family's original furnishings and artifacts. Of special note is the table where the state constitution was composed. Open May Sa & Su, open daily except Tu Jun–Aug. Call for hours. Admission charged.

Hearthstone Historic House

625 W Prospect Ave, Appleton 54911; 920-730-8204; ww.hearthstonemuseum.org

If the only thing the 1882 Queen Anne house had going for it was its majorly elegant decor, it would be worth the tour. But Hearthstone is the world's first private home powered by a central hydroelectric station. The electroliers and light switches designed by Thomas Edison are still in use today. The hands-on displays in the Hydro Adventure Center help you create enough electricity to run a model trolley. If possible, time your visit for the Christmas season as they deck the halls in award-winning Victorian style. Open Su, Tu–F. Call for hours. Admission charged. Additional fee for the Christmas exhibit. Closed mid-Jan–mid-Feb.

Honey Acres Museum & Nature Trail

N1557 Hwy 67, Ashippun; 920-474-4411

Honey Acres has been going strong since 1852. Its prime objective is public education about beekeepers and the honeymaking process. Highlights include a 20-minute video, a nature trail and a tree with a window view of busy bees at work. Sample honey, then buy some in the gift shop. Open daily May–Oct. Call for hours. Free admission.

Neville Public Museum

210 Museum Pl, Green Bay; 920-448-4460; www.nevillepublicmuseum.org

The Neville is two floors packed with exhibits displaying local art and history, natural sciences, paleontology and technology. The main draw is an impressive 7,500-square-foot diorama of a retreating glacier. The walk-through glacier traces 12,000 years of Wisconsin history. Another really interesting exhibit is the almost freakish Transparent Anatomical Mannikin (TAM). The life-size E.T. wannabe explains the parts and functions of the human body. TAM presents weekends only unless otherwise requested. While here, don't miss the breathtaking second-floor skyline view of the Fox River/Green Bay area. Open Tu-Su. Call for hours. Admission is free, but donations are welcome.

NOTE: See the Family Day chapter for more Green Bay museums.

Outagamie Museum & Houdini Historical Center

330 E College Ave, Appleton 54911; 920-733-8445

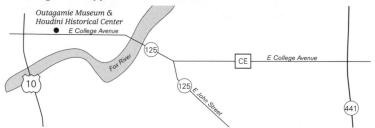

Born in Hungary in 1874, world famous magician and escape artist Harry Houdini spent most of his childhood in Appleton. He performed card tricks until perfecting his escape act. By 1900 the magician was a headliner at major theaters throughout the world. The museum carries the largest collection of Houdini memorabilia in the world, including the original leg irons and locks used in shows. The Outagamie Museum's impressive exhibits range from WW II artifacts to a history of infamous city native Joseph McCarthy to the first edition works by

Pulitzer Prize winner Edna Ferber. In the summer months actors per-form plays bringing alive the county's history. Open Tu–Su in the winter. Open daily through the summer. Admission charged.

Option: The **Fox River Mall** is the largest the state has to offer. With more than 180 stores and restaurants, you'll need to keep your buns of steel working at a steady pace to see it all. The mall is at 4301 W Wisconsin Ave and open daily. Call for hours; 920-739-4100.

Peshtigo Fire Museum

400 Oconto Ave, Peshtigo; 715-582-3244; www.peshtigocham-er.com

October 8, 1871 is the date of two fire disasters—the Chicago Fire and the Peshtigo forest fire. Almost everyone knows about the Chicago Fire and Mrs. O'Leary's cow, but few ever heard of the holocaust that destroyed over 2,400 square miles and claimed the lives of 1,200 people (900 more than the Chicago Fire). The tragedy stands as the nation's most disastrous forest fire. Precious little survived and what did is on display in the Peshtigo Fire Museum located in the first church rebuilt after the catastrophe. The adjacent cemetery contains a mass grave site with 350 unidentified victims. Open daily Memorial Day–Oct 8. Call for hours. Admission is free, but donations are appreciated.

Options: The **Badger Boardwalk** is a 10,000-square-foot play-ground with a castle-like activity area. Located within the 57-acre Badger Park, the community-wide project is along the river at the north end of Emery Ave. • The **Copper Culture State Park** is a few miles south of Peshtigo and close to the intersection of Hwy 41 and 22. The 42-acre day-use park is primarily an ancient Indian burial ground thousands of years old. The people from this time period were the first to make tools and household wares from copper. The park museum sheds some light on the Copper Culture, but is only open on weekends during summer months. Mailing address is PO Box 10448, Oconto 54307; 920-746-5112.

North

Al Capone's Hideout

12101W Cty CC, Couderay 54828; 715-945-2746; www.alcaponehideout.com

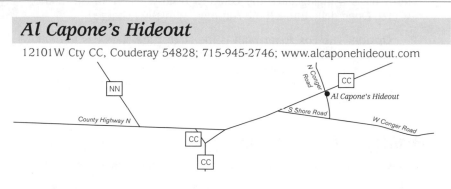

Chicago's notorious outlaw "Scarface" Al Capone got away from the daily gangster grind at his lodge in the peaceful secluded Northwoods. A tour of the Hideout reveals a massive 100-ton stone fireplace, a wooden spiral staircase custom-made in Chicago, original period furniture, an underground jail, a bunkhouse for Capone's hired thugs and a gun tower. What more could a gangster want? Full bar, gift shop and restaurant on the premises. Open daily Memorial Day–mid-Sep. Off-season hours vary; call ahead. Admission charged.

Holt & Balcolm Logging Camp

Cty F, Lakewood 54138 (east of Lakewood on Cty F, go about 1 mile, then turn south into McCauslin Brook Golf & Country Club); 715-276-7769; www.holt-balcolmloggingcamp.com

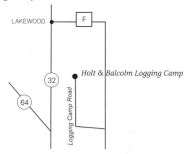

If you're up in this neck of the woods, stop in at the Holt & Balcolm Logging Camp. Built in 1880, this is North America's oldest logging camp and remarkably is still on its original site. The humble log building is the best authentic look at a logger's camp life. Open Jul & Aug Sa. Call for hours. Admission charged.

Option: For a free ½-hour guided tour of the **Mepps fishing lures plant**, stop in at **Sheldon's, Inc.**, 626 Center St, Antigo 54409;

715-623-2382; www.mepps.com. The display room houses all 4,000 lure models. The trophy room shows you what's possible if you use one. Tours are M–F year-round. Call for hours.

Museum of Woodcarving

Hwy 63, Shell Lake 54871; 715-468-7100 or 305-866-6140

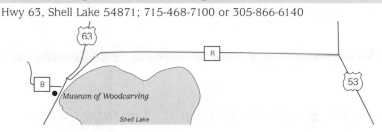

The museum is the world's largest collection of wood carvings crafted by one man, the late Joseph T. Barta. It took Mr. Barta 30 years to carve over 100 life-size figures, 400 miniatures and the amazing Last Supper. The museum has gained national recognition and was featured on *PM Magazine*. Open daily May–Oct. Call for hours. Admission charged.

> **Option:** A restored depot spotlights railroad history in twelve rooms packed to the rafters with train whistles, bells and lights. A prized artifact is the chair President Calvin Coolidge used in the presidential railcar on trips through the Spooner region. The **Railroad Memories Museum** is at 424 Front St, Spooner 54801; 715-635-3325 or 715-635-2752. Open Memorial Day–Labor Day. Call for hours. Admission charged.

National Fresh Water Fishing Hall of Fame

10360 Hall of Fame Dr, Hayward 54843; 715-634-4440; www.freshwater-fishing.org

If you ever wondered what it was like to be Jonah in the belly of the whale, a trip to the Fishing Hall of Fame is your chance to find out. Climb

the 4½-story giant muskie and peer out from his jaws at the world below. Then take a gander at the museum's hundreds of mounts, antique outboard motors and fishing accessories. There are over 5,000 lures alone! Two theaters examine the fishing industry. Throw in a line at the trout pond and try to catch the big one. Open daily mid-Apr–Oct. Call for hours. Admission charged.

Option: Scheer's Lumberjack Shows are always a good time. Watch competitive log rolling, axe throwing, climbing, chopping and sawing. They're located on Cty B, Hayward; 715-634-6923; www.scheerslumberjackshow.com. Shows are M-Sat Memorial Day–Labor Day. Call for show times and ticket prices.

Richard I. Bong World War II Heritage Center

305 Harbor View Pkwy, Superior 54880; 888-816-9944 or 715-392-7151; www.bongheritagecenter.org

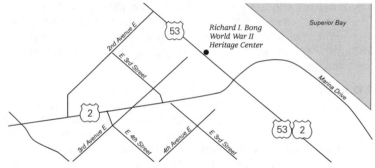

Wisconsin native and WW II hero Major Richard Bong has been called America's greatest pilot. The centerpiece of the museum is the Major's restored P-38 Lightning affectionately named "Marge" after his wife. The plane is one of only 25 remaining P-38s. Twin theaters provide a nice historical overview of Bong and the time. Ironically, the brave fighter pilot survived many air battles only to die while testing aircraft. The Heritage Center is open daily Memorial Day–Oct and Tu–Su Nov–Memorial Day. Call for hours. Admission charged.

SS Meteor Maritime Museum

Barker's Island, Superior 54880; 715-394-5712; www.ssmeteor.org

Permanently anchored at Barker's Island, the 1896 *SS Meteor* is the last remaining whaleback ship in the world. A real workhorse, it plowed through the Great Lakes with a full belly of oil and iron ore. Guided tours march from bow to stern, up and down narrow ladders and through the cargo hold. Open mid-May–mid-Oct. Call for hours. Admission charged.

Options: Vista Fleet hails from Barker's Island as well. Sightseeing packages include the Twin Harbor coal docks, Duluth Aerial Lift Bridge, dinner and moonlit cruises. Open May–mid-Oct. Call for tour schedule; 218-722-6218; www.vistafleet.com. • The **Fairlawn Mansion** is across the highway from Barker's Island; 906 E 2nd St; 715-394-5712. The 42-room, 1890 Victorian was the residence of Mayor Martin Pattison, a wealthy lumber baron and founder of Pattison State Park—the home of the state's highest waterfall (see the Waterfalls chapter). The restored building is three museums in one. The first floor offers a glimpse of the opulent Pattison lifestyle as it was at the turn of the century. The second floor is devoted to local history from the time of the Ojibwe and Sioux. The top floor contains area industry photographs and artifacts in mining, shipping, logging, etc. Fairlawn is open daily year-round Call for hours and tour schedule. Admission charged. • There's lots of antique fire fighting equipment and police memorabilia at the **Old Firehouse & Police Museum**, 23rd Ave E and 4th St; 715-392-2773. The castle-like brick museum is the original 1890 firehouse. Open summer months. Call for hours. Admission charged. • Wisconsin Point is the world's largest breakwater. It has miles of sand beach, a lighthouse (not open), an Indian cemetery, fantastic views of Lake Superior, and it's a perfect place to hunt for agates. From Superior, take E 2nd St to Moccasin Mike Rd; turn north onto Wisconsin Point Rd.

Wa-Swa-Goning

Hwy 47 and Cty H, Lac du Flambeau 54538; 715-588-2615;

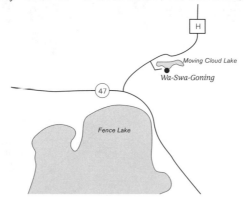

For an accurate portrayal of Ojibwe life, don't miss *Wa-Swa-Goning*, "The place where they spear fish by torchlight." An entire recreated village of birchbark lodges and wigwams sits peacefully along Moving Cloud Lake. Demonstrations during summer include birchbark canoemaking, maple syruping and weaving. Open mid-May–Sept, Tu–Sa. Call for hours. Admission charged.

> **Options:** **George W. Brown, Jr. Ojibwe Museum & Cultural Center** has one of the world's largest and finest collection of Ojibwe Indian artifacts. The gift shop showcases paintings and crafts by Ojibwe artists; 603 Peace Pipe Rd, Lac du Flambeau 54538; 715-588-333; www.ojibwe.com. Open May–Oct M–Sa, Nov–Apr Tu–Th. Call for hours. Admission charged. • The **Northwoods Wildlife Center** takes care of orphaned and injured animals. A guided tour of the hospital brings a renewed respect for all life and appreciation for the dedicated folks who work here. Find them at 8683 Blumenstein Rd, Minocqua 54548; 715-356-7400; www.minocqua.org/nwc. Open year-round. Call for hours. • Invented in 1924, see the **world's first** snowmobile at the **Vilas County Historical Society Museum**, 217 Main St, Sayner 54560; 715-542-3388. Open daily Memorial weekend–mid-Oct. Call for hours. Free admission. NOTE: The lakes in Vilas County outnumber the towns. • For even more snowmobile history, tour the **International Snowmobile Racing Hall of Fame** at 6035 Hwy 70 W, St. Germain 54558; 715-542-4488; www.snowmobilehalloffame.com. Old racing sleds, inductees and videos of famous races top the awesome list. They're open year-round M–F & most Sa, but call ahead. Free admission.

Wisconsin Concrete Park

126 Cherry St, Phillips 54555; 800-269-4505

Over 200 cement cows, horses and people perpetually graze, pull wagons or saw wood. It's sort of like Dorothy discovering the rusted Tin Man in Oz, only there's no oil can fix to get them rolling. They're part of the world's largest cement folk art collection created by the late Fred Smith. Fred also crafted a few legends such as Paul Bunyan, Abraham Lincoln and Ben Hur. The park is open daylight hours year-round. Free admission, but donations are appreciated.

Options: At a dizzying 1,951.5' above sea level, **Timm's Hill** is the **highest point in Wisconsin**. To soak up some serious scenery you're going to have to hoof it about 300 yards from the parking lot to the observation tower; you can look forward to a 100-stair climb after that. However, once you've wheezed your way to the top you're rewarded with a 30-mile panoramic view of Bass Lake and the Northwoods. Spectacular, especially during the fall colors. The park has several nice hiking trails with interpretive signs. The hilly, 10-mile Timm's Hill National Trail links the state's highest point to its longest walking path—the Ice Age National Scenic Trail. If you love to mountain bike, this is your park. It has plenty of challenging trails as well as cross-country and snowmobile trails. Timm's Hill County Park is located on Hwy 86, Ogema 54459 (take Hwy 13 to Ogema, 5 miles east on Hwy 86, then south ½ mile on Cty C, turn east ½ mile on Rustic Road 62); 800-269-4505; www.pricecountywi.net. • Built in 1991, the **Smith Rapids Covered Bridge** is at US Forest Rd 148, Pike Lake Region, Park Falls; 800-269-4505 or 715-762-2461. • The **Big White Pine** is over 300 years old and 130' tall. Find it in Flambeau River State Forest, off Cty M. If the trees look particularly tall along this ribbon of road, it's because this is the largest virgin white pine stand in the Wisconsin.

South

Fennimore Railroad Museum

610 Lincoln Ave, Fennimore 53809; 608-822-6144 or 608-822-6319;
www.fennimore.com/railroad

To service rural communities with cost-efficient transportation, railroad companies laid 150 miles of narrow-gauge tracks across the state for their miniature 15-inch gauge trains. These tiny trains looked like toys, yet the famous Fennimore-Woodman "Dinky" got the job done from 1878–1926. You can still ride a 15" gauge train at the railroad museum. Other highlights are the replica wood water tanks, remodeled depot, ticket booth, blacksmith shop and locomotives. Open daily Memorial Day–Labor Day, weekends only in Sep & Oct. Train rides on weekends. Call for hours. Admission charged.

Option: The **Fennimore Doll & Toy Museum** is at 1140 Lincoln Ave (Hwy 18 and 61); 888-867-7935 or 608-822-4100. The museum is a nostalgic blast to the past for most baby boomers. There are thousands of toys on display from the mid-twentieth century through the present—everything from tractors and trucks to Barbies, GI Joes and Nemo. Open May–Dec. Call for hours. Admission charged.

Lincoln-Tallman House

440 N Jackson St, Janesville; 800-577-1859 or 608-752-4519

Abraham Lincoln enthusiasts will not want to pass by this 26-room Italianate mansion. It's the only private Wisconsin residence in which our nation's 16th President was an overnight guest. It's also the first Janesville home to have indoor plumbing—don't know if that did it for the President or not. The mansion retained over 75 percent of its original decor and furnishings including the bed that Lincoln slept in. Open Tu–Su Jun–Sept, weekends only Feb–May and Oct. Tours begin at the Helen Jeffris Wood Museum Center, 426 N Jackson St. Call for hours. Admission charged.

> **Option:** See the world's largest known angel collection at the **Angel Museum**, 656 Pleasant St, Beloit 53512; 608-362-9099; www.angelmuseum.com. Thousands of winged seraphs, including 600 black angels donated by Oprah Winfrey, are on display in the restored former church. Open Tu–Su Jun–Aug, Tu–Sa Sep–May, closed Jan. Call for hours. Admission charged.

Milton House Museum

Five miles northeast of Janesville at the intersection of Hwy 26 and 59 in Milton; 608-868-7772; www.miltonhouse.org

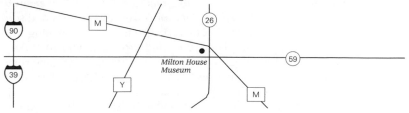

Once part of the Underground Railroad, the 20-room hexagonal Stagecoach Inn is the oldest building in the country made from poured concrete. Narrow underground tunnels connect with an 1837

log cabin. Tours of this important piece of American history take place daily, Memorial Day–Labor Day, weekends in May and by appointment Labor Day–mid-Oct.

Stonefield

Cty VV, along the Mississippi River, 1 mile north of Cassville (across from Nelson Dewey State Park); 608-725-5210; www.wisconsinhistory.org/stonefield/

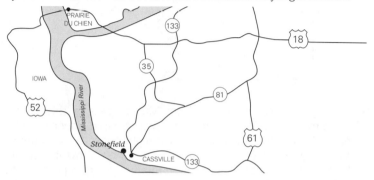

Stonefield and the buildings in the Nelson Dewey State Park are what's left of Wisconsin's first governor's estate. Cross a covered bridge into the nineteenth-century Stonefield village where costumed interpreters man reconstructed buildings and demonstrate antique equipment. Head across Highway VV for a tour of the Governor's house (a brick plantation-type spread), then drive to the top of the park for some prime Bald Eagle watching (Indian mounds bank both sides of the road). The Mississippi River valley view is outstanding from here. Stonefield is open Memorial Day–Labor Day, then weekends only until mid-Oct. Call for hours. Admission charged.

Options: **Lancaster** is east of Stonefield on Hwy 81. Once you spot the courthouse's glass and copper topper, it's pretty easy to figure out why Lancaster's called the **"City of the Dome."** The patriotic residents were the first in the country to erect a **Civil War Monument** (corner of Cherry and Madison St), and the nearby cemetery is the **final resting place of Governor Dewey** (Madison St). • The 9-vehicle **Cassville Car Ferry** is one of the remaining two on the Mississippi River. The route chugs from Cassville to Turkey Creek in Iowa. The ferry is in Riverside Park and to find it take Hwy 81 west to the river. One-way fares can be purchased. The ferry operates daily depending on river conditions; www.cassville.org. • Since you're so close to the **Dickeyville Grotto**, you better go see it. The grotto covers a full block. It was the brainchild of Father Matthias Wernerus, who began building the shrine (without a blueprint) in 1925. Colored rocks, seashells, old dishes, stalagmites, gear shift knobs donated by Henry Ford, arrowheads, Indian tools, and just about every other imaginable thing has been fashioned into permanent flowers, geometric-shaped walls and alcoves and stone-roped walkways dedicated to the patron saints as well as patriotic icons. The parish women care for the numerous gardens. The grotto is open year-round and located on the grounds of the Holy Ghost Church on Hwy 35 N in Dickeyville; 608-568-3119. Free admission, but donations are appreciated.

West

Deke Slayton Memorial Space & Bike Museum

200 W Main St, Sparta 54656; 888-200-5302 or 608-269-0033; www.dekeslayton.com

A Wisconsin native, Donald "Deke" Slayton was one of the Mercury 7—the country's first astronauts. The permanent exhibit examines Slayton's life and accomplishments. The museum's other highlights include some of the first bicycles and a quarter-scale model of the Wright Flyer. Open daily in the summer. Open M–F in the winter. Call for hours. Admission charged.

> **Options:** Sparta is the "Bicycling Capital of America" and befitting its status, it is also home to the **"World's Largest Bike."** The 30' high wheeler is at the corner of E Wisconsin and S Water St. • The 32-mile **Elroy-Sparta State Bike Trail** is the nation's first conversion of rails-to-trails. It's a fairly easy and scenic trail with three railroad tunnels, a restored caboose information center and loads of bridges and over-passes. Call 608-337-4775. • Who says religion and politics don't mix? They sure do at the **Paul and Matilda Wegner Grotto** with its religious and patriotic folk art encrusted in cement, broken glass and pottery. The site's most notable piece is the Glass Church. The Grotto is a few miles south of Cataract (Hwy 27 south, then west on Hwy 71). Open Memorial Day–Labor Day; 608-269-8680. • Take a mapped driving tour of **Fort McCoy**. This active army training facility gives you a glimpse of life as a recruit and all the tanks and equipment that go with it. Get your driver's license out and keep it out for ID; 608-388-2407; www.mccoy.army.mil. Open daily. Call for hours.

Little House Wayside

Seven miles north of Pepin on Cty CC; 800-442-3011; www.pepinwisconsin.com

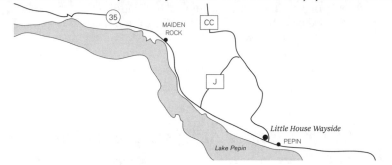

The wayside marks the birthplace of world-renowned children's author Laura Ingalls Wilder. Best known for her classic autobiographic series about pioneer life in the 1800s, Laura wrote the first of the Little House books in 1932 at the age of 65. Eight more books followed and have been translated into more than 40 languages. The book that started it all—*Little House in the Big Woods*—speaks of Laura's Pepin roots, but ironically the big woods is now prime cropland. However, beautiful Lake Pepin and the surrounding river bluffs the author so loved are still "one of the 100 most scenic sights in the world." The original Ingalls house and barn are long gone, but a log cabin replica at the wayside reveals hand-written letters from Laura and photographs of the family. There are also picnic tables, restrooms and an artesian well.

Options: Pepin is the official starting point of the **Laura Ingalls Wilder Historic Highway.** The highway travels to Wilder sites across the Upper Midwest. • Visit the **Pepin Historical Museum** to view more of the author's letters and memorabilia, along with local history. The museum is in town along Hwy 35 and open daily year-round. Call for hours; 715-442-2142. Free admission. • The **Laura Ingalls Wilder Park** is also on Hwy 35. The park has the usual picnic and playground equipment, with a completely refurbished **1886 Depot** as its center attraction. The Depot is jam-packed with steamboat and railroad history and staffed with volunteers during the summer. • While we're on the subject, did you know Pa Ingalls met wife Caroline in the adorable hamlet of Concord? Located slightly south off I-94 between Madison and Milwaukee, Concord celebrates **Laura Ingalls Wilder** with **free readings** from her books at the restored 1850s log cabin on the first Su of the month from Jun–Sep. Call 262-593-8099 for more information.

Octagon House

1004 Third St, Hudson 54016; 715-386-2654

Built in 1855, the Victorian octagon house was a popular design for the time. The eight-sided structure allowed for better lighting and airflow. Four generations lived in the house until the Historical Society purchased it in 1964. Fully restored with period furniture, take a 1-hour guided tour through the home, garden house and carriage house. Wander the beautiful gardens and sit a spell under the gazebo. Open May–Oct, Tu–Su. Late Nov–mid-Dec the house opens for special holiday tours. Admission charged. Call for hours and holiday tour information.

> **Options:** Hudson has a great **self-guided walking tour** of about a dozen historic homes and sites. Call the **Hudson Area Chamber of Commerce** for a free map; 800-657-6775; www.hudsonwi.org.
> • The **Phipps Center for the Arts** is well respected for their theater and musical performances, but they also have an impressive gallery of modern art and admission is free. Find the Phipps along the river at 109 Locust St; 715-386-2305; ticket office 715-386-8409; www.thephipps.org. See the Waterfalls chapter for more attractions in Hudson.

Old Courthouse Museum and Jail

Washington Square, Durand 54736; 715-672-5423

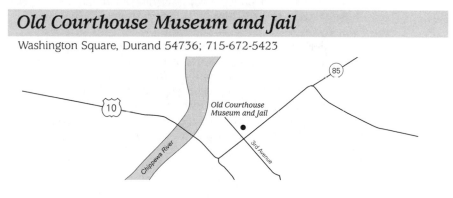

The city of Durand borders the Chippewa River and has a population of roughly 2,000 people who are incredibly supportive of all of their

217

high school teams, so don't mess with that. Durand is also the current Pepin County seat (it had been moved three times prior) and the home of the restored Old Courthouse Museum and Jail. The 1874 Greek Revival building is the **last remaining wood-frame courthouse** in Wisconsin and the site of a lynching. A self-guided tour peruses six theme rooms, the century-old sheriff's quarters and jail. Open Sa Memorial Day–mid-Oct. Call for hours and tour schedule. Admission charged.

NOTE: Internationally honored educator **Helen Parkhurst**—responsible for the Montessori movement in the US—was born in Durand. She holds the distinction of being voted "one of 100 educators of all-time." Who else is on that list? Socrates.

Options: You are in **Amish Country**. These nice folks are in the grocery stores and on the roads in their traditional horse-drawn black buggies. Most Amish farms are east of Durand on Hwy 10. Many have bakeries and furniture shops open for business. • For a taste of the local art scene, stop in at the **Accola Gallery**, 502 2nd Ave E, Durand; 715-672-8188; www.accolagallery.com. Housed in a 1929 craftsman bungalow, the gallery features all medium including Mississippi Pearl jewelry, photography, sculpture, clothing and paintings. The award-winning owner/artist, Jean Accola, works mostly in watercolor. The gallery is open Tu–Sa. Call for hours. • If you drive west on Hwy 10 from Durand, you'll land in the picturesque village of **Plum City**. Even the name is cute. The little town of 500 friendly folks has an old-fashioned hardware store with the original brass-keyed cash register and hard wood floors, a bakery loaded with charm and desserts, a couple of bar/restaurants with home-cooked food and a natural spring-fed **trout pond** filled with fat, colorful fish that like nothing better than to gobble food all day long. Fishing's a no-no; feeding only. • For the best **trout fishing** keep driving west on Hwy 10 to the **Rush River**. *Field & Stream* gave the locale two enthusiastic thumbs up. • **Nugget Lake County Park** (north off Hwy 10 on Cty CC; follow signs) is a great place for fishing, swimming, hiking, camping and panning for diamonds and gold. That's right, diamonds and gold. No one has a clue why these precious nuggets and gems are here as this is limestone country, but bring your own pan if you feel like doing a little prospecting; N4351 Cty HH, Plum City 54761; 715-639-5611.

Villa Louis

On St. Feriole Island, along the Mississippi River, Prairie du Chien 53821; 608-326-2721; www.wisconsinhistory.org/villalouis/

The opulent, 25-acre Victorian country estate rests on the site of the only western battle in the War of 1812. During the mid-nineteenth century, the Dousman's were one of the wealthiest families in the Midwest, amassing a fortune through fur trading, lumber and real estate. Hercules Dousman was the state's first millionaire. His son, Louis, spent the money on an over-the-top, nothing spared mansion. He and his wife filled it with expensive art and exquisite furniture. They traveled and entertained and lived the good life until Louis died unexpectedly, leaving a young wife and five children who could not afford the villa. Eventually the estate was turned over to the city in 1930. In 1995, the home underwent a meticulous $2 million renovation with much of the original furnishings reclaimed. It is absolutely stunning. A must-see for anyone into the Victorian era. Follow a costumed guide for an hour tour of the mansion, gardens, carriage house, War of 1812 battlefield and Fur Trade Museum. Open daily May–Oct. Tours are on the hour rain or shine. Call for hours and tour schedule. Admission charged.

Options: Take a **horse and carriage ride** through the historic St. Feriole Island district. The fellow at the reins is also your tour guide. Prairie Tales tours leave every hour. Find them in the parking lot of the American, 130 S Main; 608-326-7878. • Exhibits at the **Fort Crawford Museum at Prairie du Chien** range from clams and arrowheads to an early medical experiment documenting the human digestive system. The museum's three buildings are open May–Oct; 717 S Beaumont Rd (corner of Beaumont and Rice St); www.fortcrawfordmuseum.com. Call for hours; 608-326-6960. Admission charged.

Romance is a state of "being," not "doing." You are "being" romantic, not "doing" romantic. The five trips in this chapter have everything you need to enhance your romantic state of being. Waterfalls, wineries, champagne cruises, scenic country drives, endless hiking/cross-country trails, covered bridges, horseback riding, luxury B&B's and friendly small towns with laid-back atmospheres.

Romantic Getaways

Bayfield: Things to Do

Bayfield: The B & Bs

Lake Geneva: The Parks

Lake Geneva: The Trails

Lake Geneva: Things to Do

Romantic Getaways

Bayfield

The Bayfield Peninsula is north of "up north," along Lake Superior on Hwy 13. It is the gateway to the Apostle Islands. **Bayfield Chamber of Commerce**, PO Box 138, Bayfield 54814; 800-447-4094 or 715-779-3335; www.bayfield.org

Bayfield and the Apostle Islands are favorite Wisconsin getaways, and it's easy to see why. The picturesque peninsula and archipelago both charm and excite the visitor no matter the season. Tour six lighthouses, charter a sailboat for a sunset cruise, visit an orchard winery, explore sea caves, romance the one you love with a 5-course candlelight dinner, bike, hike, ski, shop the art scene and breathe in the beauty of Lake Superior.

Bayfield: Things to Do

Bayfield Maritime Museum

Located next to the Madeline Island Ferry Dock at 131 S 1st St, Bayfield; 715-779-9919

To get up to speed on the past 150 years of local history, take a tour of the Bayfield Maritime Museum. You'll see an authentic tugboat, various items found from lake shipwrecks and scores of displays relating to boat building, lake fishing, knot tying, marine equipment, lighthouses and more. Open daily through the summer. For off-season hours, call 715-779-3925. Admission charged.

Bayfield Winery

86565 Cty J, 54814; 715-779-5404; www.superiorviewfarm.com

The **Bayfield Winery** resides in a century-old historic barn off Cty J on the Orchard Circle drive. The view of Lake Superior from this elevation is spectacular. Bayfield Winery specializes in fruit wines such as apple and pear and they're part of **Hauser's Superior View Farms**. Hauser's is an apple orchard, thus they have an abundance of apple butter, apple jelly, fresh apples, dried apples, apple pie and apple mustard as well as a really tasty blueberry spread.

Big Top Chautauqua

Find them 3 miles south of Bayfield in Washburn; 888-244-8368; www.bigtop.org

Big Top Chautauqua means bigtime fun under an enormous blue and white tent that seats 800. National and regional acts throughout the summer include comedy, musicals and original historical theater. Tickets can be purchased on-site before the show. Concessions and souvenirs.

Boating/Sailing

There are 21 Apostle Islands and if it's not winter, the only way you're going to see them is by ferry, boat or kayak. There are more charter choices than there are probes into the late Princess Di's life. You shouldn't find it difficult to book something for fishing, sailing or touring. Here are some companies that come highly recommended.

- **Adventures in Perspective**, 866-779-9503; www.livingadventure.com (kayak)

- **Animaashi Sailing Co**, 888-272-4548; www.animaashi.com

- **Bayfield Charter**, Apostle Islands Marina; 800-567-0112; www.bayfieldsailing.com

- **Blackhawk Charters**, 800-779-3257 (fishing)

- **Catchun-Sun Charter**, 888-724-5494; www.visit-midwest.com

- **Classic Wooden Ketch-Sandpipe**r, 800-881-5903; www.thimbleberryinn.com/sandpiper

- **Dreams Afloat Charter Service**, 651-402-5884 (fishing, boat rides)

- **Roberta's Sport Fishing**, 888-806-0944; www.robertascharters.com (fishing)

- **Sailboats Inc.**, 800-826-7010; www.sailboats-inc.com

- **Superior Charters**, 800-772-5124; www.superiorcharters.com

The Chequamegon-Nicolet National Forest

1170 4th Ave S, Park Falls 54552

Looking for something outdoorsy to do? Then head to the Chequamegon-Nicolet National Forest. It has 11,000 wilderness acres, 632 miles of rivers and streams, 411 lakes, a 60-mile section of the **North Country Trail**, 200 miles of hiking trails, 200 miles of motorized trails, over 800 wetlands, 300 miles of snowmobile trails, over 50 miles of cross-country ski trails and a 12-mile horse trail (miles of forest roads also open for riding). For more information and maps, call the Chequamegon Forest Supervisor office; 715-762-2461.

Dining

- **Greunke's,** 17 Rittenhouse Ave; 715-779-5480. If you're hungry for some whitefish livers or an old-fashioned fish boil, then Greunke's won't disappoint. They've been in business forever and still pack in the local breakfast crowd with their famous blueberry pancakes. They specialize in seafood, but they've got everything else on the menu, including pizza. Open year-round.

- **Maggie's,** 257 Manypenny Ave; 715-779-564. Maggie's is to Bayfield what "Sloppy Joes" is to Key West. Filled with raging pink flamingo paraphernalia and every other kind of odd thingamabob, Maggie's is not only interesting, it serves up some tasty grub. They're open year-round for lunch and dinner.

- **Old Rittenhouse Inn,** 301 Rittenhouse Ave; 800-779-2129 or 715-779-5111; www.rittenhouseinn.com. For a very special evening, make reservations at the Old Rittenhouse Inn. For almost three decades the gorgeous Old Rittenhouse Inn has been wowing guests with palate-pleasing culinary delights such as their famous 2" thick apple-glazed pork chops, almond-crusted salmon and triple chocolate cheesecake. Open to the public daily throughout the summer (weekends in the winter). Enjoy breakfast, lunch or an elegant, 5-course candlelight dinner. Reservations are required.

Dogsledding

Mushing is a popular winter sport in the Northwoods. It's a unique and picturesque way to see the Apostle Islands as few have seen them. If you've never tried it before, this is your chance as the experienced Bayfield outfitters and guides have thousands of dogsledding miles under their belts. Trips vary from 1-day treks to week-long camping adventures.

- **Snow Ryder,** 852 Main St, La Pointe (Madeline Island) 54850; 715-747-2000; www.ontheisland.com

- **Trek & Trail Adventure Outfitters,** 7 Washington Ave, 54814; 800-354-8735; www.trek-trail.com

- **Wolfsong Adventures in Mushing,** HC 64 Box 107, 54814; 800-262-4176 or 715-779-5561; www.wolfsongadventures.com

NOTE: For more details about dogsledding and Wolfsong, see the Extreme Adventures chapter. Also, the annual Apostle Islands Sled Dog Race takes place in Feb.

Golf

- **Apostle Highlands Golf Course**, 34745 Madeline Trl, 54814; 877-222-4053; 715-779-5960; www.golfbayfield.com (18-hole, par 72)

- **Madeline Island Golf Club**, PO Box 649, La Pointe 54850; 715-747-3212; www.madelineislandgolf.com (18-hole)

Lighthouses

There are six lighthouses still in use via automated stations; all are located on the Apostle Islands and accessible by boat only. For information on touring lighthouses, check www.nps.gov/apis/table.htm

- **Devils Island**—The1898 lighthouse has a Queen Anne-style keeper's dwelling. The tower rises 82'. Devils Point is the northernmost point in Wisconsin.

- **La Pointe**—The 1895 lighthouse has a tower 67' high and is found on Long Island. There aren't any tours, but there is a dock on the island if you'd like to explore.

- **Michigan Island**—Built in 1857, the 112' tower was added in 1929.

- **Outer Island**—The 1874 lighthouse has a 90' tower. Tours are offered throughout the summer, but call ahead; 715-779-3398.

- **Raspberry Island**—Built in 1863, tour boats visit the island daily mid-Jun–Labor Day.

- **Sand Island**—The 1881 lighthouse was built by locally quarried brownstone. Tour boats dock daily late Jun–Labor Day.

Madeline Island Ferry Line

715-747-2051; www.madferry.com

Departs Bayfield and cuts through Lake Superior on a 20-minute ride to La Pointe on Madeline Island. Trips run early Apr–early Jan and every ½ hour during summer months. Fee charged.

Madeline Island Historical Museum

9 Main St, La Pointe, WI 54850; 715-747-2415

As soon as you dock the island, walk straight ahead a block or two and you'll run into what looks like an old fort. You've just found the Madeline Island Historical Museum. The museum tracks 300 years of Wisconsin history from the fur traders to the wealthy elite who claimed the island for their summer homes. Open Memorial Day–mid-Oct. Call for hours. Admission charged.

> **Options:** Rent a moped or bike at **Moped Dave's Motion To Go** (715-747-6585) and explore every nook and cranny on Madeline Island.• **Bog Lake Outfitters** on Madeline Island rents canoes, rowboats, paddleboats and cabins. Call them at 715-747-2685; winter 608-231-2174.

Orchard Circle   BIKING

Bike the hilltops above Bayfield. From this 600' vantage you have a sweeping view of the Apostle Islands. Take the Orchard Circle and stop to pick cherries, blueberries, strawberries, raspberries, apples and pears.

> **Options:** The **Iron Bridge Trail** begins at the north end of Broad St and heads into the wooded hillside with an amazing view from a 230' 1912 Iron Bridge. • **Trek & Trail** rents bikes by the hour or day (includes helmet); 7 Washington Ave, Bayfield; 800-354-8735.

Orchards

Because of the lake effect, the Bayfield area has an extended growing season perfect for fruit trees and berries. On the hills high above Lake Superior you'll find a concentrated area of orchards thicker than winter molasses. The roads that connect them are known as the **Orchard Circle**. Here's a partial listing of orchards.

- **Bayfield Apple Co**, 87540 Cty J; 800-363-4JAM; www.bayfieldapple.com. These folks have the state's largest raspberry crop. Apples, jellies and cider. Open daily. Call for hours.

- **Hauser's Superior View Farm**, 86565 Cty J; 715-779-5404; www.superiorviewfarm.com. Home of Bayfield Winery. Dried and fresh flowers, jams and jellies. Open daily May–Oct. Call for hours.

- **Highland Valley Farm**, 87080 Valley Rd; 715-779-5446; www.chequnet.net/~rdale Highland produces the state's largest blueberry crop and Bayfield's only honey. Raspberries and maple syrup. Open year-round.

- **James Erickson Orchard & Country Store**, 86600 Betzold Rd; 715-779-5438. Strawberries, apples, home bakery, log cabin antique shop. Open daily Memorial Day–Oct. Call for hours.

Skiing

The Bayfield area is a cross-country skier's paradise. There are so-o-o-o-o many outstanding trails, but some of the most thrilling involve **exploring the sea caves**. Some of the best caves are at **Meyer's Beach**, off Hwy 13, about 16 miles from Bayfield (between Bayfield and Cornucopia). For updated trail conditions call 800-234-6635; www.norwiski.com.

- **Mount Ashwabay,** off Hwy 13 on Ski Hill Rd; 715-779-3227. For downhill skiing and snowboarding, try **Mount Ashwabay**. They have 13 runs, night skiing, rentals, lessons and 25 miles of cross-country ski trails.

Tours

- **Apple Wagon Tours**, 888-806-2896. Your guide through the orchards and historic sites. Call them for more information.

- **Apostle Islands Cruise Service**, City Dock in Bayfield; 800-323-7619 or 715-779-3925; www.apostleisland.com. Narrated tour of the Apostle Islands and lighthouses. Tours run mid-May–mid-Oct. Call for a reservation.

- **Bayfield Heritage Tours**, 715-779-0299; www.bayfieldheritage-tours.com. Several unique trips that put a new spin on local history—Guided Ghost Walk, Historic Lantern Light Walk, Church & Mansion Walk. The 90-minute walks run Jun–Sep. Fee charged. Call them for more information.

- **Madeline Island Bus Tours**, 715-747-2051; www.madferry.com. Buzz around the largest of the Apostle Islands for a 2-hour history excursion. See sandstone formations and do some hiking on the nature trails. Fee charged. Make arrangements at La Pointe.

Bayfield: The B & Bs

The Bayfield area bursts with historic B&Bs and lakeshore cabins, but they fill up fast. It's always a good idea to book your stay in advance, and months in advance of the annual fall Bayfield Apple Festival. Voted one of the top ten Wisconsin festivals, the 3-day event attracts more than 50,000 people (www.bayfield.org/eve_appleFest.htm). Call the Bayfield Chamber of Commerce for more information; 800-447-4094 or 715-779-3335.

Old Rittenhouse Inn

301 Rittenhouse Ave, 54814; 800-779-2129 or 715-779-5111;
www.rittenhouseinn.com

The historic red Victorian mansion is all about pampered luxury with
Lake Superior views, wood-burning fireplaces, whirlpool baths, period antiques and spacious rooms. The Rittenhouse properties include
two mansions, a guest house and a private cottage. The main house
is a gourmet restaurant (see Dining in the Bayfield Things to Do section of this chapter). For breakfast, try the wild rice pancakes—wow!

Pinehurst Inn

83645 Hwy 13, 54814; 877-499-7651 or 715-779-3676;
www.pinehurstinn.com

The historic Pinehurst Inn has wonderful garden trails and rooms
with claw foot tubs, fireplaces and piecework quilts. The full breakfast
is entirely organic, prepared from locally grown foods. They offer
weekend retreats that vary in topic from "couples massage" to "landscape photography."

Winfield Inn & Gardens

225 E Lynde Ave, 54814; 715-779-3252; www.winfieldinn.com

Winfield Inn is actually a motel and not a B&B, so breakfast is on
your own—which isn't a problem in Bayfield. There are many great
dining options, all within walking distance. The Winfield is on the
shore of Lake Superior and has the prettiest gardens in the area. The
spacious outdoor patio overlooks the lake. It's a perfect spot to kick
back and enjoy the view.

Lake Geneva

Lake Geneva is southeast, 10 miles north of the Illinois border at the intersection of Hwy 50 and 120. Lake Geneva Area Convention & Visitors Bureau, 201
Wrigley Dr, Lake Geneva 53147 (at the lakefront downtown); 800-345-1020 or
262-248-4416; www.lakegenevawi.com

Lake Geneva is gorgeous scenery wrapped in pampered luxury. The resort
town (pop. 6,000) has long been a favored retreat for big city dwellers—more
than 60 percent of the summertime influx are Chicago citizens. The town's
focal point is Geneva Lake which is over 7 miles long and 135' deep.
Truthfully, a visit to Lake Geneva is perfect in any season, any weather. With
over 150 specialty and antiques shops, a half-dozen championship golf courses, 3 nearby state parks, a state hiking/biking trail, 5 designated rustic roads,

ski resorts, world-class spas and fine dining, there's always something to do—or not do, if that's how you like it.

Lake Geneva: The Parks

Big Foot Beach State Park

1550 Lakeshore Dr, 53147; 262-248-2528

The 270-acre park has 6 miles of hiking/cross-country skiing, and a sand beach on the shore of Geneva Lake. This is a great place to laze away the day soaking up rays while watching colorful sailboats glide by.

Richard Bong State Recreation Area

26313 Burlington Rd, Kansasville 53139 (about midway between Lake Geneva and Kenosha); 262-878-5600

If you're up for a nice little day trip within the area, head to the 4,500-acre Bong State Recreation Area. Named for the famous WW II flying ace, the park has lots of small lakes, 16 miles of hiking trails, horse trails, canoeing, a nature center, concessions, parasailing, remote-controlled planes, rocketry, dog training and falconry. It's a quirky, fun place for exploring.

Kettle Moraine State Forest—Southern Unit

Hwy 59, Eagle 53119 (can also be accessed from Hwy H, 5 miles north of Elkhorn); 262-594-6200 or 262-594-2135

There's not much you can't do in this 22,300-acre park. It's about an hour's drive north of Lake Geneva, but if you're into outdoor recreation it's worth the trip. Kettle Moraine has more than 55 miles of hiking and snowmobile trails through glacial hills and valleys. There are at least 30 miles of cross-country ski trails, another 50 miles of horse trails, fishing, swimming, a nature center and naturalist programs, mountain biking and stunning overlooks. It's also one of the few parks that has cabin rental for those with disabilities. Cross-country skis available for rent.

Lake Geneva: The Trails

Lake Walk

The 21-mile footpath around Geneva Lake is always beautiful, but especially so in the spring with the explosion of cherry and apple blossoms. But then again, a midnight stroll around the moonlit lake is perfect no matter the season.

White River State Trail

W4097 Cty NN, Elkhorn 53121; 262-741-3114

White River is a scenic, 11-mile hike (or bike) with several bridges, little towns and panoramic views. The trail begins near Elkhorn at Cty H and ends at the eastern county line. A 2-mile horse trail runs adjacent between Springfield and Lyons. Rent your bike at Pedal & Cup located on Hwy 120 in the Historic Springfield Depot (a few minutes north of Lake Geneva along the trail); www.pedalandcup.com; 262-249-1111. They serve gourmet coffees, ice cream, etc.

Lake Geneva: Things to Do

Dining

There are so many dining options in Lake Geneva and that's the problem—there are so many options. You'd like to try them all. The large resorts have their own restaurants; many have several. Here are a few unique picks.

- **Lake Geneva Pie Co.**, 150 E Geneva Sq, 262-248-5100; www.lgpie.com. For pie, hands down it's the Lake Geneva Pie Co. Bless their sweets-loving hearts, they feature over 30 varieties from fruit pies to delectable creams. They also have homemade sandwiches, quiches and soups. Open daily.

- **Annie's Ice Cream Parlor & Restaurant**, 712 Main St, 262-248-2463. Annie's deserves a plug in this dairy-loving state for scooping up more than 40 flavors of creamy Wisconsin ice cream and yogurt. Chili, sandwiches, burgers and daily specials here as well. Open year-round.

- **Kirsch's Lakeside Restaurant**, W4190 West End Rd (Hwy 50 W), 53147; 262-245-5756; www.kirschs.com. For an exquisite dining experience you won't forget, make reservations at Kirsch's. The award-winning restaurant is famous for its French cuisine with a

Hawaiian influence. They have an extensive wine list, lakeside ambience and candlelight dining. Kirsch's is the very definition of romance. You'll find them at the **French Country Inn** (a historic bed & breakfast) which features whirlpool baths, fireplaces and balconies 15' from the lake; 262-245-5220; www.frenchcountryinn.com.

Fantasy Hills Ranch

HORSEBACK RIDING

4978 Town Hall Rd (Hwy 67), Delavan; 262-728-1773; www.fantasyhillsranch.com

Go horseback riding on trails that ramble over wooded hills and deep valleys. But if you think riding a horse can't be romantic, sign up for the moonlight ride. Never learned how to ride? No problem, they'll teach you. Don't want to ride? Still no problem. Fantasy Hills has wagon, hay, carriage and sleigh rides or you can just hang out at one of their bonfires. Open year-round. Call for hours.

NOTE: Almost all of the large resorts have stables and offer seasonal horse-related rides as well.

Field Stone Farm Carriage & Pony

Corner of Broad and Wrigley Dr (down by the lake); 262-539-3620; www.fsfcarriage.com

Carriage rides are cuddly, classic and forever romantic. They're open Th–M, weather permitting.

Flat Iron Park

FREE CONCERTS IN THE PARK

Wrigley Drive in downtown Lake Geneva

Take in the **free concert** in Flat Iron Park at the lakefront. Held Th evenings Jul & Aug.

Geneva Lakes Greyhound Track & Simulcast Center

GREYHOUND RACING

1600 East Geneva Street (Hwy 50 and I-43), Delavan; 262-728-8000; www.genevagreyhounds.com

If you enjoy picking a winner—and you must, because look at the hottie you came on this trip with—then head here. This is live greyhound racing with lake views. Open daily except Tu. Call for hours. Simulcasting W–M.

233

Geneva National Golf Club

1221 Geneva National Ave S, 53147 (5 miles west of Lake Geneva on Hwy 50); reservations 262-245-7000; www.genevanationalresort.com

Geneva National Golf Club claims bragging rights to 54 holes designed by masters Palmer, Player and Trevino. Open to the public.

NOTE: The area's championship courses—and there are nine of them—are amazing. For more golf info in the Lake Geneva area: http://www.lakegenevawi.com/ or call the Chamber of Commerce at 262-248-4416.

Hogs & Kisses   DANCING

149 Broad St, (downtown); 262-248-7447

This European pub serves the usual bar fare of soups, salads and sandwiches, but its also a great place to shake your tail feather each and every night throughout the summer; weekends during the off-season. They have DJs as well as live bands year-round. Call them for a schedule. No one under the age of 21 after 5pm.

NOTE: Most of the large resorts have weekend entertainment (if not nightly).

Hot Air Balloon Rides

- **Lake Geneva Balloon Company**, 262-206-3975; www.lakegeneva-balloon.com. Does the love of your life make you feel as if you're walking on air? Show them exactly how you feel with a hot air balloon ride over Lake Geneva's picturesque countryside. A nice perk includes free transportation from most area resorts and hotels.

- **Sunbird Balloons Inc.**, 877-933-6359; www.wedofly.com. Daily sunrise and sunset champagne flights, weather permitting, from May–Oct.

Ice Skating

Again, you can't go wrong with a visit to Lake Geneva no matter the season. And what's more romantic than a few spins around an old-fashioned ice rink? It'll make those fireside brandies that much more inviting.

- **Library Park**, Wrigley Dr, If you want to stay in town, this is a scenic rink on the lake they light at night.

- **Lake Lawn Resort**, 2400 Geneva St, Delavan; 262-728-7950;

www.lakelawnresort.com. Lighted skating on the lake. Rentals also available.

Lake Geneva Animal Park & Petting Zoo

Hwy 50 and 67; 262-245-0770; www.lakegenevapettingzoo.com

The animals star at the Lake Geneva Animal Park & Petting Zoo. The place is more like a circus-zoo combo. The amazingly bright creatures range from bicycling macaws to dancing Arabian horses. Domestic farm animals look right at home with the exotics in the petting zoo. The Baby Barn houses wildlife (deer, raccoon, rabbits) and farm babies under six months of age. But the real scene stealers are the two white Bengal tigers—Sparticus and Demetrius. Open May, Sep & Oct weekends, Memorial Day–Labor Day daily except M. Shows run continuously. Call for hours. Admission charged.

Lake Geneva Cruise Line

Wrigley Dr, (Riviera Docks); 800-558-5911 or 262-248-6206; www.cruiselakegeneva.com

The absolute best way to view all the lakefront mansions—and there are gazillions of them—is a US Mailboat Tour. This 2½-hour narrated cruise boards an actual mailboat that's been in operation for more than a century. While you get the lowdown on the palatial spreads, the mailperson jumps on and off the boat delivering the mail to all the rich and famous. It's well worth the ticket price. Daily tours mid-Jun–mid-Sept. Other tours offered include luncheons, Sunday Champagne Brunches, Dixieland Dinner Cruises and Sunset Dinner Cruises. Dinner cruises require collared shirts and slacks for men, slacks or dresses for women. Call for more information.

Yerkes Observatory

373 W Geneva St, Williams Bay; 262-245-5555.

For a free tour of the world's largest refractor telescope, stop in at the Yerkes Observatory. Tours on Sa only. Call for hours.

Lake Geneva: The Resorts

There are at least a dozen B&Bs and over 100 motels, hotels, camping and resorts in the Lake Geneva area. Here are a couple of the biggies.

Abbey Resort

269 Fontana Blvd, Fontana; 800-558-2405; www.theabbeyresort.com

The Abbey has 334 rooms, several pools, tennis courts, yacht marina, a world-class European spa, exercise center, championship golf and restaurants.

Alpine Valley Resort

W2501 Cty D, Elkhorn; 800-227-9395; www.alpinevalleyresort.com

The European-style resort has indoor and outdoor pools, golf, tennis courts, exercise center, fishing, downhill skiing, cross-country skiing and rental, outdoor whirlpool and restaurants.

Grand Geneva Resort

7036 Grand Geneva Way; 888-392-8000; www.grandgeneva.com

Grand Geneva is a Triple A, Four-Diamond resort with 355 rooms/suites, a world-class spa, championship golf, indoor/outdoor water park, fitness center with climbing wall, tennis courts, riding stables, downhill skiing with 13 runs, cross-country skiing and rental, ice skating and restaurants.

Lake Lawn Resort

2400 Geneva St, Hwy 50, Delavan; 800-338-5253; www.lakelawnresort.com

Lake Lawn is another giant with a beach, golf course, tennis courts, swimming pools, health club, cross-country skiing, horseback riding and restaurants. Call the Chamber for more information about lodging.

Lake Geneva: Odds & Ends

- **AA Antique Limousine Services**, 262-245-7615; www.aaantiquelimo.com

- **A-1 Lake Geneva Limousine**, 262-248-2619; www.lakegenevalimo.com

- **Fontana Outdoor Sports**, Hwy 67, Fontana; 262-275-2220 (scuba gear, instructions, charters)

- **Jerry's Marine**, four locations, Hwy 50; 262-275-5222 or 262-248-6028; www.lakegenevawi.com/jerrys/jerrys.htm (cross-country skis, ice skates, snowmobiles, wave runners, jet boats, yachts, parasail rides, pontoons, charters)

- **LeatherLips Water Sports**, 151 Wrigley Dr (across from the Chamber of Commerce); 262-248-4142; www.genevawatersports.com (wave runners, jet boats, speedboats, deck boats)

- **Marina Bay Boat Rentals**, 300 Wrigley Dr; 262-248-4477 (wave runners, pontoons, speedboats)

- **Pedal & Cup**, 1722 Hwy 120 N, Springfield; 262-249-1111; www.pedalandcup.com (bike rentals)

- **Water Craft Rentals of Lake Geneva**, N2062 S Lake Shore Dr (across from Big Foot State Park); 262-249-9647 (wave runners, pontoons, speedboats)

New Glarus

New Glarus is south central, on Hwy 69 (slightly southwest of Madison). **New Glarus Chamber of Commerce**, 16 5th Ave, New Glarus 53574; 608-527-2095; www.swisstown.com

New Glarus is America's "Little Switzerland." "Eat, drink and yodel" is their motto. (No lie, they actually have a yodel club.) Chalet-style architecture permeates the adorable 1845 village, and window boxes overflow with red geraniums—a Swiss favorite. New Glarus (pop. 2,000) welcomes thousands of visitors annually, many from Switzerland—check out the **Swiss Church guest book** (between 4th and 5th Ave). The Swiss ties are strong in the German-Swiss dialect and the polka music. New Glarus is a romantic's dream town and not to be missed.

New Glarus: Things to Do

ARGUE-ment Golf Course

N9603 Argue Rd, 53574; 608-527-6366

The ARGUE-ment Golf Course is inarguably located in one of the most picturesque locales around. Rolling hills within a working farm setting make this 9-hole course challenging and scenic.

Dining

When in Little Switzerland, eat what the Swiss eat Kalberwurst, Wienerschnitzel, G'schnetzlets, Roesti potatoes, Spatzli dumplings, Landjaeger, cheese and beef fondues. Many of the area restaurants specialize in these ethnic dishes. Here are a few top-notch eateries right in New Glarus.

- **New Glarus Hotel**, 100 6th Ave; 800-727-9477 or 608-527-5244; www.newglarushotel.com (1853 hotel/Swiss restaurant with live polka bands F & Sa nights year-round)

- **Chalet Landhaus**, Hwy 69; 800-944-1716 or 608-527-5234; www.chaletlandhaus.com (motel with open staircase and ethnic decor; pool, pizzeria, Swiss restaurant)

- **Glarner Stube**, 518 1st St; 608-527-2216 (closed M)

- **New Glarus Bakery**, 534 1st St; 608-527-2916 (warning: if you step foot in here you may never come out again—it's that good)

  Option: **Baumgartner's** in Monroe is the state's **oldest cheese store** in continuous operation. The menu is simple: cheese, meats, beer and soft drinks—that's it. Located at Courthouse Square.

Hike/Bike

- **Sugar River State Trail**, 608-527-2334. This 23-mile trail is a multi-use railbed reaching from New Glarus to Brodhead and merging with the Ice Age Trail. Especially picturesque is the 112' covered bridge near Brodhead, constructed in 1984 with lumber used from old buildings.

- **New Glarus Woods State Park**, W5446 Cty NN, 53574; 888-947-2757 or 608-527-2335. The 431-acre state park has 7 miles of hiking and a couple miles of biking trails. They have seasonal naturalist programs and year-round camping.

The House on the Rock

The House on the Rock is at 5754 Hwy 23, Spring Green 53588; 608-935-3639; www.thehouseontherock.com

It seems the House on the Rock's late owner/builder Alex Jordan was on a mission (addict-like obsession) to gather the entire world's collection of EVERYTHING and put a roof over it. But what a roof! The complex comprises 2½ miles of space divvied over 16 buildings. Honestly, it'd probably take close to a week to really see it all. Jordan began building his amazing house in 1946. He carried masonry up a cliff strapped to his back in a wicker basket. He didn't have a plan; each room evolved from his imagination. The interior of the original 14-room house has a heavy Oriental influence, but it's also very earthy with large limestone fireplaces, wishing wells and a waterfall. The Infinity Room is the only one like it in the world and worth the price of admission. Built to withstand a tornado, the floor-to-ceiling windowed room narrows to a needle-like point, jutting over the valley treetops at a dizzying 165' aboveground. The museum is a maze of paths and turns with lots of "stuff" everywhere. The lighting is dim by design to enhance displays for certain effects, however, it's easy to get disoriented (claustrophobic). Designated areas allow for a speedy exit, should you so choose. A definite museum highlight is the world's largest carousel with 20,000 lights and 269 handcrafted animals—not one a horse. The Heritage of the Sea building spotlights a 200' Blue Whale that is 90' longer than a real one. In case you need a time-out from the unending parade of the priceless, kick back at one of the four restaurant areas or multitude of shops within the complex. It's a self-guided tour open daily mid-Mar–early Nov. Call for hours. Closed Jan & Feb. Admission is charged.

NOTE: See more than 6,000 Santas during a special scaled-back holiday tour of the house; mid-Nov–New Year's weekend. Admission charged. Call for tour times.

Mount Horeb

Nearby Mount Horeb is a fun place to nose around and spend the day. The Norwegian town of 4,000 known as the "Troll Capital" has a picture perfect main drag with a New England rotary, historic buildings and flowers.

- **Mount Horeb Mustard Museum**, 100 W Main; 800-438-6878. Over 2,000 mustards on display and is the world's the biggest mustard retailer. With more than 400 different flavors on hand, your purchasing decision should be a piece of cake. Open year-round. Call for hours. Admission is free.

- **The Grumpy Troll Brew Pub,** 105 S Second St, 608-437-2739. This pub is located in a historic 1916 creamery. Good food and a decent selection of hand-crafted ales make this a worthy stop. Watch the beermaking process through an observation window. Open daily. Call for hours.

- **Mount Horeb Area Chamber of Commerce**, 100 S First St, PO Box 84, 608-437-5914; www.trollway.com. Call the chamber for more information about the town and attractions.

  Option: Nissedahle (Valley of the Elves) is a restored Norwegian homestead, turned outdoor museum. Better known as 'Little Norway," the original 1850s log cabins and buildings showcase Scandinavian collections and antiques. The beautiful grounds at the base of Blue Mound resemble a storybook setting. Open daily May–Oct. Call for hours. Take the 45-minute tour with a costumed guide; 608-437-8211. Admission charged. To find them, exit Cave of Mounds Rd, turn right on Cty ID, go ¼ mile, then left on Hwy JG.

Museums

- **Chalet of the Golden Fleece Museum,** 618 Second St; 608-527-2614. This museum takes a thorough (three floors) look at the Swiss culture from one-of-a-kind antiques, to 2,000-year-old Etruscan earrings, to Gregorian chants on parchment (one of the oldest forms of written music). Woodcarvings, painted furniture, quilts, Swiss dolls, artwork and more. The building itself was the 1937 home of Edwin Barlow, the creator of the New Glarus version of the Wilhelm Tell drama. Open Memorial Day–Oct Tu–Su. Call for hours. Admission charged.

- **Swiss Historical Village Museum,** 612 7th Ave; 608-527-2317; www.swisshistoricalvillage.com. Swiss history further expanded, with particular focus on the birth of New Glarus. Over a dozen buildings with authentic displays simulate pioneer life in the mid-1800s. Open daily May–Oct. Call for hours. Guided tours operate continuously. Admission charged.

New Glarus Brewing Company

Cty W and Hwy 69 (off Hwy 69 at the edge of town); 608-527-5850; www.newglarusbrewing.com

Spotted Cow, Naked Cow, Fat Squirrel Nut Brown Ale, Uff Da Bock—no, these aren't secret passwords to some perverted Dairyland resort, these are a short list of outstanding beers handcrafted here. Guided tours offered Sa Jun–Aug. Admission charged and includes a commemorative glass and tasting. Self-guided tours via an observation window year-round M–F. Call for hours.

Swimming

New Glarus Community Pool, 320 2nd St, in the Village Park

Large **outdoor pool**. They don't charge much and it's a great way to wind down after a day of hiking.

Taliesin

5607 Cty Hwy C, Spring Green (2 miles south of Spring Green at the intersection of Hwy 23 and Cty C); 877-588-7900; www.TaliesinPreservation.org

Known for his "organic architecture," Frank Lloyd Wright is one of the country's greatest architects, if not the greatest. Born in 1867 in nearby Richland Center, a tour of Wright's home—Taliesin—offers more than a look at an architectural masterpiece, it's an opportunity for gaining insight into the persona of this great man. The 600-acre property includes the visitor center, Hillside Home School, Midway Farm, Tan-y-deri House and Romeo and Juliet Windmill. Architects still study and design on the grounds at the Frank Lloyd Wright School of Architecture. Taliesin is a National Historic Landmark. Open daily May–Oct. Call for hours. Several guided tours range in time, sites and admission price. The Hillside, House and Walking tours are given daily. The Estate tour takes place on Sa, Su, Tu & Th mornings. Taliesin Sunset tour is F evenings, summer months only. A video about Wright's life plays continuously at the visitor center. The center also has a gift shop and restaurant with soups and sandwiches. For an expanded list of Frank Lloyd Wright buildings and tours, see the Odds & Ends chapter.

Option: Tower Hill State Park is a few miles east of Taliesin on Cty C; 608-588-2116. The restored 1831 smelter house and 180' shot tower is open mid-Apr–Oct. Displays explain the shot-making process of dropping hot lead 180' into a pool of water, creating round pellets known as "shot."

Tyrol Basin Ski & Snowboard Area   SKIING

3487 Bohn Road, Mt. Horeb 53572; 608-437-4135; www.tyrolbasin.com
Your best bet for downhill action. They have a 300' vertical and 17 runs. For an up-to-the-minute ski report, call 608-437-4FUN.

Wine

- **New Glarus Primrose Winery**, 226 Second St, 53574; 608-527-5053. Located in a charming antiquated brick building, the winery does not have tours but does do free tastings. Open daily May–Dec, Th-Su Jan–Apr. Call for hours.

- **Maple Leaf Cheese and Chocolate Haus**, 554 First St; www.mapleleafcheeseandchocolatehaus.com; 888-624-1234 or 608-527-2000. This charming shop takes a unique stand on wines; they pair them to the cheese instead of the other way around. Owners Barb Kummerfeldt and husband Steve Wisdom believe the right wine brings out the best flavor in the cheese. The daughter of an ice cream maker, Barb travels the state teaching classes about cheese and the process of cheesemaking. Maple Leaf sells about 60 local cheeses, ice cream, specialty fudge (made by Steve), sausage and imported European products. They stock wines from around the world and hold free wine and cheese tastings Jun–Sep F or Sa, depending on the tourist crowd. Call for hours.

New Glarus: The B & Bs

Cozy, charming, friendly, hearty breakfasts, peaceful, antiques, quaint small towns, scenic countryside, romantic—the B&Bs of Green County exude these special qualities and more.

Albany House

405 S Mill St, Albany 53502; 866-977-7000 or 608-862-3636; www.albanyhouse.com

The Albany House is unique in that they special tailor "quilter's retreats." The 1908 home has 3 acres of gardens, beautiful rooms (some with fireplaces and whirlpools) and scrumptious breakfasts (crustless Jarlsberg quiche, Grand Marnier stuffed French toast, egg blossoms). Close to the Sugar River Bike Trail.

Cameo Rose Victorian Country Inn

1090 Severson Rd, Belleville 53508; 608-424-6340; www.cameorose.com.

This charming inn has been featured in numerous magazines and called one of the top fifteen B&Bs in the nation. Although it is new construction, the grounds and home have an elegant Victorian-era feel. Cameo Rose features a wrap-around porch, hammock, porch swing, gazebo and gardens, white lace, gourmet breakfasts on vintage china, antique furniture, fine linens, private baths, fireplace and whirlpool rooms, and 120 acres of private hiking and cross-country ski trails. If this sounds like your idea of a romantic getaway (and how could it not?), then give them a call.

Hoch Haus

218 Second St; 608-527-4019; www.hochhaus.homestead.com

The only B&B in New Glarus. The two upstairs rooms have a cozy "Grandma's house" feeling right down to the shared bath. The house has an open staircase and front porch swing. Since it's right in town, it's within walking distance for shopping and dining. The full breakfast includes locally made breads, cheeses and muesli. The Haus Frau is Barb Summerfield, owner of Maple Leaf Cheese and Chocolate Haus.

Osceola

Osceola is in western Wisconsin along the St. Croix River/Minnesota border (north of Hudson on Hwy 35). **Polk County Information Center,** 710 Hwy 35 S, St. Croix Falls 54024; 800-222-7655; www.polkcountytourism.com or. www.saintcroixriver.com/html_docs/towns_scvrta/osceola.html

One visit to this small town of 2,000 friendly folks and you'll be forever smitten. The main street is a charmer with its hanging baskets and storefront flower boxes. Oseola has unique gift shops and cafes, a vintage railroad and gorgeous waterfall, four nearby rustic roads and plenty of down time for relaxation and rejuvenation.

Osceola: Things to Do

Canoeing

Paddle your way along the striking St. Croix River in a canoe for two. The entire trip takes anywhere from 3–6 hours, depending on the river current and your level of ambition. Rental companies are:

- **Quest Canoe**, 340 E McKenny St, St. Croix Falls; 715-483-1692

- **Wild Mountain Boat & Canoe Rental**, 37200 Wild Mountain Rd, Taylors Falls, MN; 651-465-6315

- **Wild River Canoe Rental**, 572 Bench St, Taylors Falls, MN; 651-257-3941

NOTE: There are two nearby state parks. Willow River in Hudson has a gorgeous waterfall, so see the Waterfalls chapter for details and the Museums chapter for more Hudson attractions. Interstate in St. Croix Falls is Wisconsin's first state park and scenic abode for the world's oldest potholes. See the Family Day chapter.

Cascade Falls   WATERFALL

Downtown Osceola

Stretch the legs with a hike down 156 steps to the beautiful Cascade Falls. This is one of those perfect spots. Golden sunlight shines through a thick green canopy onto crystal clear water as it spills 25' over a limestone ledge into a shallow pool ideal for wading. Step behind the falls for an awesome view or take the footbridge and explore the woodland trails.

Cedar Lake Speedway   RACING

2275 Cty CC, New Richmond 54017 (from Hwy 64 head north on Cty C, then drive 4 miles to Cty CC, turn left, the track is 2 miles on the right); 866-425-7386 or 715-248-7119; www.cedarlakespeedway.com

If you like the sound of 700 thundering horses under the hood, then you'll love the stock car racing at the nationally recognized Cedar Lake Speedway. They boast one of the best clay tracks in the US Open most weekends Apr–Sep; tickets 612-363-0479.

Chateau Saint Croix

Along the St. Croix River at 1998 Hwy 87, St. Croix Falls; 715-483-2556;
www.chateaustcroix.com

For a little European flavor, take your sweetie to a wine tasting at the
Chateau Saint Croix. The 45-acre winery is reminiscent of an English
estate with gardens, carriage house, horse stable and picturesque
fishing pond. A 1-hour guided tour explains the winemaking process
with a visit to the aging cellar, production room and shipping area.
The tour ends in the tasting room where you'll get to sample wine
selections not available at the tasting bar. Bring a picnic lunch and
purchase a nice bottle of wine, then head off on the nature trails.
Open daily year-round except Tu. Call for hours. Closed the second
and third weeks of Feb. Tour fee charged.

Falls Theatre

105 S Main Street, River Falls (on the main drag in downtown River Falls)

The historic Falls Theatre in River Falls shows current movie releases
for 1960 prices! That's right, tickets are always $2/adult, $1/children
no matter the time, show, season or year.

Fishing

- **Star Prairie Trout Farm,** 400 Hill Ave, Osceola; 888-545-6806;
  www.starprairietrout.com. In business as a fishing farm and hatchery since 1856, Star Prairie Trout Farm is an angler's delight. Ice
  cold water flows through their facility at a rate of 1,500 gallons per
  minute, exactly what trout need to thrive. Beautiful babbling brook,
  gorgeous gardens, manicured grounds and a picnic area make Star
  Prairie a relaxing getaway. Open Sa & Su May–Sep, W Jun–Aug.
  Call for hours. There are no limits or licenses, but you may want to
  bring a cooler for your catch. You pay by the pound.

- **Kinnickinnic River.** For super serious anglers, drive south on Hwy
  35 to River Falls to the Kinnickinnic River, a Class 1 trout stream.
  For more information, contact the River Falls Area Chamber of
  Commerce; 715-425-2533; www.rfchamber.com

Gandy Dancer State Trail

www.dnr.state.wi.us/org/land/parks/specific/findatrail.html#gandy

The 98-mile **Gandy Dancer State Trail**—named after the rhythmic
sounds made by the crews working of the rail line—tracks from
St. Croix Falls to Superior. It crosses the Wisconsin/Minnesota border
twice with a breathtaking river view from a 520' bridge near

Danbury. The trail has 47 miles of bike/cross-country skiing and 66 miles of snowmobile.

Golf

Osceola has an impressive, 18-hole championship golf course open to the public. Three other courses are within a 15-minute drive.

- **Bristol Ridge**, 1978 Cty C, Somerset; 715-247-3673
- **Krooked Kreek Golf Club**, 2448 75th Ave (Cty M), Osceola; 715-294-3673
- **New Richmond Golf**, 235 S Knowles Ave, New Richmond; 800-654-6380
- **Pine Meadows**, 1139 Cty G, New Richmond; 715-246-5595

Kansas City Chiefs Training Camp   FOOTBALL

University of Wisconsin-River Falls

Watch the **Kansas City Chiefs** pro football team train for the upcoming season at the University of Wisconsin-River Falls campus. Summer camp runs mid-Jul–mid-Aug. Free admission. For more information, call 800-452-2522 (call after Jun 1 for daily practice schedule); www.uwrf.edu/chiefs

Kinni Valley Stables   HORSEBACK RIDING

1171 30th Ave, River Falls; 715-425-6184

One-hour trail rides along the scenic Kinnickinnic River. Open daily Memorial Day–Labor Day. Call for hours.

Millside Park   FREE CONCERT IN THE PARK

There's a **free concert** in the Millside Park Th evenings Jun & Jul.

The New Coffee Connection   DINING

107 N Cascade (Main St); 715-755-3833

This cozy cafe pours steaming cups of gourmet coffee along with soups, sandwiches, rolls and homemade pie. The back deck has a bird's-eye view of Cascade Falls. The swinging benches and board games beg you to linger. Open year-round, they have live music Tu evenings during the summer months.

New Richmond Heritage Center HISTORICAL SITE

1100 Heritage Dr, New Richmond 54017; 715-246-3276

The New Richmond Heritage Center is a village of about a dozen late nineteenth-century buildings open for tours and special events. The main attraction is a Victorian Italianate farmhouse. Open year-round M–F, weekends also in May–Oct. Call for hours.

Emily Olson House & Museum HISTORICAL SITE

408 River St, Osceola

Owned and operated by the Osceola Historical Society, this 1862 house is one of the oldest in town and doubles as a local history museum. Open Su Memorial Day–Oct. Call for hours. Free admission.

Osceola & St. Croix Valley Railroad TRAIN RIDE

114 Depot Rd, Osceola (off Hwy 35 just south of the railroad bridge); 715-755-3570; www.trainride.org

The wire-cut red brick, 1916 Osceola Soo Line Depot was a marvel in its day for featuring both men and ladies indoor toilets. The Osceola & St. Croix Valley Railroad departs from the depot on two regularly scheduled roundtrips aboard vintage diesel and steam powered trains. The westbound 90-minute trip traverses steep rock cliffs and an untamed river valley to the tiny village of Marine on St. Croix, MN. The shorter, 50-minute trip chugs through miles of picturesque Wisconsin dairyland to Dresser. You'll have a blast, no matter the trip. On-board bathroom and concessions should alleviate any fears of dying from hunger, thirst or embarrassment. Costumed volunteers ride along and recite local train history. Call for departure times and prices.

St. Croix ArtBarn THEATER

1040 Oak Ridge Dr, Osceola (take Hwy 35 north of town, then turn east at the Osceola High School). For a performance schedule, call 715-294-ARTS; www.stcroixartbarn.com

Whether it's a new gallery showing or a stage performance, it seems there's always something going on at the renovated century-old St. Croix ArtBarn. The 180-seat "dairy barn" theater has open rafters and pipe-fitted railing, yet still manages to feel cozy. Shows run Jun–Oct, headlining both local and worldwide talent. There's no air conditioning, so dress for the weather.

Trollhaugen Ski Area

2232 100th Ave, Dresser, 54009 (3 miles north of Osceola); 800-826-7166 or 715-755-2955
280' vertical, 10 runs, snowboarding and tubing with a conveyor lift.

Osceola: The B & Bs

Osceola has at least a half-dozen fantastic B&Bs in the area. Here are two.

Croixwood on the St. Croix River

421 Ridge Rd, Osceola; 866-670-3838 or 715-294-2894; www.croixwood.com
King beds with plush down comforters, gas fireplaces, soaking tubs, therapy jet pools and balconies with a river view you won't ever want to leave. They are pampered luxury and priced for it.

St. Croix River Inn

305 River St, Osceola; 800-645-8820 or 715-294-4248; www.stcroixriverinn.com.
A restored 1908 stone home with commanding views of the river and soaring Bald Eagles. The rooms are beautiful with private baths and whirlpool tubs. Call for reservations.

Waupaca

Waupaca is in central Wisconsin along Hwy 10 (northwest of Appleton). **Waupaca Area Chamber of Commerce**, 221 S Main St, Waupaca 54981; 888-417-4040 or 715-258-7343; www.WaupacaAreaChamber.com

The beautiful Waupaca Chain O' Lakes is resort country. People come here for the laid-back atmosphere, the hundreds of antiques shops and to fish and play in the water. Within Waupaca County's 760 square miles of rolling woodland you'll find 3 rustic roads, a state park, 280 miles of groomed snowmobile trails, 240 lakes, 79 rivers, 35 trout streams, scores of B&Bs and relaxed dining with stunning lakeshore views. Waupaca has everything you'll ever need for a memorable romantic getaway.

Waupaca: Things to Do

Antiquing

If the one you love suggests a romantic weekend in Waupaca County, what they are really saying is "Let's go antiquing." Seriously, around every bend on every road is another antiquing hot spot. That said,

247

you still have to visit the tiny village of **Rural**. The entire nineteenth-century town is on the National Register of Historic Places and is one of—if not *the* best place to find antiques. Rural is along the Crystal River a few miles southwest of Waupaca on Hwy 22.

> **Option:** Take a scenic drive along the **two Rustic Roads** (R-23 and R-24) branching out from Rural. The routes cross the river several times over stone bridges as they wind through the gorgeous countryside. Each is less than 4 miles long.

Chain O' Lakes Cruises and Charters   BOAT TOUR/CRUISE

N2757 Cty QQ (2 miles southwest of the junction of Hwy 10, 49 and 54); 715-258-2866; Clear Water Harbor 715-258-9912; www.clearwaterharbor.com

Narrated 1½-hour cruises churn the Chain O' Lake waters from Memorial weekend–mid-Oct. You have a choice of boats for tours: **The Chief**, a 60' authentic sternwheeler, chugs along 8 of the 22 lakes, or an 11-lake cruise aboard the 54' motor yacht, **Lady of the Lakes**. Sunday champagne brunches aboard the old paddleboat depart from Clear Water Harbor. Call for departure time. For lakeside dining and dancing most people go to the **Harbor Restaurant & Bar**. Their Friday night fish fries and frosted mugs of Leinie's are always a hit. Open daily the third weekend in Apr–last Su in Sep. Call for entertainment schedule.

Ding's Dock   CANOEING/TUBING

E1171 Cty Q, Waupaca; 715-258-2612; www.dingsdock.com

For a leisurely day floating on the river, go see the folks at Ding's Dock. They not only have the tubes and canoes, they give you a free boat ride to the drop off point. Ding's Dock also rents pontoons, rowboats, motorboats and cottages.

> **Options:** **Wolf River Trips and Campground** in New London rents inner tubes; 920-982-2458. Boat rentals are also available in Waupaca at **Chain O' Lakes Marine**; 715-258-8840; and **Becker Marine**; 715-258-9015.

Dutch Windmill

Clintonville

You don't see a Dutch windmill everyday, at least not in Wisconsin, but you can in Clintonville. Used for irrigation, the windmill is off Cty I (2 miles southeast of town), behind the home of owner/builder Earl Behnke. For tours call 715-823-2755.

Golf

Don't think the only activities in Waupaca involve water. They have several championship golf courses and, with any luck, you won't be playing in the water.

- **Foxfire Golf Club**, 215 Foxfire Dr, 54981; 715-256-1700 (18-hole, par 70 championship course nominated by *Golf Digest* for best new course in 1997)

- **Glacier Wood**, 604 Water St, Iola 54945; 715-445-3831 (18-hole, par 71)

- **Hidden Waters**, E4480 Hwy 22 and 54, 54981; 715-258-5054 (9-hole, par 72)

- **Royal Oaks Golf Resort**, N4440 Oakland Dr, 54981; 715-258-5103 (9-hole, par 28. Camping and swimming pool.)

- **Waupaca Country Club**, 1330 Ware St, 54981;715-258-7271 (9-hole, par 72)

Hartman Creek State Park

N2480 Hartman Creek Rd, 54981; 715-258-2372

The 1,400-acre park has 300' of sand beach, 10 miles of hiking, 7 miles of horseback riding, 9 miles of cross-country skiing, mountain bike trails, year-round camping and a nature center. A short portion of the Ice Age Trail winds through Hartman. For those craving some private time, reserve the primitive walk-in log cabin.

Ice Skating/Sliding

- **South Park**, 921 S Main; 715-258-8949. rules with its Olympic-sized ice rink in the winter and swimming beach in the summer.

- **Polliwog Park** on Clark St in nearby Manawa has pond ice skating and a steep sliding hill.

Lillie Acres Ranch

HORSEBACK RIDING

N459 Cty U, Weyauwega 54983; 920-867-2291

For a 1-hour guided trail ride head to Lillie Acres Ranch. The trail ride cost is per hour, lessons available. Open year-round. Call for hours. Reservations appreciated.

Marion A-MAZE-ment Park   MAZE

111 Industrial Dr, Marion (1 block off Hwy 45 on the northern county line;) 866-754-6293; www.marionamazementpark.com

The big draw is a huge maze, but they also have a mirror maze, rock climbing wall, 18-hole miniature golf and a game room/pool hall. Open Apr–Oct. Admission charged to the maze. Separate charge for the other activities.

Norseman Hill   CROSS-COUNTRY SKIING

Hwy 49 (5 miles north of Iola to Cty MM, then go 2 miles west)

Norseman Hill near Iola has the best cross-country trails in Wisconsin. Twenty kilometers of groomed skiing with 4 miles under lights. That's the **longest lighted trail in the state**! They have five ski jumps, rentals and a chalet with fireplace and concessions. Open daily through the winter months. Fee charged for trail use. Ski conditions hotline 715-445-3411.

> **Options:** More cross-country ski options include **Hatten Park**, New London; 920-982-5822. • **Hartman Creek State Park**, Waupaca; 715-258-2372 • **The Ice Age Trail**—connects with Hartman Creek State Park. • **Mosquito Hill Nature Center**, New London; 920-779-6433. • **Navarino Wildlife Area**, Shiocton; 715-758-6999 or 715-524-2297. • **Swan Park**, Waupaca.

Red Mill

N2190 Cty K; 715-258-7385

You might recognize the historic Red Mill. Featured in numerous magazines, it boasts Wisconsin's **largest waterwheel**. The restored mill bursts at the rafters with knick-knacks, candles, craft items and antiques (surprise!). The Crystal River runs behind the mill. A walking path crosses over a 40' **covered bridge** to the tiny **Chapel in the Woods**, which is available for weddings, should you be so inclined. Open year-round. Call for hours.

> **Option:** There's another covered bridge in the area that's 30' long. To find it take Hwy 54 east ⅓ mile from junction with Hwy 10 at the west edge of Waupaca, then drive north on Covered Bridge Rd. It's less than ½ mile to the bridge.

Waupaca: The B & Bs

The entire Waupaca County is set up for visitors. It has an easy "going to Grandma's house" hospitality and you won't have to fight bumper-to-bumper crowds to move around the county. There are hundreds of lodging options but since you're in the mood for a little romance, here are a few great B&B's.

Crystal River Inn

E1369 Rural Rd, 54981; 800-236-5789; www.crystalriver-inn.com

It's all gardens and river views at the 1853 historic Crystal River Inn. Down comforters, antique brass beds, fireplaces, whirlpools and two cottages make the inn a special retreat. The pumpkin bread seals the deal.

Ferg Haus Inn at Ferg's Bavarian Village

N8599 Ferg Rd, Manawa 54949; 920-596-2946; www.fergsbavarianvillage.com

The century-old farmstead has been in the Ferg family since 1898. No longer a working farm, the restored buildings have new lives as German gift shops and a Biergarten with German food and beer. You're going to think you're in an Alpine village with all the painted murals, flower gardens, window boxes and island gazebo. The rooms have cozy down comforters, feather beds, private baths and windows draped in lace.

Lindsay House Bed & Breakfast

539 Depot St, PO Box 304, Manawa 54949; 920-596-3643; www.lindsayhouse.com

The Lindsay House is a nicely decorated Victorian home, but it's the eight gorgeous perennial gardens and gourmet breakfast that are especially memorable. The traditional "snack" greeting is a mouth-salivating dessert that'll keep you dreaming about breakfast all night long. And you won't be disappointed. How does berry-stuffed French toast or an amaretto souffle sound? Okay. Wipe the drool. Book the stay.

Few natural wonders lure more people than a waterfall. Whether it's a roaring rush or a picturesque trickle, the waterfall is a powerful attraction. Fortunately for all of you waterfall lovers, Wisconsin virtually overflows with them. Their heights range from a staggering 165' to 12' or less. Iron and Marinette Counties boast the most falls within the shortest distance. Most of these counties are remote and rugged, but the scenery is breathtaking and so are the waterfalls.

Waterfalls

Waterfalls

Polk & St. Croix Counties

Price County

Ashland County

Brownstone Falls & Copper Falls

Copper Falls State Park, 5 miles north of Mellen; 715-274-5123

Brownstone Falls drops 30' into the Tyler Forks River, and the 40' high Copper Falls rumbles into the Bad River.

Option: The 2,700-acre **Copper Falls State Park** has year-round camping, 9 miles of hiking trails, mountain bike trails, cross-country skiing, great fishing, canoeing, a swimming beach and concessions, scenic vistas, a lookout tower, canyons, handicap accessible cabin and waterfalls.

Morgan Falls

Chequamegon-Nicolet National Forest, 12 miles west of Mellen; 715-264-2511

Morgan Falls is a small stream cascading 80' into a pool. It's not your roaring rush, but it is scenic. The ½-mile hike to the falls leaves from the parking lot. The red granite top of St. Peter's Dome is about a mile beyond the falls. It's the highest point in the Chequamegon-Nicolet National Forest. To find Morgan Falls drive northwest on Hwy 13 from Mellen to Minersville, then go west on Cty C and Midway Rd to County Line Rd, turn left (south) and drive approximately 4 miles to the parking lot. Follow signs. See map above.

Options: The **Chequamegon-Nicolet National Forest** claims more than 850,000 acres. The Ojibwe name "Chequamegon" means "Land of Shallow Waters." Although much of the land has seen the logger's saw at one time or another, there remains a few stands of 200-year-old trees. The forest is one of the best areas for birding as it is a habitat for nearly 250 species. Chequamegon-Nicolet was the first of five planned DNR-sponsored state birding trails. The Sandhill Crane logo marks the **Lake Superior/Northwoods Trail**. The forest has two National Scenic

255

Hiking Trails—the **North Country** and the **Ice Age**. There are over 800 lakes and 650 miles of rivers with Class 3 rapids. For a picturesque drive, take the **Great Divide Scenic Highway** on Hwy 77. It travels 29 miles from Glidden to Lost Lake. The **Northern Continental Divide** is a few miles north of Glidden; watch for the marker. Glidden is also the **"Black Bear Capital of Wisconsin,"** because of the record beast bagged a few years ago. For detailed maps and information, call the **Chequamegon Forest Supervisor**; 715-762-2461.

Brown County

Fonferek Falls

Fonferek Glen County Park, 4 miles south of Green Bay

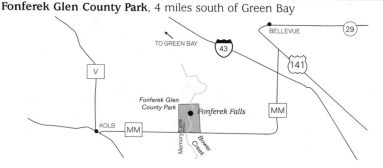

Bower Creek tumbles 30' over a limestone-walled gorge with a stone archway. The park has a gravel quarry and natural prairie. From Green Bay, take Hwy 43 S and turn right on Cty MM to Memory Ln, which is the park entrance. Follow the signs to the falls.

Douglas County

Amnicon Falls

Amnicon Falls State Park, 10 miles southeast of Superior on Hwy 2, follow signs; 715-398-3000

If you want to see a lot of waterfalls without a lot of legwork, you'll love this park. Incredibly scenic, the Amnicon River divides around an island and plunges over three waterfalls nearly 30' each. During high water the river fills another channel producing a fourth falls. A rare, 55' covered **Horton bowstring bridge** spans the river, giving access to the island. An easy ¼-mile hiking trail circles the island for a close-up view of the falls. The river's root beer color comes from the roots and decaying vegetation of nearby bogs. This gem of a park is not to be missed. Picnic grounds, camping, restrooms. View of the Lower Falls is wheelchair accessible. Open May–first weekend in Oct. Closed in winter. Park permit required.

Big Manitou Falls & Little Manitou Falls

Pattison State Park, 13 miles south of Superior on Hwy 35; 715-399-3111

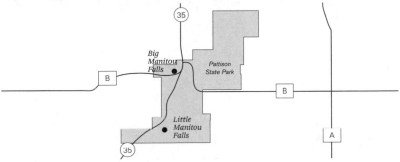

If you don't like heights—too bad, because you just have to see this waterfall. The dizzying 165' drop ranks Big Manitou Falls the thirty-ninth highest in the world and state's highest. From the overlook vantage, the Black River is nothing but a thin dark ribbon. Little Manitou Falls is 1 mile farther south on Hwy 35, measuring in at a respectable 31'. The park is open year-round. Nature center, 10 miles of hiking trails, geology walk (the area was once mined for copper), camping, fishing, swimming beach and bathhouse, picnic facilities, restrooms. Winter activities include 4½ miles of cross-country ski trails, snowshoeing, hiking and ice skating. Wheelchair accessible. Park permit required.

Iowa County

Stephen's Falls & Cox Hollow Falls

Governor Dodge State Park, 3 miles north of Dodgeville on Hwy 23;
608-935-2315

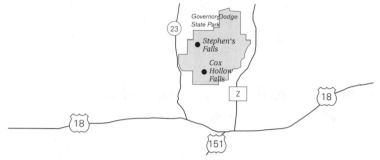

Stephen's Falls drops 15' into a shallow pool perfect for splashing around in on a hot summer's day. Take the easy ½-mile Stephen's Falls Trail. It's paved and handicap accessible. Not so easy is the 8-mile hike to Cox Hollow Falls (Enee Point). To get there, park in the lot at the west end of Cox Hollow Lake and across the road from Enee Point. Hike across the wooden bridge and veer to the right (west) along a creek which leads directly to the falls. You'll cross a snow-mobile trail when you're about ⅔ of the way there.

Options: Waterfalls are great, but the 5,200-acre **Governor Dodge State Park** has a few other attractions that may interest you. It's a wildly popular park. In fact, it's the state's third most used park with almost 30 miles of hiking, 22 miles of cross-country ski trails, horse trails and snowmobile trails. There are another 13 miles of mountain bike trails, an amphitheater and two lakes for fishing. Guided nature hikes explore caves, wildlife and ancient cultures. Cox Hollow Lake has a sand beach for swimming and sun bathing, concessions and boat rentals. The 3½-mile Mill Creek Mountain Bike Trail crosses paths with the 40-mile Military Ridge State Trail extending from Dodgeville to Fitchburg. Camping is year-round, and your horse is welcome to stay as well. If you don't have a horse but would like to ride one, **Doby Stables** can help you out. They have 1- and 2-hour guided rides in the park or a 45-minute trail ride on the ranch. Open daily May–Oct. Located right across Hwy 23 from the park; 608-935-5205.

Iron County

Iron County has the most waterfalls per county in the Midwest. It's one waterfall after another with the latest guess around 50. Most are quite spectacular, but an effort to view as they're "off the beaten path" as they say. The Iron County falls are for those of you who love adventurous hikes through thick forests and up steep climbs. Iron County has a free map to the most accessible falls. Give them a call; 715-561-2922.

Foster Falls

Located 5 miles north of Upson

Foster Falls is in a remote location (of course) and quite a scramble to get to. You've got to want to see it and you should. The falls plummets 25' into the Potato River for a robust splash. From Upson, take Hwy 122 north for 5 miles, then turn west on Sullivan Rd. It's 2 miles to the falls.

Gile Falls

Located 2 miles southwest of Hurley in the town of Gile

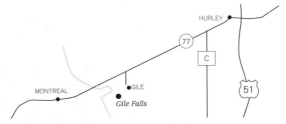

The waterfall drops 15' into the West Fork of the Montreal River. A walking trail connects with a snowmobile bridge overlooking the top of the falls. Take Hwy 77 west from Hurley to Montreal. Turn left on Kokogan Rd, then right on Gile Falls St to the overlook.

259

Kimball Park Falls

Kimball Town Park, 5 miles northwest of Hurley

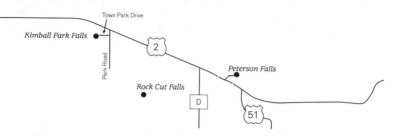

The 10' falls tumbles into the West Fork of the Montreal River. Take a walk upstream to view more falls and the a wickedly gorgeous rapids. The park has a picnic area and rustic pavilion. From Hurley, take Hwy 2 west for 3 miles. Turn south on Park Rd and continue ⅕ miles, then turn west on Town Park Rd. Enter via the one-lane bridge.

Lake of the Falls

Lake of the Falls County Park, 6 miles west of Mercer

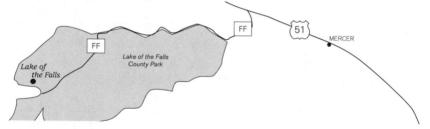

The 10' high falls rolls into the Turtle River. The park has primitive campsites and a boat landing. From Mercer, drive northwest on Hwy 51 for almost 1½ miles. Turn west on Cty FF and drive 5⅕ miles to the park.

Peterson Falls

About a mile north of Hurley

Okay, this falls is for you adventure seekers. It's in a very remote location, so bring along a map and compass. The beautiful Peterson Falls plunges 35' into the East Branch of the Montreal River. To find it, take Hwy 2 west of Hurley about ½ mile to a gravel road at the Ero Nasi Construction sign. Follow the road straight east ⅕ mile and park in a small turn-around (don't take any side roads). Take the foot path on the north side of the parking area ¼ mile to the falls. Good luck! See map above.

Potato River Falls

Located in the town park in Gurney

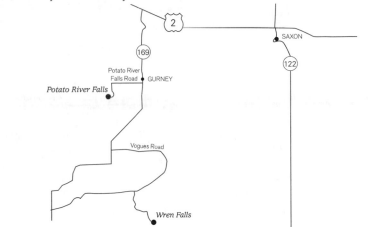

This is one of the highest and most picturesque falls in the state, rumbling 90' into the Potato River. Both upper and lower falls have scenic hiking trails. The town park has a picnic area and rustic campsites. From the intersection of Hwy 2 and 169, drive 2¾ miles south on Hwy 169 through the town of Gurney. Turn west on Potato River Falls Rd for 1½ miles.

Rock Cut Falls

Located 3 miles west of Hurley on the Montreal River

The 15' falls can be seen from a former railroad bridge on the Ironhorse ATV and snowmobile trail. One of the prettiest spots in the county, the only way to get to it is by ATV or mountain bike. See map page 260.

Saxon Falls

Three miles upstream from Superior Falls on the Montreal River; watch for signs.

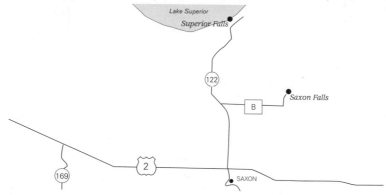

Saxon is a crazy, wild 90' waterfall. Bring your earplugs

Shay's Dam Falls

Located 6 miles northeast of Mercer

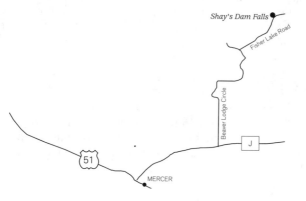

Shay's Dam drops 15' into the Turtle River. The park has a picnic area. From Mercer, drive east 2½ miles on Cty J, turn north on Beaver Lodge Circle for about 3½ miles, then turn east on Fisher Lake Rd. Drive 1⅕ miles to a side road on the left which leads to Shay's Dam. Watch for signs.

Superior Falls

Drive 1 mile east of Saxon Harbor across the Michigan state line.
  A truly spectacular falls and at 90', Superior is one of highest in the area. It literally plunges into the Montreal River near its mouth on

Lake Superior. The falls is an Iron County Heritage Site. Take Hwy 122 north of Hwy 2 about 4 miles, crossing the state border into Michigan. Continue another ½ mile, then turn left on a gravel road into a parking lot. See map page 262.

Upson Falls

Upson Community Park

Upson Falls drops 18' into the Potato River. The park has a picnic area, pavilion, playground and camping. From Hwy 77, go north at the Upson Town Park sign, take a left at the end of the street, cross the river, then turn left into the park. See map page 259.

Wren Falls

5 miles northwest of Upson

Bring your compass and fishing pole, because 15' Wren Falls are located in a remote, heavily wooded area along the Tyler Forks River. Excellent trout fishing and primitive campsites. Contact the local chamber for precise directions as many of the roads don't have signs. See map page 261.

Marinette County

Marinette County proclaimed itself "Wisconsin's Waterfall Capital." Most of the falls are within the parks system and require a daily or yearly pass for a fee. Marinette has a handy free map highlighting 14 falls. For a copy, call 715-732-7510.

Bull Falls

Located ½ mile east of Amberg on the Pike River

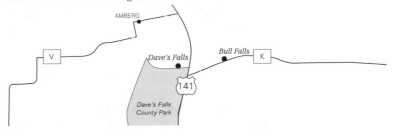

From Amberg, take Cty V to south Hwy 141, then take Cty K east for ½ mile to the power lines. Park in the right-of-way and walk a couple blocks north under the lines to the rapids on the Pike River.

Carney Rapids

Located south of Dunbar

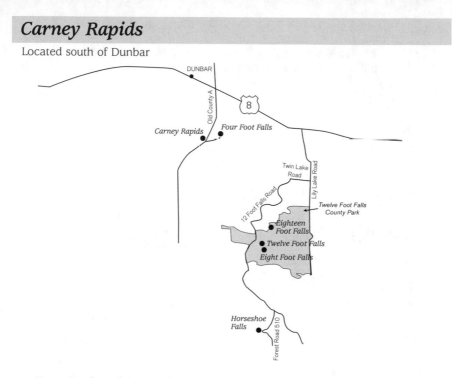

From Dunbar, drive east on Hwy 8 to Old Cty A, turn south and drive 2 miles to the bridge. The rolling rapids are to the west and visible from the road.

Dave's Falls

Dave's Falls County Park, Hwy 141 (½ mile southeast of Amberg on the Pike River)

Unusual rock formations and a series of cascades form two falls; one is accessed by a wooden bridge. The park has a picnic area, restroom and playground. See map page 263.

Four Foot Falls

North of Carney Rapids

The picturesque falls cut through large boulders. To find them, drive north of the bridge at Carney Rapids to a small dirt road. Head east about ½ mile, then park. Take the path on the right to the falls. See map above.

McClintock Falls

McClintock Park, south of Goodman on the Peshtigo River

This is an absolutely stunning series of rapids accessed by bridges and connecting miniature islands. An easy hike the kids will like and highly recommended. The park has a campground. Take Hwy 8 west to Parkway Road, drive south and watch for signs.

Piers Gorge

On the Menominee River about 9 miles north of Pembine

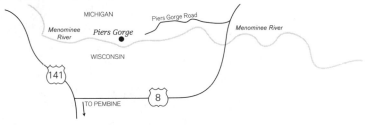

The 1¼-mile path to the falls is a sort of rough with rocks and roots, but it's not that steep and very doable with good hiking shoes. There are four lookout points or "piers" for viewing the cascading falls. For the best view take Hwy 8 into Michigan, then watch for signs to the parking lot.

Option: If you're looking for outdoor adventure, Marinette County has it. People come to fish, hike, whitewater raft, hunt, mountain bike, camp and to get away from the breakneck pace of city life. The folks at **Bjorkman Horse Outings** understand that adventurous spirit. They offer saddle horse, stagecoach and covered wagon vacations and cookouts throughout the summer and cutter and sleigh rides pulled by draft horses in the winter. Their address is W5994 Chapman Rd, Niagara 54151; 888-467-7367 or 715-251-4408; www.horsefun.net

Smalley Falls & Long Slide Falls

On the Pemebonwon River about 4 miles northeast of Pembine

Smalley Falls is not for young children. A very steep, difficult trail leads to a nasty climb downward. A precarious rock perch affords a mind-numbing, awesome view. **Long Slide Falls** is what it sounds like—a long, zigzag strip of water that rips through the rocks in a 50' drop. To get to Smalley Falls, drive north on Hwy 141/8 to Morgan Park Rd and watch for signs. For Long Slide Falls, continue on Morgan Park Rd and watch for the signs. The waterfall is an easy ¼-mile hike.

Strong Falls

Goodman Park, south of Goodman on the Peshtigo River; 715-732-7530

Easy trails trek to scenic bridges overlooking the frothy, roaring Strong Falls. Goodman Park has secluded picnic areas, a covered fire pit and children's playground. Available camping and one rental cabin that sleeps 8. Goodman Park is about 2 miles north of McClintock Park. Follow the signs. See map page 265.

Option: At about 26½ miles, R-32 is the **state's longest Rustic Road**. It traverses from Benson Lake Rd running south along the Peshtigo River to Cty W (from Strong Falls to Veteran's Falls). See numerous waterfalls, three county parks, a state forest, dense woodlands, burgeoning fern glades, lots of wildlife and several rivers. So if you're into miles of awe-inspired views, take R-32.

Twelve Foot Falls - Eight Foot Falls - Eighteen Foot Falls - Horseshoe Falls

Twelve Foot Falls County Park, southeast of Dunbar

You've hit the jackpot—four falls within the vicinity of one park. The park is on the Pike River. To get there from Hwy 8 go east to Lily Lake Rd. Go south on Lily Lake and follow the signs to the park, then turn right on Twin Lake Rd and left on Twelve Foot Falls Rd. Twelve Foot Falls is inside the park. Eight Foot Falls is a 5-minute hike through the campground. Eighteen Foot Falls is about a mile north of the park; take the second sand road on the right. Go about ½ mile and follow the path to the falls; a steep, treacherous climb. To find Horseshoe Falls drive south on Twelve Foot Falls Rd to Forest Road 510 for ½ mile to the falls turnoff. Aptly named, the falls makes a sharp bend around boulders. See map page 264.

Veteran's Falls

Veteran's Memorial Park, 10 miles west of Crivitz

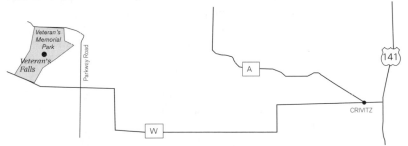

Take the steps down a steep slope that trails to an arched wooden bridge and several beautiful falls on the Thunder River. The park has a picnic area, playground and nearby camping. To find the falls, follow Cty W west from Crivitz to Parkway Rd N for 3 miles to Veteran's Memorial Park.

> **Options:** **Twin Bridge Park** is 5 miles north of Veteran's Park. The sand beach is perfect for swimming, fishing, canoeing, jet skiing and boating. The park has a large picnic area, lots of great hiking trails and camping. • For a fun evening, watch the **Crivitz Ski Cats Waterski Club** perform daring feats of skill and grace in Lake Noquebay County Park 5 miles outside of Crivitz. The shows are on W & Sa nights throughout the summer; www.marinettecounty.com/waterski.htm. Call for show times.

267

Polk & St. Croix Counties

Willow Falls

Willow River State Park, 1034 Cty A, Hudson 54016; 715-386-5931

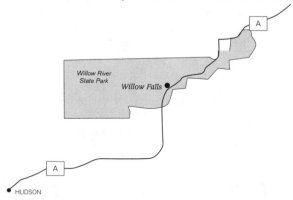

It's quite a hike to the Willow River Gorge, but worth it. Four overlooks access a series of cascading falls. The scenic 2,900-acre Willow River State Park has a campground, nature center with year-round naturalist-led programs, boat launch, fishing, 13 miles of hiking/cross-country skiing trails, canoeing, picnic area and a 400' beach. It's located 5 miles northeast of Hudson on Cty A.

NOTE: Polk County is home to the beautiful Cascade Falls in downtown Osceola. See the Romantic Getaways chapter (page 243) for more information.

Options: Located 20 minutes east of the Twin Cities (MN), Hudson is one of the state's fastest growing communities, yet nurtures a strong connection to its past. One such link is high atop the river bluffs at **Birkmose Park** on Coulee Rd. Sacred **Indian burial mounds** exist within the park. The overlook provides a breathtaking view of the St. Croix River Valley. A stone teepee marks the entrance. • If you find yourself in Hudson on a Th evening, mosey downtown to the Lakefront band shell for a **free summer concert** Jun–Aug. • Championship 18-hole golf course, hot air ballooning, theater, winter and summer tubing, antiques and specialty shops, boat cruises, fine dining, luxurious B&Bs, three Rustic Roads, tours of a buffalo farm and more await you in Hudson. Contact the **Hudson Area Chamber** for more information; 502 Second St, Hudson 54016; 800-657-6775; www.hudsonwi.org

Price County

Big Falls

Big Falls County Park, 10 miles south of Kennan on the Jump River;
715-339-6361

The Jump River cascades wildly around huge boulders forming the
Big Falls. The park has hiking, fishing, camping, playground, picnicking and swimming.

Slough Gundy

16 miles west of Phillips on the South Fork of the Flambeau River off Cty W

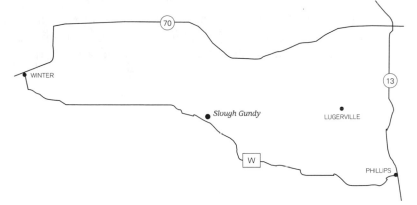

The beautiful rock canyon hosts a series of four of the steepest and
roughest rapids on the South Fork river.

The Wisconsin Dells is the Midwest's number one vacation destination, with more than 2½ million visitors annually. It has the largest indoor and outdoor water parks in America, rightly earning its status as "Water Capital of the World."

The Dells is really two places with two completely different faces. It's a gaudy, manmade, nonstop joy ride against a backdrop of natural scenery as rare and beautiful as a blushing virgin bride. Boredom is not an option. There's something here for everyone.

Wisconsin Dells

Alien Planet

228 Broadway (downtown); 608-253-5055; www.AlienPlanet.us

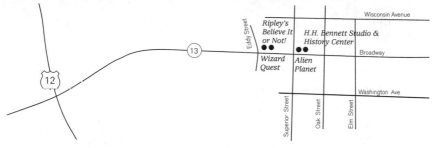

Scream your way through the 3-D Institute for Extraterrestrial Research and see more than two dozen hostile aliens. Actually, you're, um, chased by aliens, but that doesn't scare you, does it? This is super funhouse fun of the close encounter kind. Open Memorial Day–Labor Day; remainder of year F, Sa & Su. Call for hours. Admission charged.

Tommy Bartlett Show

560 Wisconsin Dells Pkwy; 608-254-2525; www.tommybartlett.com

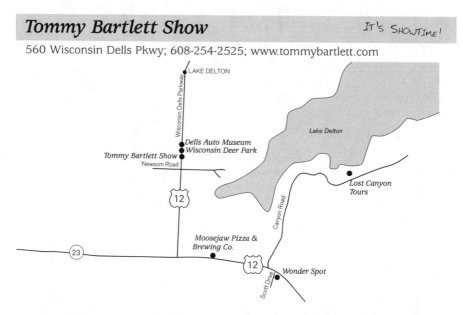

For half a century the Tommy Bartlett Show has wowed folks as Wisconsin Dells' biggest act. It's 2 hours of action-packed daredevil stunts on boats and water skis that defy gravity and sanity. There's stage comedy, and a breathtaking trapeze act performed from a helicopter. The finale is a colorful Vegas-type laser show. Daily shows Memorial Day–Labor Day. Call for show times. Admission charged. The show goes on rain or shine.

Option: Tommy Bartlett's Robot World and Exploratory is next door to the ski show. This is one cool place with more than 150 hands-on exhibits including an authentic Russian MIR space station. So if you ever wanted to be a cosmonaut, this is your chance. Test your sense of balance on the high wire SkyCycle or try out some perennial favorites such as the hydraulic backhoe and the virtual sports center. Open year-round. Call for hours. Admission charged.

Beaver Springs Fishing Park — CATCH A FISH

600 Trout Rd (1 block south of Best Western and Denny's on Trout Rd); 608-254-2735; www.beaverspringsfun.com

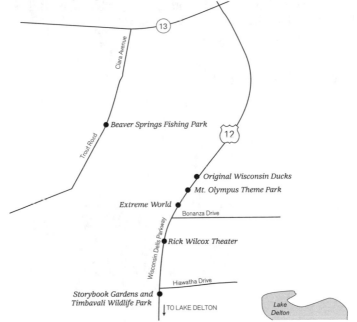

Not many attractions advertise "taxidermy service available," but you may decide that's a pretty good option when you reel in the big one at Beaver Springs Fishing Park. Bring the kids for a taste of trout fishing without any fuss on your part. They provide the equipment, bait and the cleaning and storage of your catch. You don't need a license and there's a picnic area with charcoal grills. If you don't feel like grilling your freshly caught bounty that's okay, because area restaurants will gladly do the task for you. And if you don't feel like fishing, Beaver Springs has a fabulous aquarium with over 1,000 fish and aquatic life. There's even an area for touching and feeding the fish. Open daily Apr–Oct, weather permitting Nov–Mar. General admission is free. There's a charge for fishing and a separate fee for the keepers. Aquarium admission charged.

NOTE: Beaver Springs is also a **horseback riding stable**. Call for reservations; 608-254-2735.

H.H. Bennett Studio & History Center *PICTURE PERFECT*

215 Broadway; 866-944-7483 or 608-253-3523; www.hhbennett.com

More than a century ago landscape photographer H.H. Bennett took pictures of the beautiful sandstone cliffs of the Wisconsin Dells and shared them with the world. The rest is history. Tour his former studio and have a look at the Dells as they were in the nineteenth century. The center has many interactive exhibits and displays. Gift shop. Open daily May–Sep, weekends only Oct, Nov & Feb–Apr. Call for hours. Admission charged. See map page 272.

Circus World Museum *BIG TOP FUN*

550 Water St (Hwy 113), Baraboo; 866-693-1500; www.circusworldmuseum.com

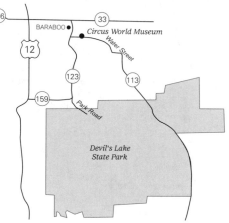

In 1884 the Ringling brothers opened their "Greatest Show on Earth" in Baraboo with a small tent, 3 horses, a hyena and a troupe of 21. Less than a quarter century later the brothers bought out the giant Barnum & Bailey Circus for $400,000—money they recouped within the first season. Circus World Museum is along the Baraboo River at the original site where the circus wintered until moving to Florida in 1918. The museum houses over 200 parade wagons and show vehicles, making it the world's largest collection of its kind. Watch the ongoing restoration process of these historic gilded beauties through an observation window. Learn everything you ever wanted to know about the brothers in the Irvin Feld Exhibit Hall and Visitor Center.

The Center has ongoing movies and displays featuring original costumes. There's also a Clown Camp, Carousel and Circus Train for the kids, but the real reason to come is for the Circus! Live 1-hour performances daily May–Sep in a real big top. Acts include clowns, elephants, ponies, hire wire, juggling and magic. Open year-round. Call for hours. Admission charged.

Options: The **Al. Ringling Theatre**, built by Al Ringling (hence the catchy name) has been in continuous operation since 1915. The decor is very fancy-schmancy, with a strong nod to the Great Opera Hall at the Palace of Versailles. Daily tours scheduled Memorial Day–Labor Day (for a fee) or take in a live performance or feature flick. Call for show/movie schedules. Find them at 136 4th Ave, downtown Baraboo; 608-356-8844; www.alringling.com.
• The **Ochsner Park Zoo** has mostly Wisconsin wildlife, but it's a clean setup and free. Corner of Hwy 33 and Park St, Baraboo.
• **Circus Royale** stars the Flying Wallendas—a family high wire act. Clowns, animal acts, acrobats and aerialists put on an entertaining 2-hour show under a big top located in the American World Resort and RV Park, Wisconsin Dells Pkwy and Cty Rd A; 866-244-8673; www.circusroyale.org

Dells Auto Museum

VROOOOMMMM!

591 Wisconsin Dells Pkwy (next to Wisconsin Deer Park); 608-254-2008

See twentieth-century muscle cars, convertibles and Indy 500 pace cars at Dells Auto Museum. For those not into hot cars, there's an extensive collection of toys, antique dolls and clothing. Gift and antiques shop. Open daily mid-May–Sep. Call for hours. Admission charged. See map page 272.

Options: For a faster pace, head to **Dells Motor Speedway** for stock car racing. Mid-Apr–Labor Day. Time trials and racing Fr & Sa evenings. Call for times. Find them at N1032 Smith Rd, Wisconsin Dells; 608-254-7822; www.dellsmotorspeedway.com.
• Still have a thrill itch you need scratched? Scratch away at **Monster Truck World**. Crush cars and climb to Killer Hill aboard a toothy beast with tires the size of small planets. Kiddie rides, too; 633 Dells Pkwy; www.monstertruckworld.biz

Devil's Lake State Park

HIKE, HIKE, SHOULD'VE BROUGHT MY MOUNTAIN BIKE

S5975 Park Rd, Baraboo (south of downtown Baraboo); 608-356-8301

Devil's Lake State Park is a must-see for rock climbers and anyone into amazing views. The bluffs tower 500' above a 360-acre lake. Every trail provides an inspired "oh, my gosh" moment. Great fishing, boating, picnicking, camping and cross-country skiing. It's situated along the Ice Age Trail (an ambitious 1,000-mile hike, of which 560 miles are complete). Full-time naturalist on duty. Park entrance fee. See map page 274.

Extreme World

ADVENTURE TO THE EXTREME

Hwy 12 (across from Treasure Island on the Dells Pkwy); 608-254-4111; www.extremeworld.com

The key word is *extreme*. If you have a need to play things safe, IBS syndrome or think Justin Timberlake is a "bad boy," then stay far away from Extreme World. Rides have cutesy names such as Ejection Seat, Terminal Velocity and Skycoaster. Bungee jump or give their indoor paintball arcade a try. Ride the Dells' fastest go-carts. A trip through their haunted house is a guaranteed heart stopper. Open year-round Memorial Day–Labor Day. Call for hours. Each attraction has its own price. See map page 273.

Fab '50s LIVE!

ELVIS LIVES!

Chula Vista Resort, 4031 River Rd; 800-388-4782 or 608-254-8366; www.fab50slive.com

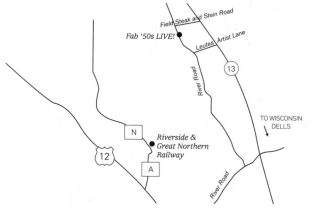

Elvis and rock 'n roll are alive and better than ever when performed by the talented cast of Fab '50s LIVE! Costumed song and dance numbers have the audience bopping in their seats. The charming Ms. Marilyn Monroe makes a sexy, breathy appearance, and the energetic score from "Grease" brings the house down. The season is mid-Jun–Labor Day daily. Call for show times and ticket prices. Dinner and show packages available.

International Crane Foundation

One of a Kind

E11376 Shady Lane Road, Baraboo; 608-356-9462

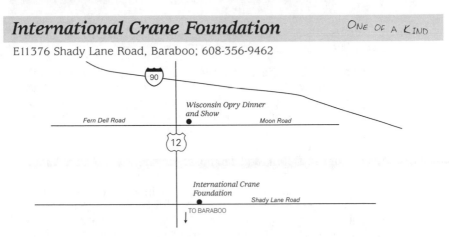

The International Crane Foundation is a one-of-a-kind, internationally-recognized center dedicated to the study and preservation of the world's largest (and rarest) flying bird—the crane. Watch as human "parents" feed and exercise the chicks. Daily guided tours Memorial Day–Labor Day, weekends only in Apr, May, Sep & Oct. Call for tour times. Self-guided tours view adult birds, marshland and restored prairie. Museum displays and videos. Admission charged.

Lost Canyon Tours

A Trot Through the Canyon

720 Canyon Rd, Lake Delton (just off I-90/94); 608-254-8757;
www.dells.com/horses/lostcanyon.htm

Enjoy a 30-minute carriage ride through stunning cliff-walled gorges. The path to the canyon is so narrow in some places that the horses and wagon barely squeeze through, but that adds to the fun. Wagons accommodate up to 15 people. Open daily Memorial Day–Labor Day. Call for hours and ticket prices. See map page 272.

Option: Lost Canyon also operates **Canyon Creek Riding Stables**. Venture through woods and streams and the "Old West" town of Tombstone. There are 3 trails to choose from and a free petting zoo. Open daily. Call for reservations; 608-253-6942 or 608-253-2781. The cost is per hour.

Moosejaw Pizza & Brewing Co.

For All That "Ales"

110 Wisconsin Dells Pkwy S (at the intersection of Hwy 12 and 23); 608-254-1122; www.moosejawbrewpub.com

Of course, the Dells has a brewpub, and by the billionth screaming roller coaster ride you'll need it. Sit back and unwind in this large, but comfortably rustic log cabin atmosphere. There are three levels to the place and each one has its own bar—you've got to like that. The brew master crafts about a dozen beers on the top level open air microbrewery. Open daily. See map page 272.

Options: Since you're so close to Reedsburg, you might as well stop in and sample the handcrafted ales at the **Corner Pub Brewery**, the oldest operating tavern in Sauk County. Watch the brew process through an observation window, but call ahead to find out when they're brewing; 100 Main St, Hwy 33/23; 608-524-8989. • The town of La Valle is just a hop, skip and jump from Reedsburg, so stop in and say howdy to the folks at **Carr Valley Cheese**. Watch the fourth-generation cheese master make his famous Cheddar through an observation window. Open M–Sa. Call for hours. They are located at S3797 Cty Hwy G, La Valle (from Reedsburg, go northwest on Hwy 23 S, right on Hwy K, right on G 1½ miles); 608-986-2781; www.carrvalleycheese.com

Mount Olympus Theme Park

GO-KART & ROLLER COASTER MANIA

Hwy 12 ; 608-254-2490; www.mtolympusthemepark.com

Formerly Known as Big Chief, this gigantic park boasts 9 go-cart tracks and 5 stomach-churning roller coasters, making it America's largest go-cart and coaster complex. The tracks rate from beginner to very difficult. The park's themed decor is straight from Greek god mythology. The tots won't get left behind either as they have their own Kiddieland with a racetrack and rides designed just for them. Open mid-Mar–Oct. Call for hours. Admission charged. See map page 273.

Original Wisconsin Ducks

DUCK, DUCK, GREEN & WHITE DUCK

1890 Wisconsin Dells Pkwy (1 mile south of the Dells on Hwy 12); 608-254-8751; www.wisconsinducktours.com

These strange WW II amphibians are what happens when you cross a fishing boat with a shuttle bus. It's a rather odd feeling to be bouncing along the wilds of Roller Coaster Hill, then splash down into the Wisconsin River for a cruise of the breathtaking Lower Dells sandstone cliffs. The narrated 1-hour tour gives a history of the Dells and points out unique rock formations. Open end of Mar–start of Nov. Call for hours. Admission charged. Wheelchair accessible. See map page 273.

Ripley's Believe It or Not!

BELIEVE IT OR NOT!

115 Broadway; 608-253-7556; www.ripleysbelieveitornotdells.com

Who ever forgets the time they saw their first shrunken head? A priceless moment. This and many more wonders are in store for all who enter the bizarro world of Ripley. Two theaters and nine galleries showcase the freaky along with artifacts from around the world. Open daily Mar–Oct, weekends only Nov–Feb. Admission charged. See map page 272.

Riverside & Great Northern Railway

CHUG-CHUG, CHOO-CHOO

N115 Cty Rd N (1 mile north of the Dells on Stand Rock Rd); 608-254-6367; www.randgn.com

It's knees up if you're riding the tiny, authentic 15-inch narrow-gauge steam train. The 3-mile roundtrip departs from the Hyde Park Depot and puffs through scenic canyons and woods. Picnic area and cafe. Open Apr–Nov weekends, Memorial Day–Labor Day daily. Call for hours and ticket prices. See map page 276.

> **Option:** You had so much fun on your train trip that you'd like to ride another one. No problem. Climb aboard a vintage train for a 50-minute ride through the Baraboo River Valley on the **Mid-Continent Railway and Museum**. There's lots to see here including original railroad cars and a wooden water tower. Trains depart daily from the 1894 depot in North Freedom. Call for departure times and coach fares (more for cab and caboose rides). Take Hwy 12 S to Hwy 136, then west to Hwy PF to North Freedom; 608-522-4261; www.midcontinent.org. Free admission to museum.

Storybook Gardens & Timbavati Wildlife Park

ONCE UPON A TIME

1500 Wisconsin Dells Pkwy; 608-253-2391; www.storybookgardens.net

Meet and greet your favorite nursery rhyme characters as they roam the gardens and pose for pictures. Opened in the 1950s, Storybook Gardens was one of the Dells' first attractions and is still going strong. The Timbavati Wildlife Park is home to exotic animals—at least for Wisconsin—including a zebra, giraffe and kangaroo. Open daily Memorial Day–Labor Day. Admission charged. See map page 273.

Rick Wilcox Theater

DO YOU BELIEVE IN MAGIC?

1666 Wisconsin Dells Pkwy; 608-254-5511; www.rickwilcox.com

Rick and Suzan Wilcox razzle-dazzle you with their amazing show of comedy and illusion. Lots of audience interaction and a magic shop make this show a family favorite. Open year-round. Call for a schedule and ticket prices. See map page 273.

Wisconsin Deer Park

PET A DEER

583 Hwy 12; 608-253-2041

The main thing to see, pet and feed here is White-tailed Deer. The park houses over 100 deer, plus bison and game birds. Take your camera. The deer are super friendly and will eat out of anyone's hand. Open May–mid-Oct. Call for hours. Admission charged. See map page 272.

Wisconsin Opry Dinner and Show

NASHVILLE IN WISCONSIN

E10964 Moon Rd, Baraboo 53913; 608-254-7951; www.wisconsinopry.com

C'mon over to the farm for some real live country music as the CMA intended it to be. It's 2 hours of opry, a hardy farmhand-type dinner and a hayride. Shop the antiques and craft barns and the weekend flea market. Open late May–mid-Sep. Wisconsin Opry headlines the occasional Grand Ole Opry star, but primarily features local talent. Showtimes M–Sa (some Su matinees). Call for dinner and show times, ticket prices and for reservations. See map page 277.

Wizard Quest

OFF TO SEE THE WIZARD

105 Broadway, downtown Wisconsin Dells (next to the River Walk); 608-254-2184

If you're looking for Harry Potter, you won't find him here. But if you're very lucky, you will find four other wizards as you journey through secret passages fighting off dragons and trolls. The interactive fantasy game will have you believing in a world beyond your mortal senses. Open year-round. Admission charged. See map page 272.

Wonder Spot

FREAK OF NATURE

100 Scott Dr, Lake Delton; 608-254-4224

Ever pour water and have it flow up? At the Wonder Spot it's a natural occurrence as is standing at weird angles and sitting on chairs with only two legs on the ground. Discovered in 1948, the Wonder Spot disputes everything you know about gravity. Open Memorial Day–Labor Day rain or shine. Call for hours. Admission charged. See map page 272.

Option: Still think you have your bearings straight? Then drive a block past the Wonder Spot for a disorienting walk through a 6,000-square-foot maze at **Corny Maze, Go-Karts and Bankshot Basketball**. Bankshot Basketball is a lot like mini-golf, only with a basketball and hoops. Find them at Hwy 12 E, Lake Delton; 608-253-7332. Admission charged.

Dells Odds & Ends

Here's a list of some other attractions and information for the Midwest's number one vacation destination. Contact the **Wisconsin Dells Visitors and Convention Bureau** at 800-223-3557 for more information.

Boat Rentals

- **Boo Canoe & Raft**, Hwy 113, Baraboo (1 mile south of Circus World Museum); 608-356-8856; www.boocanoe.com

- **Holiday Shores Water Sports Rentals**, 3901 River Rd; 608-254-2878 or 608-254-2717; www.wisvacations.com/holidayshores (parasail rides, canoes, jet boats, paddleboats, wave runners)

Boat Tours

- **Aqua Adventure Jet Airboat**, River Bay Campground, PO Box 456; www.dells-camping.com; 800-443-1112 or 608-254-7193 (only jet airboat tour of the Upper Dells)

- **Captain C.R. Soma's Dells Cruises**, Hagan's Landing, N422 Cty Rd N; www.dellscruises.com; 877-525-2628 or 608-254-2628; (May–Oct, M–Sa; tour cruise on the Upper Dells as well as sunset dinner and cocktail cruises)

- **Dells Army Duck Tours**, 1550 Wisconsin Dells Pkwy; 608-254-6080; www.dellsducks.com (Apr–Oct daily; Lower Dells tours)

- **Dells Boat Tours**, 100 block of Broadway; 608-254-8555; www.dellsboattours.com (Mar–Nov daily; Upper and Lower Dells tours; shore landing tour at Stand Rock—the sandstone formation made famous by a nineteenth-century photo; also jet boat tours)

- **Mark Twain Boat Tour**, 1550 Wisconsin Dells Pkwy; 608-254-6080; www.dellsducks.com (May–Oct daily; call for times; 1-hour tours of Upper Dells)

- **Original Wisconsin Ducks**, 1890 Wisconsin Dells Pkwy; 608-254-8751; www.winsconsinducktours.com (Mar–Nov daily; call for times; tours of Lower Dells and Lake Delton)

- **Original Dells Experience Jet Boats**, N1357 Cty Rd N, Lyndon Station; 888-538-3557 or 608-254-8246; www.dellsjetboats.com (May–Oct; call for reservations; tours the Upper Dells)

- **Wildthing Jet Boat**, 1550 Wisconsin Dells Pkwy at Dells Army Ducks; 608-254-6080; www.dellsducks.com (jet boat tour of the Upper Dells)

Golf

- **Christmas Mountain Village Golf Course**, S944 Christmas Mountain Rd; 800-289-1066 or 608-254-3971 (18-hole golf course and ski resort)

- **Fairfield Hills Golf Course**, E11345 Reedsburg Rd, Baraboo; 608-356-5524 (9-hole)

- **Pinecrest Par 3 Golf Course**, 712 Hwy 23; 608-254-2165 (9-hole, par 3 course)

- **Trappers Turn Golf Club**, 562 Trappers Turn Dr; 800-221-8876; www.trappersturn.com (27-hole award-winning course)

- **Wilderness Hotel and Golf Resort**, 511 Adams St; 608-253-9729 (open year-round; indoor water park, 18-hole championship golf course, par 3 course and resort)

Horseback Riding

- **Beaver Springs Riding Stable**, 600 Trout Rd (1 block south of Best Western and Denny's on Trout Rd); 608-254-2735; www.beaver-springsfun.com

- **Canyon Creek Stables**, 720 Canyon Rd, Lake Delton (just off I-90/94); 608-253-6942; www.dells.com/horses/lostcanyon.htm

- **OK Corral Riding Stable**, Hwy 16 E (1 mile east of downtown); 608-254-2811

Mini-Golf

- **Adventure Lagoon Outdoor Waterpark & Mini Golf**, Chula Vista Resort, 4031 River Rd; 800-388-4782 or 608-254-8366; www.chulavistaresort.com (outdoor water park and mini-golf open Memorial Day–Labor Day)

- **Old River Adventure Golf**, Eddy St, downtown Wisconsin Dells; 608-254-8336

- **Pirates' Cove Adventure Golf**, located at the Country Kitchen Corner, Hwy 12, 13, 16 and 23,; 608-254-7500 (also an amusement park)

- **Timber Falls Adventure Park**, located at the Wisconsin River Bridge and Stand Rock Rd; www.timberfallspark.com; 608-254-8414; (amusement park and miniature golf)

Mopeds

- **Uncle Gene's World of Wheels**, 1021 Stand Rock Rd (next to Timber Falls Adventure Park); www.unclegenes.com; 608-253-4230; (open Mar–Nov, Memorial Day–Labor Day)

Skiing

- **Christmas Mountain**, S944 Christmas Mountain Rd; 800-289-1066 or 608-254-3971 (7 runs)

Water parks

- **Adventure Lagoon Outdoor Waterpark & Mini Golf**, Chula Vista Resort, 4031 River Rd; www.chulavistaresort.com; 800-388-4782 or 608-254-8366; (open Memorial Day–Labor Day; outdoor water park)

- **Family Land Waterpark**, 1701 Wisconsin Dells Pkwy; 800-800-4997 or 608-254-7766; www.wisdellstreasureisland.com (open year-round; outdoor and indoor water park)

- **Kalahari Resort Convention Center & Waterpark**, 1305 Kalahari Dr; 877-253-5466 or 608-254-5466; www.kalahariresort.com (open year-round; America's largest indoor water park and resort)

- **Noah's Ark Waterpark**, 1410 Wisconsin Dells Pkwy; 608-254-6351; www.noahsarkwaterpark.com (open May–Sep; America's largest outdoor water park)

- **The Polynesian**, 857 N Frontage Rd; 800-272-5642 or 608-254-2883 (open year-round; indoor water park and resort)

- **Riverview Park & Waterworld**, 700 US Hwy 12; 608-254-2608; www.riverviewpark.com (open May–Sep; outdoor water park with amusement rides)

- **Treasure Island Waterpark Resort**, 1701 Wisconsin Dells Pkwy; 608-254-8560 (open year-round; indoor water park and resort)

- **Wilderness Hotel and Golf Resort**, 511 Adams St; 608-253-9729 (open year-round; indoor water park, 18-hole championship golf course and resort)

Here's the dilemma: Wisconsin is an amazing state with so much to see and do that it'd take at least a dozen **thick** books to do it justice. Here's the reality: No one wants to read a dozen **thick** books. Therefore, here's some valuable information that didn't make the other chapters, yet you may find helpful when planning your day trip.

Odds & Ends

Apples

More than two dozen apple varieties are grown in Wisconsin. The orchards often stock a variety of apple products from award-winning wines to jellies and juices. For a list of more than 200 apple orchards, call the **Wisconsin Department of Agriculture**; 608-224-5100; www.wisconsin.gov. For more information, write or call the **Wisconsin Apple Growers Association**, 211 Canal Rd, Waterloo 53594; 920-478-3852; www.waga.org.

Camping

The **Wisconsin Association of Campground Owners** puts out a free directory with all kinds of great campground information including camping discounts. Pick up a copy at the larger tourist information centers or call 800-843-1821; www.wisconsincampgrounds.com.

Cherries

Wisconsin ranks third nationally in cherry production. Contact **Wisconsin Red Cherry Growers Association**, PO Box 452, Egg Harbor 54209-0452; 920-839-2933; www.wisconsin-cherries.org to request a map and listing of the state's red cherry growers,

Cranberries—The State Fruit

Cranberries are native to Wisconsin and are the state's number one fruit crop. Wisconsin growers produce more than 40 percent of the nation's total. Many of the growers offer special tours of their cranberry marshes at harvest time. For more information, call the **Wisconsin State Cranberry Growers Association**; PO Box 365, Wisconsin Rapids 54495-0365; 715-423-2070; www.wiscran.org.

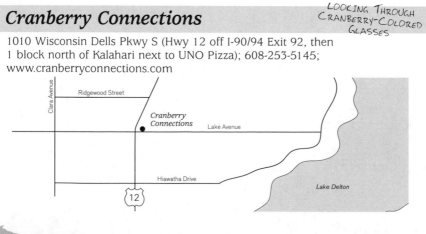

Cranberry Connections

LOOKING THROUGH CRANBERRY-COLORED GLASSES

1010 Wisconsin Dells Pkwy S (Hwy 12 off I-90/94 Exit 92, then 1 block north of Kalahari next to UNO Pizza); 608-253-5145; www.cranberryconnections.com

Cranberry Connections owner Carrie Anderson comes by the business naturally. As a sixth-generation grower, Carrie dreamed of a place where she could share her passion about cranberries with others. Established in August 2004, the 3,600-square-foot Cranberry Connections interactive exhibits feature the of business of growing and harvesting Wisconsin's number one fruit crop, as well as their health benefits. Explore the marsh culvert replica, sample gourmet products including six flavors of cranberry ice cream or enjoy a slice of cranberry pie. The gift shop includes everything cranberry—candles, candies, lotions and soaps, coffees and teas—as well as traditional gift items and souvenirs. Cranberry Connections also offers the area's largest selection of cranberry glass. A short video explains the process of adding gold to lead crystal, turning the glass pink. Open Jan-May daily, closed W. Call for hours. Admission free. Bus tours are welcome.

Covered Bridges

Wisconsin has eleven covered bridges, but only one is an authentic nineteenth-century bridge. All of them are worth seeking out.

- **Cedarburg**–Length 120', built in 1876; the state's last authentic nineteenth-century bridge. Location is across Cedar Creek, north of Cedarburg. Take Hwy 143 northwest 2 miles from junction with Hwy 57 in Cedarburg. Go north on Covered Bridge Rd for 1 mile. The bridge is on the east side.

- **Chequamegon**—Length 90', built in 1991. Location is across the

South Fork of the Flambeau River east of Fifield. Take Hwy 70 E almost 12 miles from junction with Hwy 13 in Fifield, then north on Smith Rapids Rd (Hwy 148). Go approximately to miles to the bridge.

- **Clarence**—Length 110', built in 1984. Location is across Norwegian Creek northwest of Brodhead. Take Cty E north about 2 miles from junction with Hwy 11 on the north side of Brodhead, then go west on Golf Course Rd ¼ mile to where Sugarloaf Trail crosses with the road. Park and walk about 500 yards northwest on the trail to the bridge.

- **Dorothy**—Length 50', built in 1975. Location is at the Fox Museum, northeast of Gratiot. Take Hwy 78 northeast 4 miles from junction with Hwy 11 at the east edge of Gratiot, then east on Fox Rd for about ½ mile and south on a private driveway at 7711 Fox Rd. Bridge is to the southwest.

- **Glacial River Bike Trail**—Length 51', built in 2000. Location is across the tributary of Allen Creek, southwest of Ft. Atkinson about 6 miles on the west side of Hwy 26. Built on an old railroad trestle and part of the trail.

- **James Barden**—Length 56', built in 1926; one of five authentic bow bridges—roof added in 1938. Location is across the Amnicon River northwest of Poplar (see the Waterfalls chapter). Take Hwy 2 northwest for almost 5 miles from junction with Cty D in Poplar, then go north on Cty U for ⅓ mile, then west into the park. Park entrance fee charged.

- **Pedestrian**—Location is across the Baraboo River in Elroy. Part of the Sparta-Elroy Trail, take Hwy 80 north ⅕ mile from junction with Hwy 71 in Elroy, then east on North St for 1 block to the bridge.

- **Red Mill**—Length 40', built in 1970. Location is across the Crystal River south of Waupaca. Take Hwy 22 southwest about ½ mile from junction with Hwy 10 on the south edge of Waupaca, then south on Cty K for 1⅕ miles to the Red Mill, on the east side of road (see the Romantic Getaways chapter).

- **Springwater**—Length 44', built in 1997. Location is across the Pine River west of Saxeville. Take Cty A west 1 mile from Saxeville, then south on Covered Bridge Rd.

- **Stonefield**—Length 52', built in 1962. Location is across Dewey Creek in Stonefield northwest of Cassville (see Museums chapter). Take Hwy 133 northwest for about ½ mile from the junction with Hwy 81 in Cassville, then go northwest on Cty VV for 1⅕ miles to the entrance of Stonefield, on the west side of the road.

- **Waupaca**—Length 30'. Location is across the Waupaca River at the west end of town. Take Hwy 54 east ⅓ mile from junction with Hwy 10 at the west edge of Waupaca, then go north on Covered Bridge Rd. It's less than ½ mile to the bridge.

Downhill Skiing, Snowboarding & Tubing

- **Badlands Recreation, Inc.**, 717 Badlands Rd, Hudson 54016; 715-386-1856 (snow park with tubing and snowboarding)

- **Camp 10 Ski n Snowboard**, 1604 Camp 10 Rd, Rhinelander 54501; 715-362-0506 (240' vertical, 11 runs, snowboarding, skiing free/children under age 7 if with parent)

- **Cascade Mountain**, W10441 Cascade Mountain Rd, Portage 53901; 800-992-2754 or 608-742-5588 (460' vertical, 28 runs, snowboarding, skiing free/children ages 5 and under)

- **Christie Mountain**, W13755 Cty O, Bruce 54819; 715-868-7800 (350' vertical, 21 runs, snowboarding, tubing)

- **Devil's Head Resort**, S6330 Bluff Rd, Merrimac 53561; 800-472-6670 or 608-493-2251 (500' vertical, 28 runs, snowboarding)

- **Grand Geneva (Mountain Top)**, 7036 Grand Geneva Way at Hwy 50 E and 12, Lake Geneva 53147; 262-248-8811 (211' vertical, 18 runs, snowboarding, golf, water park, spa)

- **Granite Peak**, 3605 N Mountain Rd, Wausau 54402; 715-845-2846 (700' vertical, 72 runs, snowboarding, Comet Express lifts)

- **Mount LaCrosse**, N5549 Old Town Hall Rd, LaCrosse 54601; 800-426-3665 or 608-788-0044 (516' vertical, 18 runs, snowboarding)

- **Nordic Mountain**, Mount Morris (30 miles north of Green Lake); 800-253-7266 or 920-787-3324; (265' vertical, 14 runs, snowboarding)

- **Sunburst Ski Area**, 8355 Prospect Dr, Kewaskum 53040; 414-626-8404 (214' vertical, 10 runs, snowboarding and tubing)

- **Telemark Resort**, 42225 Telemark Rd, Cable 54821; 877-798-4718 or 715-798-3999 (snowboarding, tubing, snowshoeing, ice skating, golf)

- **Trollhaugen Ski Area**, 2232 100th Ave, Dresser 54009; 800-826-7166 or 715-755-2955 (280' vertical, 10 runs, snowboarding and tubing with conveyor lift)

- **Tyrol Basin Ski & Snowboard Area**, 3487 Bohn Rd, Mount Horeb

53572; 608-437-4135 (300' vertical, 16 runs)

- **Whitecap**, Cty Rd E at Weber Lake, Montreal 54550; 800-933-SNOW or 715-561-2227 (400' vertical, 35 runs, snowboarding, golf)

- **Wilmot Mountain**, 11931 Fox River Rd, Wilmot 53192; 262-862-2301 (230' vertical, 25 runs, snowboarding)

Frank Lloyd Wright Buildings

Born in 1869 in Richland Center, the world-renowned architect lived and worked in Wisconsin for more than 60 years. Most public buildings designed by Wright are open for tours and listed here. Annually scheduled trips visit several private homes and buildings (each year is in a different locale). For more information about the trips, contact **Frank Lloyd Wright Wisconsin Heritage Tourism Program**, PO Box 6339, Madison 53716; 608-287-0339; www.WrightinWisconsin.org.

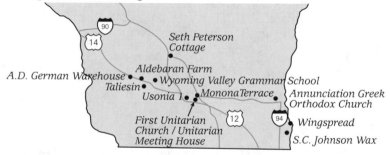

- **A.D. German Warehouse**, 300 S Church St, Richland Center; 608-647-2808 (museum and gallery; tours by appointment)

- **Aldebaran Farm**, Spring Green; 608-588-2568 (the ancestral home of Wright's uncle; call for reservations)

- **Annunciation Greek Orthodox Church**, 9400 W Congress St, Milwaukee; 414-461-9400 (tours Tu & F)

- **Monona Terrace Community and Convention Center**, One John Nolen Dr, Madison; 608-261-4000; www.mononaterrace.com (open daily, cafe open M–Sa, rooftop garden with concession cafe open daily weather permitting, gift shop, daily guided tours for a fee, call for hours)

- **S.C. Johnson Wax (Headquarters)**, 14th and Franklin St, Racine 53403; 262-260-2154; www.scjohnsonwax.com (free tours F year-round, reservations required, tours begin at Golden Rondelle Theater, 1525 Howe St)

- **Seth Peterson Cottage**, E9982 Fern Dell Rd, Lake Delton; www.SethPeterson.org (guest house totals 880 square feet, making it the architect's smallest design; for overnight rental, contact Sand County Service Co, 116 W Munroe St, PO Box 409, Lake Delton 53940; 608-254-6551; tours the second Su of the month at scheduled times; admission charged)

- **Taliesin Preservation/Frank Lloyd Wright Visitor Center**, 5607 Cty C, Spring Green; www.TaliesinPreservation.org; 608-588-7900; (Frank Lloyd Wright's home and school; cafe, movie, tours)

- **Unitarian Meeting House**, 900 University Bay Dr, Madison 53705; 608-238-1680 or 608-233-9774 (daily tours; call for tour schedule; admission charged)

- **Usonia 1 (Jacobs House)**, www.usonia1.com (for house rental contact James Dennis, 441 Toepfer, Madison 53711; 608-233-2655)

- **Wingspread**, 33 E Four Mile Rd, Racine 53402; 262-681-3353 (free tours by appointment)

- **Wyoming Valley Grammar School**, Hwy 23 (12 miles north of Dodgeville), Spring Green (2-room elementary school donated by Wright in remembrance of his mother).

Great Wisconsin Birding & Nature Trail

This new series of trails is an ambitious DNR project highlighting unique ecosystems with the best chance for viewing birds and wildlife. Still under development, the DNR plans to map five statewide regions. The first—the **Lake Superior/Northwoods**—debuted in May 2004. The Lake Superior/Northwoods Trail encompasses 18 northern counties, with 99 waypoints from the 21 Apostle Islands to the 850,000 acres of **Chequamegon-Nicolet National Forest**. Next on the slate is the **Mississippi/Chippewa Rivers Trail**. So get the binoculars out and call the Wisconsin Department of Tourism for a map; 800-432-8747; www.travelwisconsin.com. Sandhill Crane logos mark the waypoints. Visit www.wisconsinbirds.org/trail/ for more information about this project.

NOTE: Over 240 bird species breed and/or migrate through the Apostle Islands. Park rangers staff visitor centers daily Memorial Day–Labor Day.

Haunted Wisconsin

Fact: lots of places are haunted—mostly cemeteries, schools, universities, theaters, churches and dark, eerie back roads. Reason for the apparitions—who knows? But lots of people enjoy hunting the haunted. If you're one of those folks, here's a list of public places to check out the ghost vibe.

- **Bayfield—Michigan Island Lighthouse**. The ghost of a lighthouse keeper slams doors during bad storms—even when they're already bolted shut.

- **Boscobel—Hotel Boscobel**, 1005 Wisconsin Ave; 608-375-4714. Haunted by Adam Bobel, the man who built the hotel in 1863. The historic building is also the **birthplace of the Gideon Bible**.

- **Brodhead—Flynn's Steak House**, 1101 1st Center Ave. The building is one of the oldest in town and used to be a hotel. Many ghosts make noises and move objects.

- **Chippewa Falls—Sheeley House**, 236 W River St; 715-726-0561. Once a boarding house, now a bar and restaurant. Decorative roses on walls continue to reappear no matter how many times they've been painted over. Footsteps on stairs at night, closing doors; the usual mischief.

- **East Troy—Cobblestone Bar**, 2088 Church St; 262-642-3735. Constructed in the early 1800s as a hotel (President Lincoln stayed here), the bar is now haunted by the original owners.

- **Eau Claire—UW Kjer Theatre**, corner of Garfield and Park Ave; 715-836-2637. Earl Kjer, founder of the theater, messes with the lights, props, curtains, etc. You can also see him sitting in his usual theater seat.

- **Eau Claire—Vine St**. Here's a spooky one. Nearly every night in Sep (around midnight) you'll see a woman in her mid-20s out jogging. And just as you're about to pass her by, she cuts in front of your vehicle as if she's *trying* to get hit. Of course, when you look for her, she's not there.

- **Ferryville—Swing Inn**, 106 Main St; 608-734-9916. The inn is home to one ghost who walks the stairs on slow nights. Tough beat.

- **Fond du Lac—Octagon House**, 276 Linden St; 920-922-1608. A little boy ghost has the run of the place. Open Memorial Day–Labor Day M, W & F afternoons. Admission charge.

- **Green Bay—Downtown YMCA**, 235 N Jefferson St. Haunted by a murder victim.

- **Hales Corners—Whitnall Park**, Milwaukee. For a sure sighting, head to this massive park and watch for a woman in a white gown holding an infant. Sometimes she talks and sometimes the baby cries. She appears in several locations throughout the park, but for the best view stay in the parking area. She appears around 11pm.

- **Kenosha—Kemper Hall**, 121 66th St (along the lakeside). The Gothic Revival and Italianate antebellum hall was once a girls' school run by nuns. You guessed it, nuns peer out from the windows. The grounds are part of a gorgeous county park with an arboretum that showcases hundreds of roses and a herb garden designed for the blind.

- **Kewaunee—The Historic Karsten Inn**, 122 Ellis St; 920-388-3800. Four very busy ghosts vigorously haunt the inn in various ways—orbs, ectoplasm mists, unusual odors, sounds of breaking glass, flute playing, a woman crying, whispers, moving furniture—well, you get the idea. Rent a room and join the fun.

- **Lake Mills—Aztalan State Park**, 1213 S Main (east of Madison off I-94); 920-648-8774. This is the site of a twelfth-century Indian village. Many spirits roam here. Reportedly, there are also thousand-year-old pyramids at the bottom of Rock Lake. No one knows for sure why they're there, but legend has it they were built by Aztec Indians as an appeal to their gods during a long drought. Hiking trails, naturalist program, picnic areas, but no camping allowed. Park entrance fee.

- **New Richmond—Kozy Korner Restaurant**, 157 S Knowles Ave; 715-246-2220. A young boy appears here often.

- **Oshkosh—The Grand Opera House**, 100 High Ave; 920-424-2350. Haunted by Percy Keene, a stage manager from the 1960s, who won't let the show go on without him.

- **Oshkosh—Paine Art Center**, 1410 Algoma Blvd; 920-235-6903. It wasn't until after their deaths that Mr. and Mrs. Paine finally moved into their 1920s Tudor revival home. Tours given Tu–Su. If you're lucky, you may get Mrs. Paine for a guide.

- **Superior—Fairlawn Mansion**, 906 E 2nd St. (across from Barker's Island); 715-394-5712. The 42-room, refurbished 1890 mansion was once the home of Martin Thayer Pattison, a wealthy businessman who made his money in lumber and iron ore. He became the city's second mayor. The home is haunted by a former housekeeper who doubles as tour guide from time to time. Now that's dedication! Open daily. Call for hours. Admission charge.

- **Washington Island—Nelsens Hall and Bitters Pub**, Uptown on Main Rd; 920-847-2496. This is the oldest continuously operating tavern in the nation. Home to a "shoulder tapper," objects disappear and reappear. Folks think the ghost is the founder, Tom Nelsen.

- **Wisconsin Dells—The Showboat Saloon**, 24 Broadway; 608-253-2628. Several ghosts materialize in mirrors, move things around, open and close doors—general mayhem.

Hunting & Fishing

Besides all the world-renowned fame Wisconsin receives for its cheese and the Green Bay Packers, the state is a recognizable leader for top hunting and fishing opportunities. More than 5 million acres of public hunting land awaits those longing to bag White-tailed Deer, Elk, Black Bear and Wild Turkey and other game birds. Anglers never have trouble finding the perfect spot to drop a line, because the state has more than 15,000 inland lakes, 2,500 trout streams, 5,000 warm water streams, 240 miles of Mississippi riverbanks and 860 miles of Great Lakes shoreline. Wisconsin also offers special hunting and fishing opportunities for people who are legally blind or have other physical disabilities. For more information, contact the **Wisconsin DNR**; PO Box 7921, Madison 53707-7921; 608-266-2621; www.dnr.state.wi.us. For a free **Wisconsin Fishing Guide** filled with the state's hot spots and helpful tips from the pros, write 1050 E Wahner Pl, Milwaukee 53217; 414-352-2028; www.wisconsinfishingguide.net, or call the **Wisconsin Department of Tourism**; 800-432-8747.

Ice Age Trail

The Ice Age Trail is one of eight national scenic trails. It follows the path of retreating glaciers and educates on the effect the giant earth movers had on the state. Over 600 of 1,000 miles are complete. For more information about the Ice Age Trail, call 800-227-5712 or log onto www.iceagetrail.org.

Lodging

For a free town-by-town guide of the state's hotels, motels, resorts, inns, B&Bs, condos and vacation homes, contact the **Wisconsin Innkeepers Association**, 1025 S Moorland Rd, Ste 200, Brookfield 53005; 262-782-2851; www.lodging-wi.com (amenities listed).

Maple Syrup

The entire world's supply of maple syrup comes from the sugar bush—abundant stands of maple trees found in the northeastern region of North America. Wisconsin ranks fourth in the nation in maple syrup production. The sweet sap flows around Mar & Apr. Cold nights below freezing and warm days with temperatures climbing into the 40s trigger the flow. The traditional way of sap collecting is to drill a tap into the tree, then hang a bucket or plastic bag beneath it. Some people still run their syruping operation that way but many use the "gravity flow" system, funneling sap from the tree right into a holding tank where impurities are removed. The sap is then boiled down in large vats to syrup density with nothing added, then bottled and packaged. It takes about 40 gallons of sap to make one gallon of syrup. There are about as many family-owned maple syrup operations in the state as there are White-tailed Deer. You can't drive 50' without spotting a sign advertising the amber treat. Many people offer tours of their syruping operation.

Ledge View Nature Center

W2348 Short Rd, Chilton 53014 (from Appleton, take Hwy 114 to Hilbert and Hwy 57 S); 920-849-7094; www.dotnet.com/~ledge/

A hands-on event; learn to tap a tree, collect the sap, make the syrup, then eat ice cream topped with your product. Besides syruping, the nature center offers lots of other programs such as cidermaking, basket weaving and snowshoeing. There is a picnic area, nature/ski trails and a 60' observation tower. Interactive exhibits feature Wisconsin's bats, a huge aquarium, fossils of the Niagara Escarpment and caves. You must be at least 5 years old to go on the naturalist-guided 2-hour cave tour. The more adventurous can try a flashlight-led "cave crawl." Fee charged. Open year-round.

Maple Hollow

W1887 Robinson Dr, Merrill 54452; 715-536-7251; www.maplehollowsyrup.com

The award-winning, 3-generation family-owned operation has been making maple syrup since 1889. Open year-round M–F and also Sa during syruping season (Feb–May). Call for hours. They offer complimentary tours of the maple syrup process.

Mississippi Riverboat Cruises

The best view of the mighty Mississippi is from a paddleboat or luxury yacht. These tours run Jun–Oct.

- **Island Girl River Cruises**, 621 Park Plaza Dr, La Crosse 54601; 608-784-0556; www.greatriver.com/islandgirl (daily cocktail and dinner cruises aboard a luxury yacht, Su breakfast, weekend moonlight cruise)

- **Julia Belle Swain**, 227 Main St, La Crosse 54601; 800-815-1005 or 608-784-4882; www.juliabelle.com (daily excursions aboard an authentic steam-powered boat, Sunday brunch, dinner cruises, overnight trips, live music)

- **La Crosse Queen Cruises**, 405 Veterans Memorial Dr, La Crosse 54602; 608-784-8523; www.greatriver.com/laxqueen/paddle.htm (daily sightseeing tours aboard an authentic split sternwheel paddlewheeler, weekend brunch and dinner cruises)

- **Steamboat Inn River Charters**, Hwy 10 Bridge, Prescott 54021; 800-262-8232 or 715-262-5858; www.steamboatinn.com (brunch and dinner cruises aboard a river push boat)

Multi-Use, Four Season Trails

Wisconsin has four distinct seasons, each with its own blessings or curses, depending on how you feel about it. If you're an all-season fan and have a few outdoor "toys," you're probably looking for scenic trails to ride. Here are a few outstanding favorites that allow year-round use for hiking, horseback riding, biking, snowshoeing, dog sledding, cross-country skiing and snowmobiling. Almost all require trail passes. Hiking is free. **Wisconsin Department of Natural Resources Bureau of Parks and Recreation**, PO Box 7921, Madison 53707-7921; 888-WIPARKS or 608-266-2181; www.wiparks.net

- **Ahnapee State Trail**—The 30-mile trail winds northeast along the Ahnapee River from Casco to Sturgeon Bay; 3538 Park Dr, Sturgeon Bay 54235; 920-746-9959 (canoeing, tubing).

- **Chippewa River State Trail**—The 26-mile trail links the town of Eau Claire with the popular 15-mile **Red Cedar Trail** that runs from Menomonie to the Chippewa River in Downsville; 921 Brickyard Rd, Menomonie 54751; 715-232-1242 (canoeing, tubing, fishing, no horse trails).

- **Elroy-Sparta State Trail**—*The very first rails-to-trails in the US.* The 32-mile trail runs from Elroy northwest to Sparta. It has three century-old railroad tunnels—one is almost a mile long and completely black, so bring a flashlight! Mailing address PO Box 99, Ontario

54651; 608-337-4775 (fishing, but no horse trails; bike rentals available in towns along route; Kendall's historic railroad depot has electric carts for folks with disabilities).

- **Sugar River State Trail**—The 24-mile scenic trail connects New Glarus with Brodhead and features a covered bridge replica; W5446 Cty NN, New Glarus 53574; 608-527-2334 (fishing, no horse trails).

- **Wild Rivers Trail**—The 96-mile abandoned "Soo Line" railroad-grade trail begins at Rice Lake, stretches north through Barron, Washburn and Douglas Counties and ends a few miles south of Superior. City of Superior & Douglas County Visitors Center; 800-942-5313 or 715-392-2773; www.northwestwisconsin.com (96 miles of ATVing!).

NOTE: There are 33 state trails. Call the DNR and ask for the free Wisconsin State Park System brochure, which includes a complete trail list; 608-266-2621.

Round Barns

As you may surmise the Dairy State has a few barns, but not all are created equal. The round barn was a modern wonder of its time. Efficiently built, round barns used less materials and were more resistant to strong wind gusts. Some have center silos, making the feeding process less work for the farmers. Of course, there are the old tales suggesting the barns were round "so the devil can't find a corner to hide in."

There are approximately 200 round barns still standing in Wisconsin. Vernon County claims more round barns than any other county in the US. These century-old structures dot valley farms and hillside meadows with added charm and nostalgia. For a list of about 120 barns complete with pictures and detailed directions, log onto www.ohiobarns.com/index.html. Click on Round Barns, then Wisconsin.

Rustic Roads

One of the best Wisconsin day trips is a drive on a Rustic Road. Although there are 95 designated roads tallying more than 500 miles, these infrequently traveled, picturesque byways seem to be the state's best kept secret. Even Wisconsinites don't seem to have a clue about Rustic Roads, although it could be they refer to them as "Porcupine Valley" or "The Old Johnson Gulch," rather than R43, for example. The road lengths are anywhere from 2–30 miles; have a leisurely feel about them with maximum speed limits of 45mph; can be dirt, gravel or paved; and always travel through amazing terrain such as lush wooded valleys with meandering brooks or hilltop vistas with stone buildings and round barns. Keep your eyes peeled for the unique brown and yellow signs pointing the way to an authentic Wisconsin experience. For a free copy of Wisconsin's Rustic Roads with maps and descriptions, call 800-432-8747 or visit the **Wisconsin DOT's Rustic Roads** website at www.dot.state.wi.us.

Sports

Call the numbers listed below for game schedule and ticket information.

- **Duluth-Superior Dukes**, Wadc Stadium, 34th Ave W and Grand Ave, Duluth, MN; 218-727-4525; www.dsdukes.com (AA minor league baseball)

- **Elkhart Lake's Road America**, N7390 Hwy 67 (60 miles north of Milwaukee), PO Box P, Elkhart Lake 53020; 800-365-7223; www.roadamerica.com (North America's only permanent 4-mile road racing circuit, vintage cars, motorcycles, on-site driving/racing school)

- **Green Bay Packers, Lambeau Field**, 1265 Lombardi Ave, Green Bay; www.packers.com. Chances are slim to none you'll ever see the Pack play in person as the home games are sold out for something like the next 30 years, but here's a few places you can try for tickets: TicketKing 800-992-7328 or 920-405-1000; Packer Tickets and Tour Packages 800-851-7225; www.packerfantours.com

- **Milwaukee Admirals Hockey Club**, Bradley Center, 1001 N 4th St, Milwaukee 53203; 414-902-4400; www.milwaukeeadmirals.com

- **Milwaukee Brewers Baseball Club**, Miller Park, One Brewers Way, Milwaukee 53214; 414-902-4400; www.milwaukeebrewers.com

- **Milwaukee Bucks, Bradley Center**, 1001 N Fourth St, Milwaukee 53203-1312; 414-227-0500; www.bucks.com

- **Milwaukee Mile**, 7722 W Greenfield Ave, West Allis 53214; 414-453-5761; tickets 414-453-8277; www.milwaukeemile.com (state fairgrounds; high-speed auto racing)

- **Milwaukee Wave Professional Soccer**, US Cellular Arena, Milwaukee 53203; 414-224-WAVE; www.milwaukeewave.com

- **University of Wisconsin Badgers**, Camp Randall Stadium, 1440 Monroe St, Madison (Big Ten college football); ticket office 800-462-2343 or 608-262-1440; men's sports 608-262-1811; women's sports 608-263-5502; www.uwbadgers.com

- **Wisconsin Timber Rattlers**, Fox Cities Stadium, 2400 N Casaloma Dr, Grand Chute (west of Appleton); 920-733-4152; www.timber-rattlers.com (Class A baseball, affiliate of the Seattle Mariners)

State Parks

The Wisconsin State Parks welcome more than 14 million visitors each year. Vehicle permits are required inside the State Parks and can be purchased as an annual, daily or hourly permit. Senior citizens enjoy a discount. Registration plates from other states are a little higher. Call for prices. The parks system has four handicap-accessible cabins located at Buckhorn, Mirror Lake and Potawatomi State Parks and Ottawa Lake in the Southern Unit of the Kettle Moraine State Forest. Smaller rustic cabins are available at Blue Mound and Copper Falls State Parks. For cabin and camping reservations, call **Reserve America** 888-947-2757 or 800-274-7275 TTY. For information about the parks and state trails, contact the **Wisconsin Department of Natural Resources Bureau of Parks and Recreation**, PO Box 7921, Madison 53707-7921; 608-266-2181 or 608-267-2752 TTY; www.wiparks.net.

Wisconsin Department of Tourism

PO Box 7976, Madison 53707-7976; 800-432-8747; www.travelwisconsin.com

Do you want to go horseback riding? Do a little fishing? Or maybe you'd like to spend a few days on a farm helping out with chores. The folks at the **Wisconsin Department of Tourism** will point you in the right direction for these adventures and more. Give them a call or look up online.

- For a list of **farm vacations and riding stables**, ask for a free summer recreation guide.

- For **hayrides and sleigh rides**, ask for a free winter recreation guide.

- For a list of 20 fee **fishing** businesses (gear provided—no license required), ask for a free summer recreation guide.

- Wisconsin has 1,000 miles of rail-trails, 10,000 miles of roadways rated for bicycles and 26 state parks with mountain bike trails. For a free booklet with trail maps, ask for the **Wisconsin Biking Guide**.

- For a free B&B booklet, ask for **Wisconsin B&B Directory**.

NOTE: Many Chambers of Commerce offer **discount packages** for lodging, restaurants and area attractions. Contact the county or city you plan to visit and ask about these special deals.

Wisconsin Milk Marketing Board

PO Box 1012, La Crosse 54602-1012

For a free map to **62 cheese factories, 30 breweries and 12 wineries,** write to the Wisconsin Milk Marketing Board and include a self-addressed, stamped (60 cents) No. 10 envelope. The maps are also available at the larger Wisconsin tourist information centers.

World Dairy Expo

Alliant Energy Center, 1919 Alliant Energy Center Way, Madison; 608-224-6455; www.worlddairyexpo.com

One of the biggest events of the year is the World Dairy Expo held annually at the end of Sep. See top dairy cattle worth big bucks from around the world compete for blue ribbon awards.

NOTE: Nearby Fort Atkinson is the birthplace of the *Hoard's Dairyman* magazine. William Dempster Hoard was the Bill Gates of the state's dairy industry. His magazine has been in circulation since 1873. Housed in the patriarch's family home, the **Hoard Museum and Dairy Shrine** showcases everything from Wisconsin dairy history to Native American artifacts to Civil War memorabilia. The museum is at 407 Merchants Ave; 920-563-7769. Closed Su & M. Free admission.

Index

Index

Index

Index

Index